D1263171

The Gray and the Black

WINNER OF THE
JULES F. LANDRY AWARD

E 453
.D87

The
GRAY
and the
BLACK

The Confederate Debate on Emancipation

Robert F. Durden

Louisiana State University Press

BATON ROUGE

INDIANA
PURDUE
LIBRARY
MAR 1974

FORT WAYNE

WITHDRAWN

ISBN 0–8071–0244–X
Library of Congress Catalog Card Number 72–79330
Copyright © 1972 by Louisiana State University Press
All rights reserved
Manufactured in the United States of America
Printed by The Colonial Press Inc.
Designed by Dwight Agner

This book is gratefully dedicated to my friends in the Department of History of the College of William and Mary, for my appointment there as the James Pinckney Harrison Visiting Professor of History in 1970–1971 made possible the writing of THE GRAY AND THE BLACK.

Preface

THAT THE CONFEDERACY in its waning days frantically turned to the idea of arming the slaves has long been known by all close students of the Civil War. What has not been properly emphasized is that the central issue before the southern people and leaders in this last great crisis of the Confederacy was not simply the arming of the slaves, but whether or not the South itself should voluntarily initiate a program of emancipation as part of a plan to recruit black soldiers.

A proposal for Confederate emancipation was made by none other than Jefferson Davis himself. Strangely, many history books have missed a key element of the paradoxical drama that unfolded when the President of the Confederacy called for the freeing of a significant portion of the slaves.[1] Many historians may have largely missed Davis' point, but certainly his contemporaries did not. From October, 1864, until the end of the war in the following April, the Confederacy exploded in an intensely passionate debate that cut to the heart of what the Civil War was all about so far as the South was concerned. Davis and a few other leaders attempted to force the South to face the desperate alternative of sacrificing one of its war aims—the preservation of slavery—in order to make a last-ditch effort to achieve the other—an independent southern nation. Most articulate Southerners, despite

---

[1] The two most generally cited articles are N.W. Stephenson, "The Question of Arming the Slaves," *American Historical Review*, XVIII (January, 1913), 295–308; and Thomas R. Hay, "The South and the Arming of the Slaves," *Mississippi Valley Historical Review*, VI (July, 1919), 34–73. Another is Charles H. Wesley, "The Employment of Negroes as Soldiers in the Confederate Army," *Journal of Negro History*, IV (July, 1919), 239–53; much of this material is also contained in the same author's *Collapse of the Confederacy* (1937; repr. ed., New York, 1968). Following these important pioneering studies, most historians either ignore or barely mention a plan called for by Jefferson Davis, which is the focus of this book. For a fuller discussion of these matters, the reader should see the historiographical note at the end of this volume.

certain fascinating exceptions, made it tragically clear that they yet lacked, even in this ultimate crisis, the intelligence, moral courage, and imagination to begin voluntarily to abandon the peculiar institution. The South had spent forty or so years convincing itself that slavery was ordained by God as the best, indeed the only, solution to the problem posed by the massive presence of the Negro. The debate in the winter of 1864–1865 demonstrated anew and with a sad finality that many Southerners were unwilling or unable to consider voluntary alterations to the racial status quo, even as that status quo was crumbling about them in the closing phases of the Civil War. Yet Jefferson Davis, Robert E. Lee, Judah Benjamin, and a host of less famous Southerners displayed greater flexibility about and willingness to begin modifying slavery than most accounts have ever admitted.

This was probably the fullest and freest discussion of slavery in which the South as a whole ever engaged, and it was a critical turning point in southern, and indeed American, history. Yet the South refused to turn—or rather, it half turned in the chaotic closing weeks of the war and then later forgot all about the uncharacteristic flirtation with unorthodoxy. The tragedy of the unturned or half-turned corner lay not, surely, in the military outcome of the war, for the North would probably have won in any event. The whole episode shows, however, that there was yet a reservoir of good will between the white and black races in the South, which reservoir was very nearly tapped by the Confederacy. It shows too that freedom might not have been, and need not have been left as it was, solely in the gift of the Federal armies, Lincoln, and the Thirteenth Amendment.

Finally, the entire affair suggests anew what any student of American history ought to know by now: differences between North and South in fundamental matters concerning the Negro and the relations of the races have always been a matter of differences in degree, not in kind. Of course this does not mean that the differences were not important. But we have long known that wartime circumstances produced important changes in the attitudes and policies of Lincoln and the North in general concerning slavery. When one realizes that the Confederacy, led and pushed in this matter by Jefferson Davis and Robert E. Lee, verged on emancipating the slaves, surely one must recognize once and for all that, so far as our history is concerned, the Mason-Dixon line must be drawn with great care and subtlety.

Because of the centrality of this subject, not only to the Civil War but to so much of our history before and since, and because of the compelling interest of the documents, I have decided to let the Confederates speak for themselves as much as possible. But I do not wish the unwary reader to be deceived: I have had to select and edit the documents that follow from a massive number that I collected and from an even larger number that exist. I have not, certainly, achieved objectivity; I have merely tried to do so as best and fairly as I know how.

Besides my debt to the College of William and Mary, and particularly to its Department of History, which debt I have attempted to suggest by my dedication of this book, I have the largest obligation to Anne Oller Durden, my wife. She not only patiently listened as the idea developed in my mind, but she has pleasantly endured a great deal more conversation about Confederate history than she could possibly really care for. Further, she transcribed a large number of documents, many of them from half-legible newspapers, and has shared, as usual, the dubious pleasures of making an index. I thank her.

The Earl Gregg Swem Library of the College of William and Mary was a splendid home base for this undertaking. William C. Pollard, the librarian, capped a courteous reception by making available a typewriter at a critical stage, and his staff followed his example of kind helpfulness. Although the College of William and Mary has a most useful and diverse collection of Civil War newspapers on microfilm, I am particularly grateful to Mrs. Betsy Smith for her help in obtaining other microfilmed newspapers I needed through interlibrary loan.

In the William R. Perkins Library of Duke University, my friends Dr. Mattie Russell in Manuscripts and Winston Broadfoot in the Flowers Collection assisted me, as they have many times in the past; and the same is true of Dr. Carolyn Wallace in the Southern Historical Collection of the University of North Carolina Library, Chapel Hill. C. F. W. Coker in the North Carolina Department of Archives and History, Miss Jo Cille Dawkins in the Mississippi Department of Archives and History, Milton C. Russell in the Virginia State Library, Miss Eleanor Brokenbrough in the Confederate Museum in Richmond, and Roy P. Basler in the manuscript division of the Library of Congress were helpful.

Among my colleagues in the historical profession whom I thank for assistance and encouragement are Professors William Abbot, Richard Maxwell Brown, Boyd Coyner, Ludwell Johnson, Joseph Parks, Lillian Pereyra, David Roller, Willie Lee Rose, Robert Twyman, Robert Woody, and W. Buck Yearns. Dr. Edward Phifer of Morgantown, North Carolina, and Wade Boggs, Thomas Preisser, and A. M. Secrest were generous with their time and interest. Students in my classes at Duke University and at the College of William and Mary, too numerous to name here, have discussed with me many of the matters treated herein and I am grateful to them.

Charles East, director of the Louisiana State University Press, lent a sympathetic ear at a timely juncture, and I appreciate his willingness to add my name to the roster of a press that I admire.

Contents

Contents

The Gray and the Black

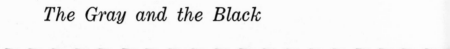

CHAPTER I

Slavery as
Confederate Cornerstone—
or Millstone?

AFTER THE CIVIL WAR ENDED, a cardinal element of the southern apologia, and an idea cherished by some Southerners well into the twentieth century, was the emphatic denial that the South's primary aim in fighting was the preservation of slavery. Liberty, independence, and especially states' rights were advanced by countless southern spokesmen as the hallowed principles of the Lost Cause. Even during the war, some Southerners minimized the defense of slavery, and thus anticipated the postwar apologia. But by and large, the Confederates themselves were not as elusive and confused on the subject as their descendants would be.

In the first place, the Confederate Constitution was not ambiguous or silent about slavery. In general the Southerners patterned their charter closely after the original model of 1787, but there were significant differences. Jefferson Davis himself italicized those portions of the Confederate document that varied from the United States Constitution, and the key passages concerning slavery are reproduced here. Perhaps the most important of these to note is in Article I, Section 9, where the Confederate Congress is explicitly prohibited from passing any law "denying or impairing the right of property in negro slaves . . . ." Because of the nature of the prolonged sectional controversy that preceded the war, no single constitutional belief held greater sway in the South of the Civil War era than the conviction that slavery in a state was exclusively the affair of that state; and nowhere was the Confederate Constitution's preamble about the "sovereign and independent character" of each state more relevant:

CONSTITUTION OF THE
UNITED STATES OF AMERICA.

We the People of the United States, in order to form a more perfect Union, establish Justice, insure domestic Tranquillity, provide for the common defence, promote the general Welfare, and secure the Blessings of Liberty to ourselves and our Posterity, do ordain and establish this CONSTITUTION for the United States of America.

Article I.

Section 2.

. . . Representatives and direct Taxes shall be apportioned among the several States which may be included within this Union, according to their respective Numbers which shall be determined by adding to the whole Number of free Persons, including those bound to Service for a Term of Years, and excluding Indians not taxed, three-fifths of all other Persons. . . .

Section 9. The Migration or Importation of such Persons as any of the States now existing shall think proper to admit, shall not be prohibited by the Congress prior

CONSTITUTION OF THE
CONFEDERATE STATES OF
AMERICA

We, the People of the *Confederate* States, *each State acting in its sovereign and independent character, in order to form a permanent Federal Government*, establish justice, insure domestic tranquillity, and secure the blessings of liberty to ourselves and our posterity—*invoking the favor and guidance of Almighty God*—do ordain and establish this Constitution for the *Confederate* States of America.

Article I.

Section 2.

. . . Representatives and direct taxes shall be apportioned among the several States, which may be included within this *Confederacy,* according to their respective numbers, which shall be determined by adding to the whole number of free persons, including those bound to service for a term of years, and excluding Indians not taxed, three fifths of all *slaves.* . . .

Section 9. The importation of *negroes of the African race, from any foreign country other than the slave-holding States or Territories of the United States of* to the Year one thousand eight hundred and eight, but a Tax or Duty may be imposed on such Importation, not exceeding ten dollars for each Person.

America, is hereby forbidden; and Congress is required to pass such laws as shall effectually prevent the same.

Congress shall also have power to prohibit the introduction of slaves from any State not a member of, or Territory not belonging to, this Confederacy.

. . . No Bill of Attainder or ex post facto Law shall be passed. . . .

. . . *No bill of attainder, ex post facto* law, *or law denying or impairing the right of property in negro slaves shall be passed. . . .*

Article IV.

Section 2. The Citizens of each State shall be entitled to all Privileges and Immunities of Citizens in the several States. . . .

Article IV.

Section 2. The citizens of each State shall be entitled to all the privileges and immunities of citizens in the several States, *and shall have the right of transit and sojourn in any State of this Confederacy, with their slaves and other property; and the right of property in said slaves shall not be thereby impaired. . . .*

No person held to Service or Labour in one State, under the Laws thereof, escaping into another, shall, in Consequence of any Law or Regulation therein, be discharged from such Service or Labour, but shall be delivered up on Claim of the Party to whom such Service or Labour may be due. . . .

No slave or other person held to service or labor *in any State or Territory of the Confederate States,* under the laws thereof, escaping *or lawfully carried* into another, shall, in consequence of any law or regulation therein, be discharged from such service or labor; but shall be delivered up on claim of the party *to whom such slave belongs, or* to whom such service or labor may be due. . . .

The Congress shall have power to dispose of and make all needful Rules and Regulations respecting the Territory or other Property belonging to the United States; and nothing in this Constitution shall be so construed as to Prejudice any Claims of the United States, or of any particular State. . . .

The Congress shall have power to dispose of and make all needful rules and regulations *concerning the property of the Confederate* States, *including the lands thereof.*

The Confederate States may acquire new territory; and Congress shall have power to legislate and provide governments for the inhabitants of all territory belonging to the Confederate States, lying without the limits of the several States; and may permit them, at such times and in such manner as it may by law provide, to form States to be admitted into the Confederacy. In all such territory, the institution of negro slavery, as it now exists in the Confederate States, shall be recognized and protected by Congress and by the territorial government; and the inhabitants of the several Confederate States and Territories shall have the right to take to such Territory any slaves lawfully held by them in any of the States or Territories of the Confederate States. . . .

Article VI.

[The Tenth Amendment of the United States Constitution was incorporated into the main body of

. . . The powers not delegated to the *Confederate* States by the Constitution, nor prohibited by it

the Confederate Constitution, as were other parts of the original Bill of Rights.] to the States, are reserved to the States, respectively, or to the people *thereof*.[1]

🖙 Underscoring the central significance of these provisions for slavery in the Confederate Constitution, newly elected Confederate Vice-President Alexander Stephens delivered a famous speech at Savannah, Georgia, on March 21, 1861. He was elucidating what he regarded as "improvements" in the southern charter that had been drawn up earlier in that month:

. . . The new constitution has put at rest, *forever,* all the agitating questions relating to our peculiar institution—African slavery as it exists among us—the proper *status* of the negro in our form of civilization. This was the immediate cause of the late rupture and present revolution. Jefferson in his forecast, had anticipated this, as the "rock upon which the old Union would split." He was right. What was conjecture with him, is now a realized fact. But whether he fully comprehended the great truth upon which the rock *stood* and *stands,* may be doubted. The prevailing ideas entertained by him and most of the leading statesmen at the time of the formation of the old constitution, were that the enslavement of the African was in violation of the laws of nature; that it was wrong in *principle,* socially, morally, and politically. It was an evil they knew not well how to deal with, but the general opinion of the men of that day was that, somehow or other in the order of Providence, the institution would be evanescent and pass away. This idea, though not incorporated in the constitution, was the prevailing idea at that time. The constitution, it is true, secured every essential guarantee to the institution while it should last, and hence no argument can be justly urged against the constitutional guarantees thus secured, because of the common sentiment of the day. Those ideas, however, were fundamentally wrong. They rested upon the assumption of the equality of races. This was an error. It was a sandy foundation, and the government built upon it fell when the "storm came and the wind blew."

Our new government is founded upon exactly the opposite idea; its foundations are laid, its corner-stone rests upon the great truth, that

[1] Jefferson Davis, *The Rise and Fall of the Confederate Government* (1881; repr. ed., with foreword by Bell I. Wiley, 2 vols.; New York, 1958), I, 648–73.

the negro is not equal to the white man; that slavery—subordination to the superior race—is his natural and normal condition. [Applause.]

This, our new government, is the first, in the history of the world, based upon this great physical, philosophical, and moral truth. This truth has been slow in the process of its development, like all other truths in the various departments of science. It has been so even amongst us. Many who hear me, perhaps, can recollect well, that this truth was not generally admitted, even within their day. The errors of the past generation still clung to many as late as twenty years ago. Those at the North, who still cling to these errors, with a zeal above knowledge, we justly denominate fanatics. . . . They assume that the negro is equal, and hence conclude that he is entitled to equal privileges and rights with the white man. If their premises were correct, their conclusions would be logical and just—but their premise being wrong, their whole argument fails. . . .

In the conflict thus far, success has been on our side, complete throughout the length and breadth of the Confederate States. It is upon this, as I have stated, our social fabric is firmly planted; and I cannot permit myself to doubt the ultimate success of a full recognition of this principle throughout the civilized and enlightened world.

. . . Many governments have been founded upon the principle of the subordination and serfdom of certain classes of the same race; such were and are in violation of the laws of nature. Our system commits no such violation of nature's laws. With us, all of the white race, however high or low, rich or poor, are equal in the eye of the law. Not so with the negro. Subordination is his place. He, by nature, or by the curse against Canaan, is fitted for that condition which he occupies in our system. The architect in the construction of buildings, lays the foundation with the proper material—the granite; then comes the brick or the marble. The substratum of our society is made of the material fitted by nature for it, and by experience we know, that it is best, not only for the superior, but for the inferior race, that it should be so. It is, indeed, in conformity with the ordinance of the Creator. It is not for us to inquire into the wisdom of his ordinances, or to question them. For his own purposes, he has made one race to differ from another, as he has made "one star to differ from another star in glory."

The great objects of humanity are best attained when there is conformity to his laws and decrees, in the formation of governments as well as in all things else. Our confederacy is founded upon principles in strict conformity with these laws. This stone which was rejected by the first builders "is become the chief of the corner"—the real "corner-stone"—in our new edifice. [Applause.]

I have been asked, what of the future? It has been apprehended by some that we would have arrayed against us the civilized world. I care not who or how many they may be against us, when we stand upon the eternal principles of truth, *if we are true to ourselves and the principles for which we contend,* we are obliged to, and must triumph. [Immense applause.] . . .[2]

⬯ Corroborating Stephens' viewpoint and illustrating the general southern thinking about slavery at the time, an editorial from the New Orleans *Bee* (March 16, 1861), which was also published in a French-language edition, reiterates one critical ingredient of the proslavery argument, the alleged racial inferiority of the Negro. The editorial also illustrates the widespread but erroneous belief that the general northern attitude toward the Negro differed fundamentally from that of the South:

One salutary result of the movement in favor of Southern independence has been the awakening of certain intelligent and thoughtful minds in the North to the consideration of the true relations existing between the negro and the white man. There have not been wanting sound philosophical thinkers who have labored earnestly to disabuse public opinion at the North of its prevailing fallacies on this subject, but either their numbers were few, or the prejudices of those they addressed were too inveterate to be easily overcome. But since the

[2] Professor James Rabun was kind enough to call my attention to a handy source for this speech: Henry Cleveland, *Alexander Stephens in Public and Private* . . . (Philadelphia, 1866), 721–23, which reprints the impromptu address, or the reporter's version of it, from the Savannah (Ga.), *Republican.* The speech is also available in the Macon (Ga.), *Telegraph,* March 25 and 26, 1861, and in the Columbus (Ga.), *Enquirer,* March 26, 1861. The italics are in the original here and throughout. To argue that slavery was, as Stephens said, the cornerstone of the Confederacy is not, of course, to say that each individual Confederate soldier, or even most of them, consciously fought for slavery. Hudson Strode, the most recent biographer of Jefferson Davis, tells a relevant story in this connection about a puzzled Federal officer who asked a ragged Confederate prisoner, clearly no slaveowner, why on earth he was fighting. The "Johnny Reb" eyed his interrogator coolly and replied: "Because y'all are down here." Strode, *Jefferson Davis: Confederate President* (New York, 1959), xvi–xvii.

South has shown her determination to sever all political connection with the North, precisely on account of the persistence of the latter in cherishing these pernicious views, there has been some disposition manifested to bestow dispassionate investigation on the negro question. We have recently perused interesting disquisitions from Northern men on the capacity of the black man, on his condition in a state of involuntary servitude, on the benefits accruing to him from his position as a chattel, and on the unwise and dangerous tendency of all efforts at his emancipation. In a late number of the Philadelphia *Inquirer*—a Republican journal of some fairness and moderation—there is a capital article on the fitness of the negro for freedom in the midst of the white race. The ground is taken that the abstract right of personal freedom, like that of political self-government, is conditioned upon fitness. If this were otherwise, every nation would be justified in organizing the same political institutions. Now what sort of republicans could be manufactured out of Russian serfs, or the subjects of the Emperor of China? Has not France twice tried a republic, and twice replaced it by a monarchy?

The idea of the equality of race is a figment. Neither politically nor socially, nor legally can it be said to exist. Mentally or physically the weak are ever subjugated by the strong, and the grades of society are as numerous as the rounds of a ladder. We are told that a man has a right to his own bones and muscles, his mental and moral powers. This is a favorite axiom of the Abolitionists, and is undoubtedly true, but he must be a man, neither an idiot nor a child, as the *Inquirer* very forcibly declares. It may happen, too, that the right of a man to his bones and muscles becomes purely nominal. In our elaborate system of sociology a white laborer, with the unrestricted command of all his physical energies, may be exposed to starvation, because nobody is inclined to use and pay for them; whereas the black laborer, whose thewes [sic] and sinews are the property of his master, is certain at all times of food, shelter, and clothing, and generally of kind treatment.

The entire theory of negro slavery is founded upon certain truths as familiar as household words to Southern minds, but which until very recently were utterly unknown to the North. It is based on the native and unchangeable characteristics of the African race itself. The black man in his own home is a barbarian and a beast—often a slave, and then the most abject and wretched of beings, liable at any moment to be knocked on the head or tortured to death at the caprice of his master. In America he is subjected to every possible influence adapted for the melioration of his condition. He learns something of civilization and of Christianity; the better traits of his nature are developed, while his lower instincts are perpetually repressed. Good example and constant guidance combat and overcome his dominant propensity to relapse into barbarism. He rises as high in the social scale as it is possible for him to do; but it is impossible for him to soar beyond his level. Why is it that the negro thrives in servitude, multiplies in numbers, and improves from generation to generation? Simply because while his will is good, enabling him readily to imbibe habits of docility and obedience, his understanding is feeble and needs control. Left to himself, the negro would perish if placed in conflict with the white man, and this is what is gradually taking place in the North. When emancipated and removed from the crushing competition of a superior race he demonstrates his utter incapacity for self-restraint, grows idle and thriftless, indulges his passions without the slightest check, descends step by step down to the original depths of his ignorant and savage instincts, and at length is debased to nearly the state in which he is found in the wilds and jungles of Africa. To this complexion is he approximating in Hayti. Hence the normal condition of the negro is servitude, and he is happiest when he alternately labors and rests under the firm and unrelaxed, but not ungentle government of his owner.

The reverse of the peculiarities which qualify the negro for his existing relations to the white man are discernible in the Indian. With the latter the intellect is often more expanded and comprehensive. He is capable of acquiring knowledge; but his will is as inflexible as adamant. He cannot be subdued; he cannot be brought under the modifying influences of civilization. He resists all encroachment upon his sovereignty of the wilderness; if conquered, he sullenly retires before the advance of the hated pale face. He would rather perish than surrender a jot of his independence, and perish he does.

☛ At the opposite end of the South from New Orleans, Virginia still hung precariously between seceding or remaining in the Union. Yet one strong bond with the new Confederacy was slavery. The Richmond *Dispatch* (March 23, 1861), which was clearly in favor of Virginia's joining her sister states of the Deep South, emphasized the peril it saw to the peculiar institution if the Old Dominion dallied too long:

Since the world began there has been no system of labor comparable, in productive efficiency, with the slave system of the Southern States. If we look back through the ages, we shall discover no great achievement of human toil but such as was the product of slave labor. In modern times two competitors have appeared to contest the palm of productive capacity with the slave—the machine, and the cooley [*sic*]; but the machine can be employed to advantage only in manufactures, and the cooley only as an indifferent substitute to supply the want of slaves. The immense demands of modern civilization for labor have called forth these new agencies of production; but except the machine for particular branches of industry, no equivalent has yet been discovered for the slave laborer. Slave labor is the foundation of productive power—the other agencies are but auxiliaries.

The commerce and wealth of a country depend upon its surplus products. If a man makes only what he consumes, he may be very comfortable, very tidy in his person and his form, very independent; but he cannot grow richer. A country made up of rich citizens may be very populous, very beautiful in all its features and departments, and very powerful for its own defense; but it can have no foreign commerce of importance, and cannot grow a whit in external influence, power or consideration.

The only States, of what were the late United States, which produced surpluses for exportation and foreign commerce, were the slaveholding ones. The exports of the Union were four hundred millions of dollars, the great bulk of which were the peculiar production of these States. There were also exported grain, provision stuffs, and other products, such as are produced alike by slaveholding and non-slaveholding States; but the quantity of those that went abroad scarcely equalled the amount of the same articles which were sent from the South to the North, so that it may be said with truth, that *the whole foreign exportation of the Union went, directly or indirectly, exclusively from the slaveholding States.* In other words, the slaveholding section of the Union furnished all the surplus products that constituted the basis of the foreign commerce of the country, while the non-slave-holding section furnished nothing, but consumed all that it produced.

The most fortunate condition of a community for prosperity is where slave labor is largely engaged in the production of articles valuable for importation, at the same [time] that machinery and intelligent free labor may be employed in manufactures and the more highly paid branches of industry; and both of these conditions exist under circumstances, geographical and political, favorable to the growth of external and internal commerce.—Precisely in this fortunate relation to all these subjects does Virginia stand at this hour. But the substratum and foundation of her whole power and wealth of resources, is her system of slave labor. She is the largest slaveholding State in the Union; Eastern Virginia the largest slaveholding community in the world. Blot this slave system of Virginia out of existence, and at the same time cut her off from trade with the productive, wealth-teeming, because slaveholding, South, and she becomes a vast waste, with here and there a cluster of counties cut up into small farms, tenanted by owners, well fed, comfortably clad, and independent it may be, but whose whole business of life consists in making the two ends of the year meet.

To show the value of the slave system of Virginia, we have only to adduce the single subject of annual taxation; although the bulk of the white population of the State resides in the West, the great bulk of her taxable values, which are the result of the labor of the slaves, is found in the East. Taxed according to white population, the West would have to pay the larger portion of the public revenues. Taxed, however, as the fact is, according to the values of the State, and the burden falls two to one upon the East; for while Tidewater and Piedmont paid last year, of the taxes locally levied, $2,104,386, the Valley, Northwest and Southwest, paid only $1,216,599. Of the taxes of a general character, amounting additionally to three-quarters of a million dollars, much the larger portion is paid by the East; so that in truth, while the West pays of the annual taxation of the State only about a million and a half dollars, the East pays more than two millions and a half, or two for one.

Now, it is proposed to destroy the slave system of Virginia—which contributes so much to her general wealth, and discharges so large a portion of her annual taxation—by two processes, to wit: first, by adhering to the North in the division of the Union that has taken place, which puts our slave system at the mercy of an abolition majority; and, secondly, by taxing the slaves in three forms—that is to say, by not only taxing the values which they produce, and taxing them *per capita*, as is already done, but also by taxing their individual value, as represented by the cash prices they would bring in the market.

Disunion being a fact accomplished; two Confederacies being now in existence, the one non-slaveholding at the North, the other slaveholding at the South; the alternative presented to Virginia is, whether to *affiliate* with the North or the South, which carries also the question, with which she shall *assimilate* her institutions. The question is secession or emancipation. It is whether she shall destroy or preserve her slave system of labor—the grandest and most efficient agency of wealth ever enjoyed by any community on the globe. The Republicans of the North would have her to cling to them, in order that they may vote her slave system out of existence. A few demagogues from her western districts declare that, secede or not secede, they will tax Virginia slavery out of existence. Between the two enemies of the institution the choice is tweedle-dum or tweedle-dee.

With the beginning of the war at Fort Sumter still more than a week in the hidden future, the Richmond *Dispatch* (April 2, 1861) boasted that if war should come, slavery would indeed add to the strength of the South:

There never was a period in the history of the country when there was more perfect order and quiet among the servile classes, than at this time, when, according to the Black Republican thieves, we should have insurrectionary volcanoes everywhere in full blast.—But the experiment at Harper's [*sic*] Ferry ought to have satisfied them that the Southern negro has no sympathies with Northern abolitionists. . . . Both our wars with England and the whole history of the world, demonstrate that a slave population is an element of strength in war, and not of weakness or insecurity.

In March, 1861, there were none to dispute the Richmond *Dispatch*, Alexander Stephens, and the other champions of slavery, save a relatively small group of abolitionists in the North. The newly inaugurated Abraham Lincoln denied, repeatedly and emphatically, any intention of attempting to tamper in any way with slavery in the states. This emerged as a paramount element of his policy before the war began in April, 1861, and, despite mounting pressures for a change, continued as his policy through the first year and a half of the war, that is, until September, 1862. The South, in other words, might champion slavery as much as it wished, but with the North, through President Lincoln, refusing to attack it, the issue could hardly be drawn.

Perhaps the earliest indications to southern leaders that the vaunted cornerstone might also pose something of a problem came from the Confederacy's first diplomatic envoys to Britain and France. They reported to Richmond some five weeks after the war began:

. . . We are satisfied that the public mind here is entirely opposed to the Government of the Confederate States of America on the question of slavery, and that the sincerity and universality of this feeling embarrasses the Government in dealing with the question of our recognition. We are fully convinced, however, that the leading public men of all parties look to our recognition as certain, unless the fortune of war should be against us to such an extent as to destroy all reasonable hope of our permanency. . . .[3]

Once in Europe and out of the parochial, ultradefensive atmosphere that surrounded the question of slavery in the South, other Confederate emissaries repeatedly tackled the task of telling the Richmond government unwelcome truths about European antislavery sentiment. In Paris, John Slidell, the Confederate envoy to the government of Napoleon III, confessed that he tried his best to avoid even discussing the subject with Europeans:

. . . I have scarcely conversed with any foreigner who has not expressed a decided partiality for our cause and a degree of prejudice, amounting to bitterness, against our Northern foes. This uniform current of public opinion among the intelligent classes, of all nationalities, can not fail to exercise a salutary influence on their respective Govern-

[3] William L. Yancey and A. Dudley Mann to Secretary of State Robert Toombs, May 21, 1861, in *Official Records of the Union and Confederate Navies in the War of the Rebellion* (31 vols.; Washington, 1895–1929), Series II, Vol. III, 216, hereinafter cited as *O.R.N.*

ments, and stimulate them to earlier favorable action than they would be disposed to adopt, if the tendency and force of that opinion were more doubtful. It is true that you often hear expressed the regret that slavery exists amongst us, and the suggestion of a hope that some steps may be taken for its ultimate but gradual extinction, but, so far as my experience extends, this is never done in any offensive way, and the conversation is easily diverted to other and more agreeable topics. I make it a rule to enter into no discussion on the subject, for many of our best friends, who heartily advocate our cause, have theoretical views on the subject which in general it is not worth while to combat. . . .[4]

✿ At the height of the critical period in the early fall of 1862, when England came closest to recognizing the Confederacy and before it had received news of the South's reversal at Antietam and Lincoln's subsequent switch to an emancipation policy, Slidell reported a significant conversation to the Confederate secretary of state, Judah P. Benjamin:

. . . The Earl of Shaftesbury passed through Paris about 10 days since on his way from Spa to London, and called to see me for the purpose of talking of our affairs. His peculiar position as the leader of an extensive and influential class in England and the son-in-law of Lady Palmerston gives a value and significance to his opinions beyond that of a simple member of the House of Lords, and I therefore think it proper to put you in possession of them.

He opened the conversation by saying that from the commencement of our contest his sympathies had been decidedly with the South, and that everything that had since occurred had but served to confirm and strengthen them. That at first he was almost alone in his opinions among those with whom he habitually acted; that they considered the war as one between slavery and freedom. He, on the contrary, viewed it as a struggle, on the one hand, for independence and self-government, on the other, for empire, political power, and material interests.

That in this respect there had been a complete revolution in public sentiment in England, and especially among those who had most at heart the abolition of slavery, the great body of ''dissenters,'' their eyes had been opened by the course of Mr. Lincoln, and especially by

[4] John Slidell to Robert M. T. Hunter, February 11, 1862, *ibid.*, 336.

16

his recent speech to the delegation of colored men from New York and his letter to Horace Greeley.[5]

That they were now satisfied that the chances of negro emancipation were much better if we were left to ourselves than if we had remained in the Union. In this I concurred with him, for then the solution of the question would depend on a calm and dispassionate consideration of the economical and social advantages or disadvantages of the system.

If the day should ever arrive when slave labor ceased to be profitable and the slave could safely be liberated, slavery would soon cease to exist. That day would be retarded—it certainly could never be advanced—by foreign intervention in any form, or by foreign suggestions, advice, or remonstrance.

The Earl of Shaftesbury asked if the [Confederate] President could not in some way present the prospect of gradual emancipation. Such a declaration coming from him unsolicited would have the happiest effect in Europe, lead immediately to recognition, and, if necessary or desirable, to more decided measures to put an end to the war. I said that this was a matter appertaining exclusively to the States; that ours was a constitutional Government in spirit as well as form; and that no President could take upon himself to speak on the subject, even in the way of counsel. . . .[6]

☞ Henry Hotze, one of the most astute of the Confederate agents in Europe, published a newspaper in London, the *Index*. He made for Benjamin a shrewd analysis of certain differences between the antislavery sentiment of Britain and that of France:

. . . There are two phases under which the antislavery prejudice confronts you. One is the English phase, in which it feels itself constantly under the necessity of self-assertion, of propagandism, of offensive demonstrations. With this phase, by preserving one's temper, provoking the ill-temper of antagonists, and carefully watching for opportunities, it is possible to maintain an even contest and even to hope

---

[5] The reference is to Lincoln's urging the unhappy Negro spokesmen to join him in supporting a policy of separating the white and black races by the voluntary colonization of the latter outside of the United States; and to Lincoln's famed reply to Greeley's plea for an emancipation policy that whatever he did or did not do as President concerning slavery was governed by his primary object of preserving the Union.

[6] John Slidell to Judah P. Benjamin, September 29, 1862, *O.R.N.*, Series II, Vol. III, 546.

for ultimate victory. Here the events of this war have done more for us than all the arguments of our ablest and most judicious advocates.

The other phase, far more dangerous and difficult to deal with, is where the prejudice has passed into, or has not yet ceased to be, one of those fixed principles, which neither individuals nor nations permit to be called in question. This is actually the case in France and continental countries generally. There no such violent antislavery demonstrations are made as in England, simply because there is no one against whom to make them. Slavery is there classed with atheism, socialism, or other topics, on which however eccentric one's views may be or however certain one is of the secret sympathy of one's hearers, it is a rule of decency and decorum not to make them the subject of argument or to obtrude them upon well-bred ears. I have entered into this seemingly uncalled-for disquisition because I fear that, judging only from a distance and from outward appearances, you may mistake the relative strength of the prejudice in England and in France. In the latter country it is infinitely more unanimous and unassailable. With the exception of the Emperor and his nearest personal adherents, all the intelligence, the science, the social respectability, is leagued with the ignorance and the radicalism in a deep-rooted antipathy, rather than active hostility, against us. This is what has paralyzed the wise intentions of the Emperor heretofore, and what paralyzes them still. It is much easier for the English, accustomed to a hierarchy of classes at home and to a haughty dominion abroad, to understand a hierarchy of races than it is for the French, the apostles of universal equality and who have sacrificed so much to their creed. Few of our friends understand the full force of this fact in its bearings upon the political action of the Government. The Emperor, from the very magnitude of his power, can not afford to offend so universal a feeling, and he can not act as he wishes unless by conciliating that feeling with manifest and dazzling material advantage, or by creating such a situation as to give him the excuse of necessity. I regret being obliged to take a less sanguine view of our expectations from France, than may possibly reach you through other channels, but it is above all my duty to write you what I believe to be the truth in reference to the currents of public opinion. . . .[7]

[7] Henry Hotze to Judah P. Benjamin, September 26, 1863, *ibid.*, 916–17.

🐍 Secretary of State Benjamin himself was much more cosmopolitan and sophisticated than most Americans of his day, South or North. He agreed with the analysis presented by Hotze and was clearly among the vanguard of certain southern leaders who were secretly beginning to entertain some highly unorthodox, even revolutionary ideas concerning slavery:

. . . Your appreciation of the tone and temper of public opinion in France . . . , although not in accordance with the views of the other correspondents of the Department, concurs entirely in the conclusions to which I had arrived from the perusal of the principal organs of French journalism. It has been impossible to remain blind to the evidence of the articles which emanate from the best-known names in French literature. In what is perhaps the most powerful and influential of the French periodicals, La Revue des Deux Mondes, there is scarcely an article signed by the members of its able corps of contributors which does not contain some disparaging allusion to the South. Abolition sentiments are quietly assumed as philosophical axioms too self-evident to require comment or elaboration, and the result of this struggle is in all cases treated as a foregone conclusion, as nothing within the range of possibility except the subjugation of the South and the emancipation of the whole body of the negroes. The example of St. Domingo does not seem in the least to disturb the faith of these philanthropists in the entire justice and policy of a war waged for this end, and our resistance to the fate proposed for us is treated as a crime against liberty and civilization. The Emperor is believed by us to be sincerely desirous of putting an end to the war by the recognition of our independence, but, powerful as he is, he is too sagacious to act in direct contravention of the settled public opinion of his people while hampered by the opposition of the English Government. . . .[8]

🐍 Benjamin, like many other secretaries of state, found himself painfully squeezed between foreign and domestic realities. One of the most influential of the prosouthern books on the American crisis that appeared in Britain was *The American Union* by James Spence, a highly literate merchant in Liverpool. Spence's

---

[8] Benjamin to Hotze, January 9, 1864, *ibid.*, 993–94.

work came out in November, 1861. Although it went through numerous reprintings in England, was translated into German, and was published in Richmond in 1863, the book reflected the early period of the war when not only did Lincoln refuse to touch slavery, but when the United States Congress had passed and submitted to the states a Thirteenth Amendment (never ratified) that would bar any future amendment giving Congress the power to abolish slavery within the states.

To the embarrassment of the Confederates, however, their friend Spence dared to couple his sympathy for the South with an outspoken, even if moderate, plea for emancipation. Despite this fact Davis and Benjamin appointed Spence as a financial agent of the Confederacy. The Richmond *Enquirer,* which ultimately would drastically alter its own tune, attacked the Confederate state department because of Spence's appointment and growled (September 5, 1863) that it "could not remain silent when an accredited agent in Europe published his offensive reflections against our institutions; we could not believe the services of any abolitionist necessary to our cause."

Among the passages in Spence's book that offended sensitive Southerners was this carefully expressed hope—that the South itself might choose to conciliate the opinion of the "great civilized powers":

. . . If the Southern Confederacy maintain its independence, it will become its strongest desire to be received into the family of independent powers. It will clearly be allowable to our government when acknowledging that independence to obtain engagements in relation to slavery. Apart from the difficult subject of absolute emancipation (and in any rational view of the case, as necessary preliminaries to it), there are many less striking, but really important changes, which are clearly practicable, and which would ameliorate at once the condition of the slave, lessen his degradation, and educate him for further advances toward freedom. These changes could be made, too, without appreciable loss to the owner.

An exchange from slavery into serfdom would involve no insuperable difficulties. To prevent the separation of husband from wife, or parent from child; to substitute taskwork for unmeasured labor; to devise means for the prevention of cruel treatment—in short, to end the barbarities of the system of slavery, all this could be done with immeasurable advantage to the negro, and no real detriment to the owner. . . .

To any such suggestion to the government of a reconstructed Union the reply may be easily predicted. We should be warned of the presumption of attempting to interfere in matters entirely domestic; we should be reminded of the condition of various classes at home; some allusion might be made to the Declaration of Independence—possibly to Ireland; finally, the star spangled banner would wave over the whole. Let us suppose the same suggestions to be made to the government of the new power [the Confederacy]. If made in an earnest, and yet friendly tone, the probable reply would be: "Our system of labor, right or wrong, we have no immediate power to alter. But we desire to obtain the respect of other states, and especially of those whose good will is essential to our welfare, by making at once those amendments in it that are within our reach. We cannot desire a state of permanent conflict with the opinions of all the great civilized powers. We inherit a position we have not made and cannot escape from at will; but as far as our means extend we will endeavor to respond to the suggestions of friendly powers, and to enter into accordance with the spirit of the age."[9]

🐦 Antislavery sentiment such as expressed even by a southern partisan like Spence was by no means the only obstacle to the Anglo-French recognition that was so crucial to the Confederacy. But it was clearly an important complicating factor. It became even more of one when Lincoln announced in September, 1862, that as of the first day of 1863 he would, as commander in chief, take the step of declaring free the slaves of rebels. Consequently, on January 1, 1863, he issued his proclamation:

. . . Now, therefore, I, Abraham Lincoln, President of the United States, by virtue of the power in me vested as Commander-in-Chief of

[9] James Spence, *The American Union* (Richmond, 1863; 1st American ed., printed from 4th English ed.), 108–109.

the Army and Navy of the United States in time of actual armed rebellion against the authority and government of the United States, and
as a fit and necessary war measure for suppressing said rebellion, do
. . . order and designate as the States and parts of States wherein the
people, thereof, respectively, are this day in rebellion against the
United States the following, to wit: [the names of ten Confederate
states follow; excepted from the proclamation were Tennessee, thir-
teen reconquered parishes in Louisiana, forty-eight counties "designated as West Virginia," and seven counties in eastern Virginia that
were held by Federal authorities].

And by virtue of the power and for the purpose aforesaid, I do order
and declare that all persons held as slaves within said designated
States and parts of States are, and henceforward shall be, free; and
that the executive government of the United States, including the military and naval authorities thereof, will recognize and maintain the
freedom of said persons.

And I hereby enjoin the people so declared to be free to abstain
from all violence, unless in necessary self-defense; and I recommend
to them that, in all cases when allowed, they labor faithfully for reasonable wages.

And I further declare and make known that such persons of suitable
condition will be received into the armed service of the United States
to garrison forts, positions, stations, and other places, and to man ves-
sels of all sorts in said service.

And upon this act, sincerely believed to be an act of justice, warranted by the Constitution upon military necessity, I invoke the considerate judgment of mankind and the gracious favor of Almighty
God.[10]

☞ The various military, political, and diplomatic pressures that impelled Lincoln to alter his initial stand and to embrace emancipation as a means, a weapon, in his struggle to preserve the Union
need not be explored here. The point for this study is that now, as
Lincoln certainly intended, the South's problems were considerably compounded. Diplomatically, England and France no longer
faced the choice between a proslavery South and a North that
was neutral or silent concerning slavery in the states. In short,

[10] Henry Steele Commager (ed.), *Documents of American History* (2 vols.; New
York, 1935), 420–21.

Lincoln had made it more difficult for the European nations to consider the recognition of the Confederacy.

Politically, Lincoln's move struck a sensitive nerve in the South, for it spotlighted the difference in "interests" between the majority of the southern whites (and the larger part of the Confederate army) who owned no slave property and the powerful minority who did. In other words, until Lincoln made the war one partially but significantly against slavery, Southerners really had had no occasion to ponder and debate the question of whether they were or were not fighting to protect the property of a distinct minority of the white population. Lincoln's emancipation action, however, added a new element to the controversy within the Confederacy over the law exempting from conscription a planter, or his overseer, who had at least fifteen (later changed to twenty) slaves to supervise. Ever-present class tensions, tensions that were only partially patched over by white racial solidarity, grew sharper as the war dragged on; and grumbling increased within the Confederacy about its being a rich man's war but a poor man's fight.

Most important of all, Lincoln's simultaneous programs of emancipation and recruitment of Negro soldiers threatened to weaken the South militarily as they also opened a significant new reservoir of manpower for the Union army. The role of the Negroes in the Federal armies of the Civil War has become widely known through several fine studies. One of the best and more recent of these is *The Negro's Civil War* by Professor James McPherson. It vividly demonstrates that a large number of blacks actively participated in the war to preserve the Union and end slavery. This was particularly true of nearly two hundred thousand who were recruited into the Federal army, mostly from among the slaves freed by Union forces in conquered portions of the South.

By the late summer of 1864, Lincoln could answer the racist taunts of his political foes in the North with an assertion that was widely reported and commented upon in the South: "No human power can subdue this rebellion without using the Emancipation lever as I have done. Freedom has given us the control of 200,000 able bodied men, born & raised on southern soil. It will give us more yet. . . . My enemies condemn my emancipation policy. Let them prove by the history of this war, that we can restore the Union without it.'' [11]

Certainly in early 1863, neither Lincoln nor Jefferson Davis could envision the full impact that the new northern policies of emancipation and recruiting Negro soldiers would have. A few days after Lincoln's final proclamation of January 1, 1863, Davis in his message to the Confederate Congress could only declare in cold fury that Lincoln was desperately trying to encourage insurrections among the slaves:

The public journals of the North have been received, containing a proclamation, dated on the 1st day of the present month, signed by the President of the United States, in which he orders and declares all slaves within ten of the States of the Confederacy to be free, except such as are found within certain districts now occupied in part by the armed forces of the enemy. We may well leave it to the instincts of that common humanity which a beneficent Creator has implanted in the breasts of our fellowmen of all countries to pass judgment on a measure by which several millions of human beings of an inferior race, peaceful and contented laborers in their sphere, are doomed to extermination, while at the same time they are encouraged to a general assassination of their masters by the insidious recommendation ''to abstain from violence unless in necessary self-defense.'' Our own detestation of those who have attempted the most execrable measure recorded in the history of guilty man is tempered by profound contempt for the impotent rage which it discloses. . . .

In its political aspect this measure possesses great significance, and to it in this light I invite your attention. It affords to our whole people the complete and crowning proof of the true nature of the designs of the party which elevated to power the present occupant of the Presidential chair at Washington and which sought to conceal its purpose by every variety of artful device and by the perfidious use of the most solemn and repeated pledges on every possible occasion. . . .

The people of this Confederacy, then, cannot fail to receive this proclamation as the fullest vindication of their own sagacity in foresee-

[11] Lincoln interview of August 19, 1864, as reported in diary of Joseph T. Mills, in Roy P. Basler (ed.), *The Collected Works of Abraham Lincoln* (9 vols.; New Brunswick, N.J., 1953), VII, 507.

ing the uses to which the dominant party in the United States intended from the beginning to apply their power, nor can they cease to remember with devout thankfulness that it is to their own vigilance in resisting the first stealthy progress of approaching despotism that they owe their escape from consequences now apparent to the most skeptical. This proclamation will have another salutary effect in calming the fears of those who have constantly evinced the apprehension that this war might end by some reconstruction of the old Union or some renewal of close political relations with the United States. These fears have never been shared by me, nor have I ever been able to perceive on what basis they could rest. But the proclamation affords the fullest guarantee of the impossibility of such a result; it has established a state of things which can lead to but one of three possible consequences —the extermination of the slaves, the exile of the whole white population from the Confederacy, or absolute and total separation of these States from the United States.

This proclamation is also an authentic statement by the Government of the United States of its inability to subjugate the South by force of arms, and as such must be accepted by neutral nations, which can no longer find any justification in withholding our just claims to formal recognition. It is also in effect an intimation to the people of the North that they must prepare to submit to a separation, now become inevitable, for that people are too acute not to understand a restoration of the Union has been rendered forever impossible by the adoption of a measure which from its very nature neither admits of retraction nor can coexist with union.[12]

☞ Echoing Davis, the Confederate Congress in a later address to the southern people displayed the obsession with the past, with history, that was already a hallmark of much southern thinking:

. . . These cruelties and atrocities of the enemy have been exceeded by their malicious and bloodthirsty purposes and machinations in reference to the slaves. Early in this war President Lincoln averred his constitutional inability and personal unwillingness to interfere with the domestic institutions of the States and the relation between master and servant. Prudential considerations may have been veiled

[12] James D. Richardson (ed.), *The Messages and Papers of Jefferson Davis and the Confederacy* (with introduction by Allan Nevins, 2 vols.; New York, 1966), I, 290–93.

under conscientious scruples, for [Secretary of State] Seward, in a confidential instruction to Mr. Adams, the minister to Great Britain, on 10th of March, 1862, said:

If the Government of the United States should precipitately decree the immediate abolition of slavery, it would reinvigorate the declining insurrection in every part of the South.

Subsequent reverses and the refractory rebelliousness of the seceded States caused a change of policy, and Mr. Lincoln issued his celebrated proclamation, a mere *brutum fulmen* liberating the slaves in the "insurrectionary districts." On the 24th of June, 1776, one of the reasons assigned by Pennsylvania for her separation from the mother country was that in her sister colonies the "King had excited the negroes to revolt" and "to imbrue their hands in the blood of their masters in a manner unpracticed by civilized nations." This, probably, had reference to the proclamation of Dunmore, the last royal Governor of Virginia, in 1775, declaring freedom to all servants or negroes, if they would join "for the reducing the colony to a proper sense of its duty." The invitation to the slaves to rise against their masters, the suggested insurrection, caused, says Bancroft, "a thrill of indignation to run through Virginia, effacing all differences of party, and rousing one strong, impassioned purpose to drive away the insolent power by which it had been put forth." A contemporary annalist, adverting to the same proclamation, said, "It was received with the greatest horror in all the colonies."

"The policy adopted by Dunmore," says Lawrence in his Notes on Wheaton, "of arming the slaves against their masters was not pursued during the war of the Revolution; and when negroes were taken by the English they were not considered otherwise than as property and plunder." Emancipation of slaves as a war measure has been severely condemned and denounced by the most eminent publicists in Europe and the United States. The United States, "in their diplomatic relations, have ever maintained," says the Northern authority just quoted, "that slaves were private property, and for them, as such, they have repeatedly received compensation from England." Napoleon I was never induced to issue a proclamation for the emancipation of the serfs in his war with Russia. He said:

I could have armed against her a part of her population by proclaiming the liberty of the serfs. A great number of villages asked it of me, but I refused to avail myself of a measure which would have devoted to death thousands of families.

In the discussion growing out of the treaty of peace of 1814 and the proffered mediation of Russia, the principle was maintained by the United States that "the emancipation of [an] enemy's slaves is not among the acts of legitimate warfare." In the instructions from John Quincy Adams, as Secretary of State, to Mr. Middleton, at Saint Petersburg, October 18, 1820, it is said:

The British have broadly asserted the right of emancipating slaves (private property) as a legitimate right of war. No such right is acknowledged as a law of war by writers who admit any limitation. The right of putting to death all prisoners in cold blood, and without special cause, might as well be pretended to be a law of war, or the right to use poisoned weapons, or to assassinate.

Disregarding the teachings of the approved writers on international law, and the practice and claims of his own Government in its purer days, President Lincoln has sought to convert the South into a San Domingo, by appealing to the cupidity, lusts, ambition, and ferocity of the slave. Abraham Lincoln is but the lineal descendant of Dunmore, and the impotent malice of each was foiled by the fidelity of those who, by the meanness of the conspirators, would only, if successful, have been seduced into idleness, filth, vice, beggary, and death.

But we tire of these indignities and enormities. They are too sickening for recital. History will hereafter pillory those who committed and encouraged such crimes in immortal infamy. . . .[13]

☞   To the great satisfaction of the Confederates, and the dismay of at least some Northerners, no significant slave insurrection occurred. This was certainly not because the slaves were happy in their bondage, as white Southerners constantly reassured themselves. The reasons for the absence of insurrections, even after Lincoln's proclamation, are complex and not of principal concern here. But surely a major factor was the ambivalence that characterized the slave's relationship to the master and to the master's family. That is, as Professor Eugene Genovese, a prominent his-

---

[13] "Address of Congress to the People of the Confederate States, January 22, 1864," in *The War of the Rebellion: A Compilation of the Official Records of the Union and Confederate Armies* (73 vols., 128 parts; Washington, 1880–1901), Series IV, Vol. III, 132-33, hereinafter cited as *O.R.*

torian of slavery, has recently pointed out, many slaves could, and clearly did, accept or at least tolerate their masters as human beings but at the same time fiercely hate the fact of bondage.[14] Needless to say, this was an insight which few nineteenth century white Southerners seemed capable of gaining, or if they did gain it, they certainly never expressed it publicly until, as will be discussed below, a few bold leaders did so toward the end of the war.

Furthermore, if the "grapevine" system of spreading news and rumors among the slaves functioned as well as many historians now believe it did, the blacks may well have realized, however dimly, that at the same time Lincoln held out the promise of emancipation with one hand, with the other he offered colonization of the Negroes outside of the United States as the best solution to the problem of racial adjustment. And to nervous northern whites, who generally lived none too happily with the approximately 1 percent of the northern population that was black, Lincoln explained in his second annual message of December, 1862, that emancipation would actually lessen the number of Negroes who might wish to flee North. "And in any event," he coldly concluded, "can not the North decide for itself whether to receive them?"[15]

At any rate, blacks neither resorted to insurrection nor did they, even when opportunities arose, evince any burning zeal to go North. But, as mentioned earlier, they did join the Union army, and their gradually increasing military significance by no means went unnoticed in the South.

[14] Eugene Genovese, "American Slaves and Their History," *New York Review of Books*, December 3, 1970, pp. 34–43.
[15] Fred L. Israel (ed.), *The State of the Union Messages of the Presidents* (3 vols.; New York, 1966), II, 1,082–1,083.

≈§ CHAPTER II §≈

Early Proposals
for a Change

WITH THE YANKEES increasingly resorting to the use of Negro soldiers in 1863, numerous but scattered Confederates began to suggest in the newspapers and in letters to officials in Richmond that the South should make greater military use of adult male slaves. Paradoxically, in light of the Deep South's historic reputation for crying "Never!" to any demand for racial change, the first calls for a Confederate policy of emancipation came from Mississippi, Alabama, and Louisiana.

Undoubtedly the triumph of Federal armies in that region and the miserable devastation that war left behind were major influences toward unorthodox thinking. Federal forces captured New Orleans in the spring of 1862 and began steadily expanding their control of the Mississippi River. Long before Vicksburg fell to General Grant on July 4, 1863, much of Mississippi had been overrun by Union armies and the capital, Jackson, had been captured in May, 1863. "Mississippi's heart was broken but not its spirit," according to one historian of the war in that state.[1] Perhaps, too, the very real but still unthinkable possibility of defeat—unless drastic steps were taken—began to lurk in the minds of men in that part of the Confederacy. At any rate the Jackson *Mississippian* (as reprinted in the Montgomery, Alabama, *Weekly Mail*, September 9, 1863) dared to say aloud that slavery should be sacrificed for the sake of the South's national independence:

[1] John K. Bettersworth, *Mississippi in the Confederacy* (1961; repr. ed., New York, 1970), 142.

EMPLOYMENT OF NEGROES IN THE ARMY.

. . . We must either employ the negroes ourselves, or the enemy will employ them against us. While the enemy retains so much of our territory, they are, in their present avocation and status, a dangerous element, a source of weakness. They are no longer negative characters, but subjects of volition as other people. They must be taught to know that this is peculiarly the country of the black man—that in no other is the climate and soil so well adapted to his nature and capacity. He must further be taught that it is his duty, as well as the white man's, to defend his home with arms, if need be.

We are aware that there are persons who shudder at the idea of placing arms in the hands of negroes, and who are not willing to trust them under any circumstances. The negro, however, is proverbial for his faithfulness under kind treatment. He is an affectionate, grateful being, and we are persuaded that the fears of such persons are groundless.

There are in the slaveholding States four millions of negroes, and out of this number at least six hundred thousand able-bodied men capable of bearing arms can be found. Lincoln proposes to free and arm them against us. There are already fifty thousand of them in the Federal ranks. Lincoln's scheme has worked well so far, and if no[t] checkmated, will most assuredly be carried out. The Confederate Government must adopt a counter policy. It must thwart the enemy in this gigantic scheme, at all hazards, and if nothing else will do it—if the negroes cannot be made effective and trustworthy to the Southern cause in no other way, we solemnly believe it is the duty of this Government to forestall Lincoln and proceed at once to take steps for the emancipation or liberation of the negroes itself. Let them be declared free, placed in the ranks, and told to fight for their homes and country.

We are fully sensible of the grave importance of the question, but the inexorable logic of events has forced it upon us. We must deal with it, then, not with fear and trembling—not as timid, time-serving men —but with a boldness, a promptness and a determination which the exigency requires, and which should ever characterize the action of a people resolved to sacrifice everything for liberty. It is true, that such a step would revolutionize our whole industrial system—that it would, to a great extent, impoverish the country and be a dire calamity to both the negro and the white race of this and the Old World; but better this than the loss of the negroes, the country and liberty.

If Lincoln succeeds in arming our slaves against us, he will succeed in making them our masters. He will reverse the social order of things at the South. Whereas, if he is checkmated in time, our liberties will remain intact; the land will be ours, and the industrial system of the country still controlled by Southern men.

Such action on the part of our Government would place our people in a purer and better light before the world. It would disabuse the European mind of a grave error in regard to the cause of our separation. It would prove to them that there were higher and holier motives which actuated our people than the mere love of property. It would show that, although slavery is one of the principles that we started to fight for, yet it falls far short of being the chief one; that, for the sake of our liberty, we are capable of any personal sacrifice; that we regard the emancipation of slaves, and the consequent loss of property as an evil infinitely less than the subjugation and enslavement of ourselves; that it is not a war exclusively for the privilege of holding negroes in bondage. It would prove to our soldiers, three-fourths of whom never owned a negro, that it is not "the rich man's war and the poor man's fight," but a war for the most sacred of all principles, for the dearest of all rights—the right to govern ourselves. It would show them that the rich man who owned slaves was not willing to jeopardize the precious liberty of the country by his eagerness to hold on to his slaves, but that he was ready to give them up and sacrifice his interest in them whenever the cause demanded it. It would lend a new impetus, a new enthusiasm, a new and powerful strength to the cause, and place our success beyond a peradventure. It would at once remove all the odium which attached to us on account of slavery, and bring us speedy recognition, and, if necessary, intervention.

We sincerely trust that the Southern people will be found willing to make any and every sacrifice which the establishment of our independence may require. Let it never be said that to preserve slavery we were willing to wear the chains of bondage ourselves—that the very avarice which prompted us to hold on to the negro for the sake of the money invested in him, riveted upon us shackles more galling and bitter than ever a people yet endured. Let not slavery prove a barrier to our independence. If it is found in the way—if it proves an insurmountable obstacle to the achievement of our liberty and separate nationality, away with it! Let it perish. We must make up our minds to one solemn duty, the first duty of the patriot, and that is, to save ourselves from the rapacious North, WHATEVER THE COST.

☞ Seeing themselves directly in the path of unchecked Federal armies, Alabamians were no less inspired, or frightened, than their neighbors to the west. The Montgomery *Weekly Mail* (September 2, 1863), while dodging the question of emancipation, urged that the time to arm the slaves had come.

The Report from the [legislature's] Committee on Federal Relations urging that it is the duty of Congress to provide by law, for the employment in the military service of the Confederate States, in such situations, and in such numbers, as may be found necessary, the able bodied slaves of the country whether as pioneers, sappers, and miners, cooks, nurses, teamsters, or as soldiers, was debated in the [Alabama] House on Friday. The chief objection to the bill was made on the ground that negroes employed as soldiers would not be reliable. Mr. Clarke of Lawrence, stated the case of his own servant who had grown up with him from boyhood, who had gone with him to the army and had shared with him, share and share alike, every article of food and clothing, had seized the first opportunity which presented of deserting him, and joining the Yankees. He inferred from this that negroes, even those who had been treated the most favorably by their masters, were so ungrateful, that they would desert in the hour of danger and difficulty. Mr. Bethea, who warmly advocated the measure reported by the committee, said that he had every confidence in the faithfulness and devotion of the negroes to their masters; that the love of home with the negroes was a peculiar feature in their nature, and that when it became a question of defending these homes from the ravages of the enemy, the negroes would, if employed as soldiers, aid their masters in repelling the Yankees. In the case mentioned by Mr. Clarke, he said, that if Mr. Clarke had treated his negro boy as a servant and not as a companion, the result would have been different. The proper way to manage negroes, he contended, was to treat them as servants, and if you do this, you may always depend upon their faithfulness and obedience.

But little was said in the debate about our historical position on the slavery question. The argument which goes to the exclusion of negroes as soldiers, is founded on the status of the negro. It is stated that the people of the Confederate States have been accustomed to regard the African race as inferior to the Caucasian or white race, born to servitude and not entitled to equality; that the proposition to make them soldiers is a practical ignoring of their normal and actual status, as maintained by Southern statesmen and the Southern people; that it is a practical acknowledgment of equality, from which we cannot escape in our dealings with the enemy, however much we may strive to qualify and explain; that so far as we should adopt the policy, we would be compelled to consent to the exchange of black prisoners for white, man for man, and what would that be but a practical equalization of the races?

Now we acknowledge the force of these objections. But what are we to do in the present emergency? We must deal with facts as we find them, and as they are at work in the operations of this infernal war. We may reason forever about the difference of races, but that is not really the question which we have to encounter and overcome. The question is, how are we to meet the enemy in the new phase which he has given to this war by the employment of negro troops? . . . We are forced by the necessity of our condition—by the insolence and barbarity of the enemy—by his revengeful and demoniacal spirit—to take a step which is revolting to every sentiment of pride, and to every principle that governed our institutions before the war. But the war has made great changes, and we must meet those changes, for the sake of preserving our very existence. It is a matter of necessity, therefore, that we should use every means within our reach to defeat the enemy. One of these, and the only one which will checkmate him, is the employment of negroes in the military service of the Confederacy. Their employment in this capacity will relieve the present difficulty about exchanges, for then black will be exchanged for black, and we shall not suffer the exquisite mortification of having our gallant soldiers hanged, in retaliation for the hanging of a Yankee black-guard.

We have long believed it impolitic for the South to employ negroes in the army, and up to the time that the committee made its report, we were averse to a measure which was apparently fruitful of injury to our cause. But when we take into consideration the actual condition of

things—the sanguinary character of the war in which we are engaged
—the employment of negro troops by the enemy—his stealing our
slaves and converting them into soldiers—we reach the conclusion that
it is better for us to use our negroes for our defense than that the
Yankees should use them against us. Can any man say how long South
Alabama will be sacred from the presence of the enemy? We know
that Grant is about to press upon us from the Mississippi river, and
that Rosecrans is menacing us with an advance from the Tennessee.
The enemy have raiding parties organizing in North Mississippi and
North Alabama. This presents a perilous picture. The figures in that
picture are full of meaning to us, who dwell near the banks of the
Alabama. Should the enemy penetrate to this section of the State, what
becomes of our negroes? Shall we run away with them, as many of the
Mississippians did with their slaves, and if we do where shall we run
to? Georgia? There may be as much peril in Georgia as in Alabama.
What then? The enemy will seize the negroes everywhere, and organize them as soldiers, to burn and desolate the country, and extirpate
their masters. This will certainly be the consequence of a Yankee invasion of our section. But may we not arrest this catastrophe by avail-
ing ourselves of the services of these negroes? They must be used for or
against us. There is no alternative. To this complexion must it come,
and if this be a true picture of the condition of the South whenever
the Yankee army has made its appearance, why should we claim an
exemption for Alabama? It occurs to us that the Legislature should
have taken some action on the subject irrespective of Congress. The
time calls for action, and we should be ready to respond by meeting the
danger boldly.

☞ As the Montgomery newspaper suggested, the Alabama legislators, although no doubt as enamored of states' rights as most
other Southerners, looked to the Confederate government in
Richmond for leadership and action in the matter of the military
utilization of the slaves:

. . . That in the opinion of this General Assembly public sentiment
and the exigencies of the country require that all able-bodied men in
the service of the Confederate States as clerks, or employed in any
other capacity in any of the quartermaster or commissary departments

of the Government, should be put in active military service without delay, and that their places be filled with soldiers or citizens who are unfit for active military service.

Second. *Be it further resolved,* That this General Assembly are of the opinion that the details of soldiers from the Army to labor in workshops, foundries, and other places, and upon railroads, have been entirely too numerous, and in many instances useless, and that in the opinion of this body slaves should be required by the Confederate States to take [the] places of all those soldiers who are detailed to labor in the places herein mentioned, when it can be done without prejudice to the service, and that prompt and efficient measures should at once be adopted to effect these purposes.

Third. *Be it further resolved,* That this General Assembly earnestly calls the attention of the President and Secretary of War of the Confederate States to this subject as requiring immediate and energetic action on the part of the Government.

Fourth. *Be it further resolved,* That this General Assembly recommend to Congress such a modification of the exemption law as will correct the evils herein named, and thereby increase the strength of our military force.

Fifth. *Be it further resolved,* That in view of the fact that the Government of the United States has determined to put in the field negro soldiers, and are enlisting and drafting the slaves of the people of the South, this General Assembly submits for the consideration of Congress the propriety and policy of using in some effective way a certain percentage of the male slave population of the Confederate States, and to perform such services as Congress may by law direct.

Sixth. *Be it further resolved,* That the Governor transmit a copy of these resolutions to the President of the Confederate States, the Secretary of War, and a copy to each of our Senators and Representatives from this State in the Confederate Congress.[2]

☞ A few political leaders were beginning to share the unconventional ideas expressed by the *Mississippian* and the *Weekly Mail.* John B. Jones, the war clerk and diarist in Richmond, commented

[2] Joint Resolutions of the Alabama Senate and House of Representatives, August 29, 1863, in *O.R.,* Series IV, Vol. II, 767.

on a letter from Alabama that he apparently did not take too seriously:

July 31st [1863].—Hon. E. S. Dargan, member of Congress [from Alabama], writes from Mobile that Mississippi is nearly subdued, and Alabama is almost exhausted. He says our recent disasters, and Lee's failure in Pennsylvania [at Gettysburg], have nearly ruined us, and the destruction must be complete unless France and England can be induced to interfere in our behalf. He never believed they would intervene unless we agreed to abolish slavery; and he would embrace even that alternative to obtain their aid. He says the people are fast losing all hope of achieving their independence; and a slight change of policy on the part of Lincoln (pretermitting confiscation, I suppose) would put an end to the revolution and the Confederate States Government. Mr. D. has an unhappy disposition.[3]

☞ Writing gloomily of desperate conditions and drastic policies in a private letter, as Congressman Dargan had done, was one thing. But "speaking right out in meeting" was another. James L. Alcorn, prominent Whig leader in Mississippi and vociferous critic of Jefferson Davis and his administration, did just that in an address to the legislature of his state:

. . . Secession, he said, was purely a matter of principle in the outset, [but] now its success was a question of life and death. The Southern people had no hope except in the Confederate Government. If they were base enough to ask a restoration of the relations which existed with the North before the war, Lincoln would not permit them to come back, he would receive them only as crouching menials, divested of property, honor and hope for the future. All therefore, he could promise himself or his children for the future must come from the Confederate Government.

The Administration had blundered—in fact it had been a series of blunders. We do not endorse this assertion in its full extent but, unfortunately, there is more truth in it than is palatable. Lincoln had completely out-generaled the President of the Confederate States in the field of diplomacy. While our commissioners had persistently held out the idea that the war waged against us was for the purpose of dis-

[3] John B. Jones, *A Rebel War Clerk's Diary* (2 vols.; Philadelphia, 1866), I, 391.

turbing our rights and abolishing the institution of slavery, Lincoln as persistently denied it. The more Lincoln proclaimed in the beginning that he did not intend to interfere with slavery, the more we and our commissioners vociferated that the war was for the sole purpose of abolishing slavery. This sort of diplomacy on our part had the effect of prejudicing us in the eyes of Europe. We struggled to make it appear to the world that it was a war on our part exclusively and solely to preserve slavery, forgetting that this was exactly the thing France and England were hostile to—exactly the thing to set them against us. Lincoln at length saw the point. He accepted the issue we had, both at home and abroad, so pertinaciously insisted upon. He issued his proclamation of emancipation, and at one blow blasted all our hopes of recognition by either France or England.

The mistake was, we placed the cause of the war upon a false ground. It was not exclusively to save slavery. It had a higher purpose—the vindication of the sovereignty of the States and our inalienable rights purchased by the blood of our forefathers—the right to govern ourselves according to our own wishes.

Gen. Alcorn contended that the power of diplomacy might yet be made available. We might agree to submit the adjustment of the slavery question to foreign nations with the understanding that emancipation should be postponed at least twenty years. By that time the interest and justice of the institution would become apparent to the world, and even abolition England and France would find it adverse to their interests and convictions of humanity to emancipate at all. If otherwise, if the whole world are irrevocably set against slavery and remains firm in its convictions, we must make up our minds to fight the world as legal slavery is made the corner-stone of our republic.

If the Southern people fail in establishing their independence it would not be through any want of courage and zeal on their part. It would be from either a want of statesmanship or a want of generalship on the part of our leaders. The slavery question, as at present understood, is an insurmountable barrier to recognition. If we do not overcome it, or pal[l]iate it by diplomacy, we must go on an unrecognized nation, and fight against the physical power of the North and the moral force of Europe. The question should be met by our Government.

These are forcible suggestions—they bear the stamp of a clear, a bold and sagacious mind. It may be, however, that we have not given Gen. Alcorn's idea on this subject with perfect accuracy. We heard him at a disadvantage, and write only the impression made upon our minds by this part of his speech.[4]

☞ Alcorn's views, so heretical to most Southerners, did not go unchallenged. An incensed letter-writer ("J. H.") to the Mobile, Alabama, *Register and Advertiser* (November 25, 1863) flailed out at those Southerners who would do any thing other than defend to the death the institutions that "the Lord has given to us":

'Tis a base abandonment of reason to resign our right of thought; 'tis a base abandonment of a righteous cause to advocate its success on false grounds, or under false pretences. This idea is suggested on reading a synopsis of Gen. Alcorn's speech before the General Assembly of Mississippi. He is said to take the ground [that] whereas Lincoln by diplomatic strategy, or in other words, by pretending one thing when he meant another, managed to outgeneral our Commissioners at foreign courts, that now we should pursue the same course. That because our Commissioners manfully, truthfully and persistently alleged that "the war against us was for the purpose of disturbing our rights and abolishing the institution of slavery"—a fact patent to all the world from the platform on which he was elected, and the declaration made by him that "the Union cannot exist half slave and half free, and that it must be all one or the other"—and that thereby the sympathies of foreign nations have been alienated from us, on account of their anti-slavery bias, *we* should now take the cue from him—stultify our cause and falsify every argument and plea we have made, surrender the principle that a people have "a right, and it is their duty to institute government in *such form as to them shall seem best,*" and that a free people cannot admit interference with its internal affairs and cravenly say to European nations, "we abandon the right of self-government and will submit our views of right, our ideas of independence, our

[4] Jackson *Mississippian*, November 20, 1863 (?). A xeroxed copy of her transcript of an undated clipping from the *Mississippian* was kindly furnished by Professor Lillian A. Pereyra, whose *James Lusk Alcorn: Persistent Whig* (Baton Rouge, 1966), I have found helpful. My dating of this clipping is based partly on the document that follows next.

freedoms to your dictation.'' And for what? Ay, what is to be gained by our ignoring everything we have been and are struggling for? Gen. Alcorn's proposition is that ''the power of diplomacy may yet be made available'' (that sort of diplomacy now known, in the nations where we are advised to use it, by its synonym of Sewardism). ''We might agree to submit (ay, that's the word that tells its nature, *submit*) the adjustment of the slavery question to foreign nations, with the understanding that emancipation should be postponed twenty years,'' &c.— O, most gracious counsellor, a very Daniel come to judgment! And then what? Having *submitted* to a fanatical idea, instead of manfully battling it with the force of justice and of truth, having surrendered the freedom we claim as a free people to ''institute government as to us shall seem best,'' what is the boon so precious we are to look for in return? Why, ''by that time (those precious 20 years that foreign nations, through our own connivance, have magnanimously *postponed* emancipation to) the interest and justice of the institution would become apparent to the world, and even abolition England and France would find it adverse to their interests and convictions of humanity to emancipate at all''!! Was ever such sagacity seen before?—such deep subtility?—such profound wisdom? Surely the spirit of a Machiavelli is among us. . . .

But from such a man, in such a position, the promulgation of such views is too serious for mere badinage. Slavery, as it exists with us, is either wrong or right. If wrong, if not warranted of God, if not sanctioned by the great teacher of Christianity, if not consistent with good morals, if not beneficial as a system of labor to the laborerer [*sic*], for his physical and moral welfare, let us, ourselves, without diplomatic chicanery or Seward-like attempts at over-reaching, amend the wrong, and, as fast as possible, free the slave. *That* would be magnanimous and noble. But if it be right—and we are firmly convinced it is so; if it be, as we deem it, a trust placed in our hands by the All-wise; if sanctioned, as we believe it to have been, by the Saviour, the teacher of faith, hope and charity, of the reciprocal duties of the master and servant, of the bond and free; if it tends, as those who have most carefully noted its working feel is demonstrated, to the physical, moral and mental welfare of the race; if, as a system of labor, it be, as no one can deny who will faithfully compare it with other ''hewers of wood and drawers of water,'' the most conducive to the happiness, comfort and enjoyment of the laborer; if the relation between master and slave be generally that of patriarchal and child-like affection, and if the interests of both are improved and elevated by it, it would be a "base abandonment" of duty, honor and the trust God has placed in our hands, to ignore its obligations, or to desert its custody or defense. If it be wrong, away with it! If it be right, defend it, our cause and our country, to the last. If it be a trust from God, as we religiously believe, *He* will "give us strength to push down those who rise up against us," and in His own good time, and in His own way, will give to us the victory. No compromise, therefore, but a stern, unbending, inflexible determination to do our duty, and defend that which the Lord has given to us.

☞   As the above letter shows, the Mobile *Register* opened its columns to those who placed slavery at the heart of the southern cause. The influential editor of the newspaper, John Forsyth, did not share that viewpoint. Destined to be one of the major supporters in the Deep South of President Davis' later program for employing slaves militarily, the Mobile *Register* (November 13, 1863) foreshadowed legislation soon to be enacted by the Confederate Congress:

It has been a subject of frequent remark, in Alabama as well as elsewhere, where negroes were needed for work upon the military defences, that planters should show so great a reluctance to furnishing them. Fortifications are essential to the successful prosecution of war; or, at least, if they are dispensed with, a larger force of soldiers is needed to occupy and protect exposed positions. Taking the works at Mobile for an example, we feel secure behind them because we know that the enemy are aware of our well fortified positions; whereas, if this point were left exposed, an army of thirty thousand men would not have been more than [would be] necessary to secure us from an attack by the enemy after the fall of Vicksburg. For every negro, then, that the planter fails to furnish for the work of constructing fortifications, not merely one, but several soldiers have to be added to the defensive force —in other words, the planter is more ready to contribute his sons than his slaves to the war; for it amounts to this.

It is true the planters do not view the subject in this light, but they offer divers excuses, more or less plausible, for their reluctance, the most prominent of which is the inequality of the burden, it being made to bear upon those who are willing to aid the country, while others escape. If, in consequence of their delinquency, the negroes are not forthcoming, and impressment has to be resorted to, complaints of unfairness are made; and finally all the sickness and mortality which occurs among the negro laborers is charged by the masters to neglect on the part of superintendents and physicians.

As far as the question of sickness is concerned, there is no doubt that the way the business is managed increases it; for instead of a force of thoroughly seasoned negroes being constantly employed, hardly have they become acclimated before the term for which they were drafted expires, and a new levy is made, of men who have to go through the seasoning process before their full efficiency can be made available. There are other objections to the practice of impressing negroes for a limited time, the only one of which that we will advert to being the expense of transportation back and forward.

It has been suggested that a better arrangement in all respects, would be to make a permanent levy or draft of a certain proportion of the slave population, to be organized as a corps of sappers, for service during the war. To the negroes thus employed, the Confederate authorities would furnish rations and clothing, and pay their masters at the rate of say $11 a month for ordinary laborers, and for mechanics as high as $30 [? figure blurred]. The negroes should be examined by a medical officer, and if unsound, should be rejected. Such as were approved should be appraised by two persons, one on behalf of the Confederate States, the other on that of the master, and in case of death while in the service, the appraised value should be paid to the master.

By a comparison of the last census with the preceding, and a proper allowance for the increase during the last three years, it will be found that a levy of one tenth of the male slaves in Alabama between the ages of 18 and 45, would give a force of upwards of 6,000 for this purpose.

The advantages of the plan are manifold. First, it would work equitably; next, the expense of transporting negroes back and forward every sixty days would be done away with; third, the negroes once acclimated would be healthier than when employed as they now are; fourth, after being properly trained to the work which they would have to perform, they would be more efficient; and finally, the quasi military discipline to which they would be made to conform would increase that efficiency. Indeed, it is not easy to enumerate all the advantages of such a system.

Such a plan is certainly worthy the consideration of our legislators, for as things are now managed, much dissatisfaction exists, not to speak of the expensive nature of the arrangement. Had such a system been in operation a year and a half ago, there is little doubt that the works around our city would have been constructed at half the expense which has actually been incurred.

☞ Probing deeper, the *Register* (November 26, 1863) chose to deny that slavery was the rock-bottom cause of the war. It also compared and contrasted, from a southern vantage point, of course, the North's and the South's attitudes toward and relationships with the Negroes:

The idea has been prevalent to both belligerent sections that the present war had its origin in the existence of negro slavery at the South. This is a plausible but mistaken notion. It was the occasion and the ostensible subject of dispute, but not the cause. The causes lay far deeper, and were to be found in antagonism of character and interest; in distinctive differences of habit, character, modes of thought, political dissent, and ideas of government radically and irreconcilably opposed. These had produced long since a general alienation of feeling. The Yankee regarded the Southron with envy and malignant dislike; the Southron regarded the Yankee with suspicion and contempt. This state of things was tacitly but universally recognized. The Southron bore himself proudly in conscious dignity and honor; abode by the faith of compacts, and maintained the supremacy of law. The Yankee plied his genius of invention; out-traded, out-voted, and out-managed the Southron. When territory was to be pre-occupied, he sent out the scum of Europe to prevent the more tardy march of Southern agricultural enterprise. He took bounties by legislation, and pleaded for liberality and concession. He stole the negro because he hated and envied his master. He invoked the mob and defied the law. He educated his children to hate the people of the South. His literature, his religion, his pulpit ministrations, his politics, and his commerce were converted into so many engines to diffuse the leaven of deadly hate against his Southern brethren. He bided his time to be strong enough to disfranchise the South by the *forms* of law. He had proclaimed a purpose to environ our land with a cordon of hostile States, and cause our *institution* to sting itself to death, like a scorpion encircled with fire!

When he got the negro, he wronged him, cheated him, starved him, and abandoned him to die in sickness. He has shown himself as cruel to the slave as he was vindictive toward the master. With such a people it was impossible to live under the same government. We were in feeling as much bound to the Austrian as to the Yankee; and he loved any people on earth more than the people of the South. Negro slavery was a very attractive and popular, and convenient bone of contention. But some other bone would have been found if this had been wanting. This special bone combined many advantages. It united religious fanaticism and political licentiousness. It acquired some countenance from Europe. And this, therefore, was made the keystone of the coalition. But all elements of opposition and hate already and antecedently existed, and it was a foregone determination to put down the South, and have dominion over her people and her property.

We protest against the theory that this is a war for the negroes; it is a war for constitutional liberty, and the rights of self-government. Our revolutionary sires never endured the one-tenth degree of the provocation and injustice from the British government which the South had already endured at the hands of the Yankee. With any foreign power we would have dared a war for the same reasons, any given year of the last dozen years. It was not domestic slavery in itself, but it was intolerable injustice; never-ceasing abuse and misrepresentation; and the most shameless and flagrant disregard of the faith of solemn covenants. But the negro is still made the object of discussion.—The foe not only steals the negro for the purpose of robbery, but he has determined as far as practicable to convert him into a Yankee soldier for the subjugation of his master.

Now, this scheme is fraught with more practical danger to the South than our people seem yet to have apprehended. *It must be prevented at all hazards.* We do not hesitate to affirm that our Government ought to have adopted, regardless of consequences, such retaliatory measures as would have intimidated our foe. Is there not good reason to believe that if the Government delays to adopt a policy bold enough, and stern enough, and efficient enough, to put a stop at once to this uncivilized, unwarrantable and infernal scheme of the Yankees, the Southern armies will do it for themselves, and for their wives and children, without further consulting our weak kneed representatives at Richmond? It were better that the *black flag* were raised, and war to the *knife* proclaimed, than to permit the foe to adopt the means to force our sons to meet their own slaves on the field, fighting for the cowardly cutthroats who thus mean to destroy us, and occupy our land!

But with respect to the military use to be made by the South of her slave population there is some difference of opinion. Some hold that it is not safe, in any event, to employ our slaves as soldiers, and that such a proceeding would be incompatible with the maintenance of the institution itself. The answer to this is that Yankee success is death to the institution, as well as to its masters, and that any peril should be confronted to avoid it. So that it is a question of necessity—a question of a choice of evils at last. We hold that it is not only legitimate but a safe and prudent policy to fight an enemy whose purpose is our ruin with every weapon which God and Nature has placed in our hands— with fire and water, with steel and powder and ball, and with our household servant and plantation hands, if they prove necessary to avert from us the supreme calamity of subjugation. If they send the negro to confront our sons and brothers in battle, why not, if necessity requires, meet them with the same fighting material? Here at least we can beat them in recruiting, and outnumber them in reinforcements. We can also make them [the Negroes] fight better than the Yankees are able to do. Masters and overseers can marshal them for battle by the same authority and habit of obedience with which they are marshalled to labor. If then, (and we would only employ them in case of clear necessity) negro soldiers are needed to beat the enemy and conquer independence and peace, there is no argument of doubtful expediency to counterbalance the superlative end.

But meantime we can press into service a number sufficient for teamsters, cooks, and fatigue duty; and thus relieve many thousand soldiers, and put them in the ranks. This ought to be done. Slave owners, if patriotic, will not object to this—and if they do object, they are madmen, and their objections will avail nothing. Let this be done. Let the army ask for it, and it will be done. . . .

  ⭰ Confederate leaders in Richmond were undoubtedly aware of the political dynamite with which certain Mississippians and Alabamians were beginning to toy. Richmond newspapers, however, the most brilliantly edited and influential in the South, paid scant attention to the distant ferment. As 1863 closed, perhaps a more typical expression of the South's thinking about slavery— albeit with an interesting speculation about hidden misgivings— appeared in the Memphis *Appeal* (December 23, 1863; refugee- ing in Atlanta, Georgia) :

We often hear such remarks as that slavery is doomed; that, though the South achieve her independence, she will lose slavery; and that the negro and cotton are already obsolete, or, at least, pretermitted issues. Now, we confess we have never heard such remarks without the suspi- cion that the party using them had some motive personal to himself, and that they proceeded from those who never felt any great deal of interest in slavery—their prejudices of interest or feeling lying out- side of it; from those who were opposed to war or separation, for any cause, or from those who, disappointed in the success of the war, so far, or suffering in the sensitive point, from the effects of invasion, have a feeling of despair or despondency akin to recklessness.

With all the forensic confidence exhibited by the South in times past, in slavery, as an institution, moral and social, we always enter- tained a hidden suspicion that a majority of slaveholders themselves, were not exactly morally satisfied with it, but had doubts and misgiv- ings as to its real lawfulness, proved to us by the fact that they never stood squarely up for its constitutional rights when its issues were to be made the subjects of decisive legislation in Congress, or of popular arbitrament between sections in the great quadrennial canvasses for the presidency. While in legislation they would trim and compromise, in elections they adopted equivocal platforms, or voted for questionable candidates, as if either afraid of the North, or deterred or frightened by the lurking ghost of some question of conscience, whose shadowy outlines were not clearly seen, or palpably defined to their trembling moral sense. . . .

No doubt much of the misgiving of the people in times past upon the subject of slavery was the result of political management upon the part of those who desired or expected to be President; but after making all due allowances, there has been but too much exhibition unmistakable, of diffidence, of want of confidence or courage in meeting the issue, or facing its alternatives; and no doubt this it is, in part at least, which prompts the exclamations of despondency or despair alluded to above. Now, while we do not believe that slavery is the real political issue with the Northern Government, and believe that it was only a suggestive issue with us—the Patroclus of a controversy involving other and more logical or important questions connected with political truth or human rights—yet we believe that slavery is an integral in our social and political system, as it is of all good or wise, or republican government, which it is vital to retain, and which it would be fatal to abandon. . . .

While the introduction of African slavery into the American colonies was in some sense the suggestion of climate, and other causes purely topical, its logical value was in supplying a controllable labor to agriculture, in lieu of the feudal relations of service left by the colonists behind. And when by the revolution we got free government, there was to the agricultural necessity for controllable labor, to a country destined in much the largest proportion to be agricultural, added a high political motive or necessity for its continuation. While it is always true that labor, to be profitable, must be controllable, it is equally true that the subordinate and unintelligent offices of society will devolve upon a naturally philosophical principle, on the inferior or least intelligent classes, and that, if possible, the franchises of a free political society—bestowed upon the presumption of enlightened moral and intellectual character—should not be degraded by association with menial or servile employment; it has been found equally true that the best way to subserve all purposes, social and political, is to devolve the servile duties of life upon those of a different race from those holding the property, and managing the great political interests of the country. This is, and has been, met in our country by the employment of the African, for while his physical nature makes him a good laborer isothermally, and his intellectual nature makes him politically and socially unambitious, his color meets the great political want of a free government in creating a line of separation between the dominant political, and the inferior social classes.

In a society like ours, franchises can never be degraded, or brought into contempt by degrading association. The ballot box provides very effectually against that, and the consequence has been, that there is no country in the world, in which the white man is so white, or so free, as in these States. The European States, with all their mawkish sentimentality about African slavery, keep franchises from the degradation of servile association by tabooing the subordinate, or laboring classes of the prevalent race, in denying to them the right of suffrage, by one form, or motive of legislation or another.

No. Slavery is not doomed, nor shall be. Every motive, political or social, should animate us to maintain it, and preserve it under all circumstances. What we lose by war below our necessities, must be supplied. It is demanded by every consideration, political, social, industrial, by our own wants, by the wants of the world, by the adaptation of our country to tropical productions, which England is seeking to monopolize, by the destruction of our system of labor. Let us, therefore, be neither yielding, despondent, nor even doubtful, but maintain it as a part of our political inheritance and rights.

☞ The *Appeal* might exhort the faithful to stand fast all it wished, but the ferment of change, a by-product of the war, was at work in the South. How the Negroes themselves reacted to the possibility of their playing a larger, or more military, role for the Confederacy is a difficult question to answer. At the beginning of the war, Louisiana had accepted the offer of some fourteen hundred free Negroes in New Orleans to serve in the state militia. Although many of the Louisiana blacks ultimately entered the Union service after the Federals captured New Orleans, free Negroes in both Tennessee and Alabama, among other southern states, were regarded as acceptable for the states' forces.[5] As for the slaves, only indirect evidence is available. But what there is suggests that if freedom were anywhere in prospect, some blacks were indeed willing to become Confederates. The New Orleans *Bee* (November 23, 1863) furnished one clue:

An occasional correspondent of the New York *Tribune*, writing recently from Washington, relates a conversation between himself and an English surgeon who had spent some time in the South, where he had been attached to military hospitals, and where he professed to have enjoyed unusual facilities for obtaining important social and political information.

In reply to a question about the rumored project for emancipating

[5] Bell I. Wiley, *Southern Negroes, 1861–1865* (New Haven, 1938), 147–48.

and arming the slaves, the correspondent's informant is reported to have said:

The work of emancipation is not now in the hands of the Central Government, but in the hands of the States. The States, in their sovereign capacity, have, unwittingly no doubt, done already a great deal for this unfortunate race. They have conscripted many free colored men, and impressed thousands and thousands of slaves. By calling upon the free colored population for their services in the army, they have begun to break down the social prejudices existing against color, and open the gate of military distinctions and honors to men who had hitherto been deprived of all advantages attached to public life, and of all the political rights common to the whites. As to the blacks who have served in the army as body servants, pioneers and sappers, there is but one opinion concerning their future position. These men will be made free at the end of the war. National vanity, in the absence of a better motive, will prompt the States to propose the emancipation of the slaves who have served in the army during the war by means of an indemnity which will be determined by their Legislatures. The blacks with whom I had an opportunity to converse, live in the hope that all of those of their race who had the chance of serving Master Jeff, will receive their freedom and a patch of ground with a house upon it. This expectation has caused them to look with jealousy upon the favored ones who, by order of their master, are delivered up to the Recruiting Sergeant, and the privilege of joining the army was regarded as a great boon by all the blacks I have seen.

☞ The immediate upshot of the proposals in late 1863 for a change in Confederate policy concerning slavery was a law enacted in February, 1864, authorizing the War Department to impress free Negroes for various noncombatant military duties and, if necessary, to impress as many as twenty thousand slaves for the same purposes. This measure was anticipated by the report of Secretary of War James A. Seddon to President Davis in November, 1863:

. . . To some extent, likewise, the necessity of details might be obviated by some organized system of impressing or engaging the labor of free negroes and slaves where they could be made available. The effort

48

to do this, by the temptation of interests of owners, has been generally found to be unavailing. In many of the Government works, where the unskilled labor of slaves would be most available, exposure to the seductions or attacks of the enemy are dreaded by owners, who are averse to having them removed from their personal supervision and influence. To command slaves, therefore, in anything like the number required for the many works of Government to which they could be applied, compulsion in some form would be necessary. The use of negroes may, likewise, swell the number of men in arms in the field by substituting teamsters, cooks, and other camp employés, who are now largely supplied from the ranks. This policy has heretofore met the approbation of Congress, and been embodied in the act approved April 21, 1862. No provision, however, was made to procure the negroes for these offices, and from the causes mentioned, although their utility has been recognized, they could not be obtained by voluntary engagements of service or hire from their owners.

There may be difficulties and embarrassments in enforcing the service of slaves, but they might be overcome on the principle of impressing them as property, or of requiring contributions from their owners of certain quotas for public service, as has been done for works of public defense. The wickedness and malignity of our enemies have certainly placed [a] considerable number of negroes, almost of necessity, at the control of our Government. To favor the pusillanimity of their people, as well as the better to advance the nefarious ends of their unjust warfare, they have adopted as their deliberate policy the employment of the slaves as soldiers in their Army. They have already formed numerous regiments of the slaves they have seduced or forced from their masters, and the statement has been boastfully made in their public prints that they have already some 30,000 negro troops in arms. It is now an ascertained fact that as they overrun any portion of our territory they draw off, often by compulsion, the most efficient male slaves and place them in their negro regiments; and when they have established anywhere a temporary occupation, they practice a regular system of compulsory recruiting from the slaves within their reach. Not merely, therefore, for the purpose of preserving to the Confederacy this valuable labor, thus abstracted, but from the plainer necessity of preventing the enemy from recruiting their armies with our slaves, it becomes a clear obligation on the military authorities of the Confederacy to remove from any district exposed to be occupied or overrun by the enemy the effective male slaves. . . .[6]

☞ In the portion of his message to the Confederate Congress in December, 1863, that dealt with the army's increasingly critical need for more men, Davis only briefly alluded to the legislation that he desired concerning the slaves. But he seized the occasion to lambaste the enemy for alleged mistreatment of Negroes:

. . . If to the above measures be added a law to enlarge the policy of the act of the 21st of April, 1862, so as to enable the Department to replace not only enlisted cooks, but wagoners and other employés in the Army, by negroes, it is hoped that the ranks of the Army will be so strengthened for the ensuing campaign as to put to defiance the utmost efforts of the enemy.

. . . I cannot close this message without again adverting to the savage ferocity which still marks the conduct of the enemy in the prosecution of the war. . . .

Nor has less unrelenting warfare been waged by these pretended friends of human rights and liberties against the unfortunate negroes. Wherever the enemy have been able to gain access they have forced into the ranks of their army every able-bodied man that they could seize, and have either left the aged, the women, and the children to perish by starvation, or have gathered them into camps where they have been wasted by a frightful mortality. Without clothing or shelter, often without food, incapable without supervision of taking the most ordinary precautions against disease, these helpless dependents, accustomed to have their wants supplied by the foresight of their masters, are being rapidly exterminated wherever brought in contact with the invaders. By the Northern man, on whose deep-rooted prejudices no kindly restraining influence is exercised, they are treated with aversion and neglect. There is little hazard in predicting that in all localities where the enemy have gained a temporary foothold the negroes, who under our care increased six-fold in number since their importation into the colonies by Great Britain, will have been reduced by mortality during the war to no more than one-half their previous number.

[6] James A. Seddon to Jefferson Davis, November 26, 1863, in *O.R.*, Series IV, Vol. II, 998–99.

Information on this subject is derived not only from our own observation and from the reports of the negroes who succeed in escaping from the enemy, but full confirmation is afforded by statements published in the Northern journals by humane persons engaged in making appeals to the charitable for aid in preventing the ravages of disease, exposure, and starvation among the negro women and children who are crowded into encampments. . . .[7]

☞ The act providing for the Confederate impressment of as many as twenty thousand slaves was mainly important because of the fact that the central government itself had finally moved, however circumspectly, into the area of slavery. It was an essential first step toward a much bolder policy that Jefferson Davis would call for before the year ended. Although he ultimately conceded that the law had not worked well, Davis approved the act on February 17, 1864:

AN ACT TO INCREASE THE EFFICIENCY OF THE ARMY
BY THE EMPLOYMENT OF FREE NEGROES AND SLAVES
IN CERTAIN CAPACITIES.

Whereas, the efficiency of the Army is greatly diminished by the withdrawal from the ranks of able-bodied soldiers to act as teamsters, and in various other capacities in which free negroes and slaves might be advantageously employed: Therefore,

The Congress of the Confederate States of America do enact, That all male free negroes and other free persons of color, not including those who are free under the treaty of Paris of eighteen hundred and three, or under the treaty with Spain of eighteen hundred and nineteen, resident in the Confederate States, between the ages of eighteen and fifty years, shall be held liable to perform such duties with the the Army, or in connection with the military defenses of the country, in the way of work upon fortifications or in Government works for the production or preparation of material of war, or in military hospitals, as the Secretary of War or the commanding general of the Trans-Mississippi Department may, from time to time, prescribe, and while engaged in the performance of such duties shall receive rations and clothing and compensation at the rate of eleven dollars a month, under such rules

[7] Davis to Confederate Congress, December 7, 1863, *ibid.*, 1,041, 1,047.

and regulations as the said Secretary may establish: *Provided,* That the Secretary of War or the commanding general of the Trans-Mississippi Department, with the approval of the President, may exempt from the operations of this act such free negroes as the interests of the country may require should be exempted, or such as he may think proper to exempt, on grounds of justice, equity, or necessity.

SEC. 2. That the Secretary of War is hereby authorized to employ for duties similar to those indicated in the preceding section of this act, as many male negro slaves, not to exceed twenty thousand, as in his judgment, the wants of the service may require, furnishing them, while so employed, with proper rations and clothing, under rules and regulations to be established by him, and paying to the owners of said slaves such wages as may be agreed upon with said owners for their use and service, and in the event of the loss of any slaves while so employed, by the act of the enemy, or by escape to the enemy, or by death inflicted by the enemy, or by disease contracted while in any service required of said slaves, then the owners of the same shall be entitled to receive the full value of such slaves, to be ascertained by agreement or by appraisement, under the law regulating impressments, to be paid under such rules and regulations as the Secretary of War may establish.

SEC. 3. That when the Secretary of War shall be unable to procure the service of slaves in any military department in sufficient numbers for the necessities of the Department, upon the terms and conditions set forth in the preceding section, then he is hereby authorized to impress the services of as many male slaves, not to exceed twenty thousand, as may be required, from time to time, to discharge the duties indicated in the first section of this act, according to laws regulating the impressment of slaves in other cases: *Provided,* That slaves so impressed shall, while employed, receive the same rations and clothing, in kind and quantity, as slaves regularly hired from their owners; and, in the event of their loss, shall be paid for in the same manner and under the same rules established by the said impressment laws: *Provided,* That if the owner have but one male slave between the age of eighteen and fifty, he shall not be impressed against the will of said owner: *Provided further,* That free negroes shall be first impressed, and if there should be a deficiency, it shall be supplied by the impressment of slaves according to the foregoing provisions: *Provided further,*

That in making the impressment, not more than one of every five male slaves between the ages of eighteen and forty-five shall be taken from any owner, care being taken to allow in each case a credit for all slaves who may have been already impressed under this act, and who are still in service, or have died or been lost while in service. And all impressments under this act shall be taken in equal ratio from all owners in the same locality, city, county or district.[8]

☞ Davis, the political leader, moved cautiously, as did his opposite number in Washington. But a brilliant and gallant major general in the Confederate army, Patrick R. Cleburne, suffered no such inhibitions as did well-seasoned and constitutionally minded politicians. Common knowledge to historians today, Cleburne's proposal for freeing all the slaves and arming some of them was known at the time to only a handful of top Confederate leaders, and even for some thirty years after the war it was "lost" to history.[9]

Born and educated in Ireland, Cleburne came to America in 1849 and prospered as a druggist, then as a lawyer and landowner in Helena, Arkansas, for a decade before the war. A zealous convert to the southern cause, Cleburne served with renowned distinction in the Confederate army, but by late 1863 he had caught the sense of desperation that some Mississippians and Alabamians had begun to articulate. Cleburne, fresh from the humiliating Confederate defeat at Chattanooga and in winter quarers in northern Georgia, brooded about the extensive preparations General Sherman was making and the large army he was

[8] *Ibid.*, III, 208. The best older studies of this matter are Wiley, *Southern Negroes*, 110–33; and Harrison A. Trexler, "The Opposition of Planters to the Employment of Slaves as Laborers by the Confederacy," *Mississippi Valley Historical Review*, XXVII (September, 1940), 211–24. A fine new study, though limited to a single state, is James A. Brewer, *The Confederate Negro: Virginia's Craftsmen and Military Laborers, 1861–1865* (Durham, 1969). Although the matter is tangential to his concern, Professor Brewer (pp. 160–61) quotes a passage from President Davis' message of November 7, 1864, and characterizes it as perhaps the "strangest of all" the various incentives that Confederates extended to Negroes in an effort to identify them with the southern war effort.

[9] The best source on Cleburne and his plan was written by an officer who served under him, Irving A. Buck, *Cleburne and His Command* (New York, 1908). I am also indebted to Miss Barbara Ruby, who wrote a paper on this topic in my seminar at Duke University, May, 1970. Thomas L. Connelly, *Autumn of Glory: The Army of Tennessee, 1862–1865* (Baton Rouge, 1971), is helpful for the tangled politics of the Army of Tennessee and Cleburne's role therein.

gathering for the spring campaign. At the same time, the ranks of the strife-torn Army of Tennessee, now commanded by General Joseph E. Johnston, steadily dwindled because of death, disability, and desertion. Realizing the critical need to recruit men for the exhausted Confederate ranks and ignoring the cautionary warnings of his friends, Cleburne cut boldly to the core of the southern dilemma in what is surely one of the most fascinating documents of the Civil War era:

[JANUARY 2, 1864.]
COMMANDING GENERAL, THE CORPS, DIVISION, BRIGADE,
AND REGIMENTAL COMANDERS OF THE ARMY OF TENNESSEE:

GENERAL: Moved by the exigency in which our country is now placed, we take the liberty of laying before you, unofficially, our views on the present state of affairs. The subject is so grave, and our views so new, we feel it a duty both to you and the cause that before going further we should submit them for your judgment and receive your suggestions in regard to them. We therefore respectfully ask you to give us an expression of your views in the premises. We have now been fighting for nearly three years, have spilled much of our best blood, and lost, consumed, or thrown to the flames an amount of property equal in value to the specie currency of the world. Through some lack in our system the fruits of our struggles and sacrifices have invariably slipped away from us and left us nothing but long lists of dead and mangled. Instead of standing defiantly on the borders of our territory or harassing those of the enemy, we are hemmed in to-day into less than two-thirds of it, and still the enemy menacingly confronts us at every point with superior forces. Our soldiers can see no end to this state of affairs except in our own exhaustion; hence, instead of rising to the occasion, they are sinking into a fatal apathy, growing weary of hardships and slaughters which promise no results. In this state of things it is easy to understand why there is a growing belief that some black catastrophe is not far ahead of us, and that unless some extraordinary change is soon made in our condition we must overtake it. The consequences of this condition are showing themselves more plainly every day; restlessness of morals spreading everywhere, manifesting itself in the army in a growing disregard for private rights; desertion spreading to a class of soldiers it never dared to tamper with before;

military commissions sinking in the estimation of the soldier; our supplies failing; our firesides in ruins. If this state continues much longer we must be subjugated. Every man should endeavor to understand the meaning of subjugation before it is too late. We can give but a faint idea when we say it means the loss of all we now hold most sacred—slaves and all other personal property, lands, homesteads, liberty, justice, safety, pride, manhood. It means that the history of this heroic struggle will be written by the enemy; that our youth will be trained by Northern school teachers; will learn from Northern school books their version of the war; will be impressed by all the influences of history and education to regard our gallant dead as traitors, our maimed veterans as fit objects for derision. It means the crushing of Southern manhood, the hatred of our former slaves, who will, on a spy system, be our secret police. The conqueror's policy is to divide the conquered into factions and stir up animosity among them, and in training an army of negroes the North no doubt holds this thought in perspective. We can see three great causes operating to destroy us: First, the inferiority of our armies to those of the enemy in point of numbers; second, the poverty of our single source of supply in comparison with his several sources; third, the fact that slavery, from being one of our chief sources of strength at the commencement of the war, has now become, in a military point of view, one of our chief sources of weakness.

The enemy already opposes us at every point with superior numbers, and is endeavoring to make the preponderance irresistible. President Davis, in his recent message, says the enemy "has recently ordered a large conscription and made a subsequent call for volunteers, to be followed, if ineffectual, by a still further draft." In addition, the President of the United States announces that "he has already in training an army of 100,000 negroes as good as any troops," and every fresh raid he makes and new slice of territory he wrests from us will add to this force. Every soldier in our army already knows and feels our numerical inferiority to the enemy. Want of men in the field has prevented him from reaping the fruits of his victories, and has prevented him from having the furlough he expected after the last reorganization, and when he turns from the wasting armies in the field to look at the source of supply, he finds nothing in the prospect to encourage him. Our single source of supply is that portion of our white men

55

fit for duty and not now in the ranks. The enemy has three sources of supply: First, his own motley population; secondly, our slaves; and thirdly, Europeans whose hearts are fired into a crusade against us by fictitious pictures of the atrocities of slavery, and who meet no hindrance from their Governments in such enterprise, because these Governments are equally antagonistic to the institution. In touching the third cause, the fact that slavery has become a military weakness, we may rouse prejudice and passion, but the time has come when it would be madness not to look at our danger from every point of view, and to probe it to the bottom. Apart from the assistance that home and foreign prejudice against slavery has given to the North, slavery is a source of great strength to the enemy in a purely military point of view, by supplying him with an army from our granaries; but it is our most vulnerable point, a continued embarrassment, and in some respects an insidious weakness. Wherever slavery is once seriously disturbed, whether by the actual presence or the approach of the enemy, or even by a cavalry raid, the whites can no longer with safety to their property openly sympathize with our cause. The fear of their slaves is continually haunting them, and from silence and apprehension many of these soon learn to wish the war stopped on any terms. The next stage is to take the oath to save property, and they become dead to us, if not open enemies. To prevent raids we are forced to scatter our forces, and are not free to move and strike like the enemy; his vulnerable points are carefully selected and fortified depots. Ours are found in every point where there is a slave to set free. All along the lines slavery is comparatively valueless to us for labor, but of great and increasing worth to the enemy for information. It is an omnipresent spy system, pointing out our valuable men to the enemy, revealing our positions, purposes, and resources, and yet acting so safely and secretly that there is no means to guard against it. Even in the heart of our country, where our hold upon this secret espionage is firmest, it waits but the opening fire of the enemy's battle line to wake it, like a torpid serpent, into venomous activity.

In view of the state of affairs what does our country propose to do? In the words of President Davis "no effort must be spared to add largely to our effective force as promptly as possible. The sources of supply are to be found in restoring to the army all who are improperly absent, putting an end to substitution, modifying the exemption law, restricting details, and placing in the ranks such of the able-bodied men now employed as wagoners, nurses, cooks, and other employés, as are doing service for which the negroes may be found competent.'' Most of the men improperly absent, together with many of the exempts and men having substitutes, are now without the Confederate lines and cannot be calculated on. If all the exempts capable of bearing arms were enrolled, it will give us the boys below eighteen, the men above forty-five, and those persons who are left at home to meet the wants of the country and the army, but this modification of the exemption law will remove from the fields and manufactories most of the skill that directed agricultural and mechanical labor, and, as stated by the President, ''details will have to be made to meet the wants of the country,'' thus sending many of the men to be derived from this source back to their homes again. Independently of this, experience proves that striplings and men above conscript age break down and swell the sick lists more than they do the ranks. The portion now in our lines of the class who have substitutes is not on the whole a hopeful element, for the motives that created it must have been stronger than patriotism, and these motives added to what many of them will call breach of faith, will cause some to be not forthcoming, and others to be unwilling and discontented soldiers. The remaining sources mentioned by the President have been so closely pruned in the Army of Tennessee that they will be found not to yield largely. The supply from all these sources, together with what we now have in the field, will exhaust the white race, and though it should greatly exceed expectations and put us on an equality with the enemy, or even give us temporary advantages, still we have no reserve to meet unexpected disaster or to supply a protracted struggle. Like past years, 1864 will diminish our ranks by the casualties of war, and what source of repair is there left us? We therefore see in the recommendations of the President only a temporary expedient, which at the best will leave us twelve months hence in the same predicament we are in now. The President attempts to meet only one of the depressing causes mentioned; for the other two he has proposed no remedy. They remain to generate lack of confidence in our final success, and to keep us moving down hill as heretofore. Adequately to meet the causes which are now threatening ruin to our country, we propose, in addition to a modification of the President's plans, that we retain in service for the war all troops now in service, and that we immediately commence training a large reserve of the most courageous of our slaves, and further that we guarantee freedom within a reasonable time to every slave in the South who shall remain true to the Confederacy in this war. As between the loss of independence and the loss of slavery, we assume that every patriot will freely give up the latter—give up the negro slave rather than be a slave himself. If we are correct in this assumption it only remains to show how this great national sacrifice is, in all human probabilities, to change the current of success and sweep the invader from our country.

Our country has already some friends in England and France, and there are strong motives to induce these nations to recognize and assist us, but they cannot assist us without helping slavery, and to do this would be in conflict with their policy for the last quarter of a century. England has paid hundreds of millions to emancipate her West India slaves and break up the slave-trade. Could she now consistently spend her treasure to reinstate slavery in this country? But this barrier once removed, the sympathy and the interests of these and other nations will accord with our own, and we may expect from them both moral support and material aid. One thing is certain, as soon as the great sacrifice to independence is made and known in foreign countries there will be a complete change of front in our favor of the sympathies of the world. This measure will deprive the North of the moral and material aid which it now derives from the bitter prejudices with which foreigners view the institution, and its war, if continued, will henceforth be so despicable in their eyes that the source of recruiting will be dried up. It will leave the enemy's negro army no motive to fight for, and will exhaust the source from which it has been recruited. The idea that it is their special mission to war against slavery has held growing sway over the Northern people for many years, and has at length ripened into an armed and bloody crusade against it. This baleful superstition has so far supplied them with a courage and constancy not their own. It is the most powerful and honestly entertained plank in their war platform. Knock this away and what is left? A bloody ambition for more territory, a pretended veneration for the Union, which one of their own most distinguished orators (Doctor Beecher in his Liverpool speech) openly avowed was only used as a stimulus to stir up the anti-slavery crusade, and lastly the poisonous and selfish interests which are the fungus growth of the war itself. Mankind may fancy it a great duty to destroy slavery, but what interest can mankind have in upholding this remainder of the Northern war platform? Their interests and feelings will be diametrically opposed to it. The measure we propose will strike dead all John Brown fanaticism, and will compel the enemy to draw off altogether or in the eyes of the world to swallow the Declaration of Independence without the sauce and disguise of philanthropy. This delusion of fanaticism at an end, thousands of Northern people will have leisure to look at home and to see the gulf of despotism into which they themselves are rushing.

The measure will at one blow strip the enemy of foreign sympathy and assistance, and transfer them to the South; it will dry up two of his three sources of recruiting; it will take from his negro army the only motive it could have to fight against the South, and will probably cause much of it to desert over to us; it will deprive his cause of the powerful stimulus of fanaticism, and will enable him to see the rock on which his so-called friends are now piloting him. The immediate effect of the emancipation and enrollment of negroes on the military strength of the South would be: To enable us to have armies numerically superior to those of the North, and a reserve of any size we might think necessary; to enable us to take the offensive, move forward, and forage on the enemy. It would open to us in prospective another and almost untouched source of supply, and furnish us with the means of preventing temporary disaster, and carrying on a protracted struggle. It would instantly remove all the vulnerability, embarrassment, and inherent weakness which result from slavery. The approach of the enemy would no longer find every household surrounded by spies; the fear that sealed the master's lips and the avarice that has, in so many cases, tempted him practically to desert us would alike be removed. There would be no recruits awaiting the enemy with open arms, no complete history of every neighborhood with ready guides, no fear of insurrection in the rear, or anxieties for the fate of loved ones when our armies moved forward. The chronic irritation of hope deferred would be joyfully ended with the negro, and the sympathies of his whole race would be due to his native South. It would restore confidence in an early termination of the war with all its inspiring consequences, and even if contrary to all expectations the enemy should succeed in overrunning the South, instead of finding a cheap, ready-made means of holding it down, he would find a common hatred and thirst for vengeance, which would break into acts at every favorable opportunity, would prevent him from settling on our lands, and render the South a very unprofitable conquest. It would remove forever all selfish taint from our cause and place independence above every question of property. The very magnitude of the sacrifice itself, such as no nation has ever voluntarily made before, would appal[1] our enemies, destroy his spirit and his finances, and fill our hearts with a pride and singleness of purpose which would clothe us with new strength in battle. Apart from all other aspects of the question, the necessity for more fighting men is upon us. We can only get a sufficiency by making the negro share the danger and hardships of the war. If we arm and train him and make him fight for the country in her hour of dire distress, every consideration of principle and policy demand that we should set him and his whole race who side with us free. It is a first principle with mankind that he who offers his life in defense of the State should receive from her in return his freedom and his happiness, and we believe in acknowledgment of this principle. The Constitution of the Southern States has reserved to their respective governments the power to free slaves for meritorious services to the State. It is politic besides. For many years, ever since the agitation of the subject of slavery commenced, the negro has been dreaming of freedom, and his vivid imagination has surrounded that condition with so many gratifications that it has become the paradise of his hopes. To attain it he will tempt dangers and difficulties not exceeded by the bravest soldier in the field. The hope of freedom is perhaps the only moral incentive that can be applied to him in his present condition. It would be preposterous then to expect him to fight against it with any degree of enthusiasm, therefore we must bind him to our cause by no doubtful bonds; we must leave no possible loop-hole for treachery to creep in. The slaves are dangerous now, but armed, trained, and collected in an army they would be a thousand fold more dangerous; therefore when we make soldiers of them we must make free men of them beyond all question, and thus enlist their sympathies also. We can do this more effectually than the North can now do, for we can give the negro not only his own freedom, but that of his wife and child, and can secure it to him in his old home. To do this, we must immediately make his marriage and parental relations sacred in the eyes of the law and forbid their sale. The past legislation of the South concedes that a large free middle class of negro blood, between the master and slave, must sooner or later destroy the institution. If, then, we touch the institution at all, we would do best to make the most of it, and by emancipating the whole race upon reasonable terms, and within such reasonable time as will prepare both races for the change, secure to ourselves all the advantages, and to our enemies all the disadvantages that can arise, both at home and abroad, from such a sacrifice. Satisfy the negro that if he faithfully adheres to our standard during the war he shall receive his freedom and that of his race. Give him as an earnest of our intentions such immediate immunities as will impress him with our sincerity and be in keeping with his new condition, enroll a portion of his class as soldiers of the Confederacy, and we change the race from a dreaded weakness to a position of strength.

Will the slaves fight? The helots of Sparta stood their masters good stead in battle. In the great sea fight of Lepanto where the Christians checked forever the spread of Mohammedanism over Europe, the galley slaves of portions of the fleet were promised freedom, and called on to fight at a critical moment of the battle. They fought well, and civilization owes much to those brave galley slaves. The negro slaves of Saint Domingo, fighting for freedom, defeated their white masters and the French troops sent against them. The negro slaves of Jamaica revolted, and under the name of Maroons held the mountains against their masters for 150 years; and the experience of this war has been so far that half-trained negroes have fought as bravely as many other half-trained Yankees. If, contrary to the training of a lifetime, they can be made to face and fight bravely against their former masters, how much more probable is it that with the allurement of a higher reward, and led by those masters, they would submit to discipline and face dangers.

We will briefly notice a few arguments against this course. It is said Republicanism cannot exist without the institution. Even were this true, we prefer any form of government of which the Southern people may have the molding, to one forced upon us by a conqueror. It is said the white man cannot perform agricultural labor in the South. The experience of this army during the heat of summer from Bowling Green, Ky., to Tupelo, Miss., is that the white man is healthier when doing reasonable work in the open field than at any other time. It is said an army of negroes cannot be spared from the fields. A sufficient number of slaves is now administering to luxury alone to supply the place of all we need, and we believe it would be better to take half the able-bodied men off a plantation than to take the one master mind that economically regulated its operations. Leave some of the skill at home and take some of the muscle to fight with. It is said slaves will not work after they are freed. We think necessity and a wise legislation will compel them to labor for a living. It is said it will cause terrible excitement and some disaffection from our cause. Excitement is far preferable to the apathy which now exists, and disaffection will not be among the fighting men. It is said slavery is all we are fighting for, and if we give it up we give up all. Even if this were true, which we deny, slavery is not all our enemies are fighting for. It is merely the pretense to establish sectional superiority and a more centralized form of government, and to deprive us of our rights and liberties. We have now briefly proposed a plan which we believe will save our country. It may be imperfect, but in all human probability it would give us our independence. No objection ought to outweigh it which is not weightier than independence. If it is worthy of being put in practice it ought to be mooted quickly before the people, and urged earnestly by every man who believes in its efficacy. Negroes will require much training; training will require much time, and there is danger that this concession to common sense may come too late.

P. R. Cleburne, major-general, commanding division; D. C. Govan, brigadier-general; John E. Murray, colonel Fifth Arkansas; G. F. Baucum, colonel Eighth Arkansas; Peter Snyder, lieutenant-colonel, commanding Sixth and Seventh Arkansas; E. Warfield, lieutenant-colonel, Second Arkansas; M. P. Lowrey, brigadier-general; A. B. Hardcastle, colonel Thirty-second and Forty-fifth Mississippi; F. A. Ashford, major Sixteenth Alabama; John W. Colquitt, colonel First Arkansas; Rich. J. Person, major Third and Fifth Confederate; G. S. Deakins, major Thirty-fifth and Eighth Tennessee; J. H. Collett, captain, commanding Seventh Texas; J. H. Kelly, brigadier-general, commanding Cavalry Division.[10]

In orthodox southern eyes at the time, perhaps Cleburne's most heretical idea, and one that Jefferson Davis himself would eventually advance, was the candid recognition that the Negro wished to be free. Even so, as the names above attest, some dozen or so of his fellow officers endorsed the proposal. General Joseph E. Johnston, however, refused to forward it to Richmond on the grounds that "it was more political than military in tenor." [11] One of Cleburne's associates, Brigadier General Patton Anderson, was so distressed by the proposal that he sought confidential advice from another highly placed Confederate, Lieutenant General Leonidas Polk:

After you have read what I am about to disclose to you, I hope you will not think I have assumed any unwarrantable intimacy in marking this communication as confidential.

My thoughts for ten days past have been so oppressed with the weight of the subject as to arouse in my mind the most painful apprehensions of future results, and has caused me to cast about for a friend of clear head, ripe judgment, and pure patriotism with whom to confer and take counsel. My choice has fallen upon you, sir, and I proceed at once to lay the matter before you. On the 2d of January I received a circular order from the headquarters, Hindman's Corps, informing me that the commanding general of the army desired division commanders to meet him at his quarters at 7 o'clock that evening. At the hour designated I was at the appointed place. I met in the room General Johnston, Lieutenant-General Hardee, Major-Generals Walker, Stewart, and Stevenson, and in a moment afterwards Major-Generals Hindman and Cleburne entered, Brigadier-General Bate coming in a few moments later—the whole, with the general commanding, embracing all the corps and division commanders (infantry) of this army except Major-General Cheatham, who was not present. In a few minutes General Johnston requested Lieutenant-General Hardee to explain the object of the meeting, which he did by stating that

[10] *O.R.*, Series I, Vol. LII, Pt. 2, pp. 586–92.
[11] Buck, *Cleburne and His Command*, 213.

Major-General Cleburne had prepared with great care a paper on an important subject addressed to the officers of this army and he proposed that it now be read. General Cleburne proceeded to read an elaborate article on the subject of our past disasters, present condition, and inevitable future ruin unless an entire change of policy might avert it. That change he boldly and proudly proposed to effect by emancipating our slaves and putting muskets in the hands of all of them capable of bearing arms, thus securing them to us as allies and equals, and insuring a superiority of numbers over our enemies, &c.

Yes, sir; this plain but, in my view, monstrous proposition was calmly submitted to the generals of this army for their sanction and adoption, with the avowed purpose of carrying it to the rank and file. I will not attempt to describe my feelings on being confronted by a project so startling in its character—may I say so revolting to Southern sentiment, Southern pride, and Southern honor. And not the least painful of the emotions awakened by it was the consciousness which forced itself upon me that it met with favor by others besides the author in high station then present. You have a place, general, in the Southern heart perhaps not less exalted than that you occupy in her Army. No one knows better than yourself all the hidden powers and secret springs which move the great moral machinery of the South. You know whence she derived that force which three years ago impelled her to the separation, and has since that time to this present hour enabled her to lay all she has, even the blood of her best sons, upon the altar of independence, and do you believe that that South will now listen to the voices of those who would ask her to stultify herself by entertaining a proposition which heretofore our insolent foes themselves have not even dared to make in terms so bold and undisguised? What are we to do? If this thing is once openly proposed to the Army the total disintegration of that Army will follow in a fortnight, and yet to speak and work in opposition to it is an agitation of the question scarcely less to be dreaded at this time, and brings down the universal indignation of the Southern people and the Southern soldiers upon the head of at least one of our bravest and most accomplished officers. Then, I repeat, what is to be done? What relief it would afford me to talk to you about this matter! but as that may not be, do I go too far in asking you, to write to me? I start in a few days to my home in Monticello, Fla., where I expect to spend twenty days with my family, and I assure you, general, it would add much to the enjoyment of my visit if you would favor me by mail with some of the many thoughts which this subject will arouse in your mind.[12]

☞ If another of Cleburne's associates, Major General W. H. T. Walker, had not been so indignant that he took it upon himself to inform the President directly, Richmond might never have heard of the proposal:

I feel it my duty as an officer of the Army to lay before the Chief Magistrate of the Southern Confederacy the within document, which was read on the night of the 2d of January, 1864, at a meeting which I attended in obedience to the following order:

Headquarters Hardee's Corps,
Dalton, Ga., January 2, 1864.

Major-General Walker:
Commanding Division:
GENERAL: Lieutenant-General Hardee desires that you will meet him at General Johnston's headquarters this evening at 7 o'clock.
Very respectfully, your obedient servant,

D. H. Poole,
Assistant Adjutant-General.

Having, after the meeting adjourned, expressed my determination to apply to General Cleburne for a copy of the document to forward to the War Department, some of the gentlemen who were present at that meeting insisted upon their sentiments on so grave a subject being known to the Executive. I informed them that I would address a letter to each of the gentlemen present at the meeting, which I did. I addressed a note to General Cleburne, asking him for a copy of the document, informing him that I felt it my duty to forward it to the War Department; that should he do so I would, of course, give him a copy of the indorsement I made on it. He furnished me with a copy, and avowed himself its author. I applied to the commanding general for permission to send it to the War Department through the proper official channel, which, for reasons satisfactory to himself, he declined to do; hence the reason for it not reaching you through the official channel. The gravity of the subject, the magnitude of the issues involved, my strong convictions that the further agitation of such senti-

---

[12] Patton Anderson to Leonidas Polk, January 14, 1864, in *O.R.*, Series I, Vol. LII, Pt. 2, 598–99.

ments and propositions would ruin the efficacy of our Army and involve our cause in ruin and disgrace constitute my reasons for bringing the document before the Executive.[13]

☞ Wary about publicity concerning Cleburne's revolutionary ideas, President Davis immediately replied to General Walker:

I have received your letter, with its inclosure, informing me of the propositions submitted to a meeting of the general officers on the 2d instant, and thank you for the information. Deeming it to be injurious to the public service that such a subject should be mooted, or even known to be entertained by persons possessed of the confidence and respect of the people, I have concluded that the best policy under the circumstances will be to avoid all publicity, and the Secretary of War has therefore written to General Johnston requesting him to convey to those concerned my desire that it should be kept private. If it be kept out of the public journals its ill effect will be much lessened.[14]

☞ General Johnston dutifully sent the order suppressing Cleburne's plan down the chain of command:

LIEUTENANT-GENERAL HARDEE, MAJOR-GENERAL CHEATHAM, HINDMAN, CLEBURNE, STEWART, WALKER, BRIGADIER-GENERALS BATE AND P. ANDERSON:

GENERAL: I have just received a letter from the Secretary of War in reference to Major-General Cleburne's memoir read in my quarters about the 2d instant. In this letter the honorable Secretary expresses the earnest conviction of the President "that the dissemination or even promulgation of such opinions under the present circumstances of the Confederacy, whether in the Army or among the people, can be productive only of discouragement, distraction, and dissension. The agitation and controversy which must spring from the presentation of such views by officers high in the public confidence are to be deeply deprecated, and while no doubt or mistrust is for a moment entertained of the patriotic intents of the gallant author of the memorial, and such of his brother officers as may have favored his opinions, it is requested that you communicate to them, as well as all others present

---

[13] W. H. T. Walker to Jefferson Davis, January 12, 1864, *ibid.*, 595.
[14] Davis to Walker, January 13, 1864, *ibid.*, 596.

on the occasion, the opinions, as herein expressed, of the President, and urge on them the suppression, not only of the memorial itself, but likewise of all discussion and controversy respecting or growing out of it. I would add that the measures advocated in the memorial are considered to be little appropriate for consideration in military circles, and indeed in their scope pass beyond the bounds of Confederate action, and could under our constitutional system neither be recommended by the Executive to Congress nor be entertained by that body. Such views can only jeopard among the States and people unity and harmony, when for successful co-operation and the achievement of independence both are essential."

Most respectfully, your obedient servant,

J. E. Johnston,
General.

P. S.—Major-General Cleburne: Be so good as to communicate the views of the President, expressed above, to the officers of your division who signed the memorial.

J. E. Johnston.[15]

⌾   Given the realities of the Confederate Constitution and, more important, the dominant southern thought-patterns about slavery, Jefferson Davis probably did the only thing he could have done in suppressing Cleburne's proposal. For the one crucial weakness in Cleburne's otherwise brilliantly incisive and logical argument was this: How could Jefferson Davis, or any other human being for that matter, convince eleven sovereign southern states, some of them led by such recalcitrant figures as Governor Joe Brown of Georgia and Governor Zebulon Vance of North Carolina, to abandon slavery? Truly Davis might as well have urged the sun not to rise or the ocean tides to cease and desist.

Yet even as he killed all consideration of Cleburne's plan, Davis may have been frantically casting about in his own mind for a less grandiose but more practical and workable scheme of emancipation. No one knows. What is known is that events in 1864, the fourth year of the most agonizing war in our history, seemed to push the Confederacy closer to the precipice. In Janu-

---

[15] Joseph E. Johnston to William H. Hardee, et al., January 31, 1864, ibid., 608.

ary, when Davis suppressed the Cleburne document, General Grant had not yet begun his relentless, bloody hammering at Lee's army. By November that onslaught had been intermittently raging for some six months, and General Lee had been forced to make this candid assessment to President Davis:

I had the honour to receive last evening your letter of the 31st. . . .

The information contained in the notes you enclosed me, I hope is exaggerated as regards to numbers. Grant will get every man he can, & 150,000 men is the number generally assumed by Northern papers & reports. Unless we can obtain a reasonable approximation to his forces I fear a great calamity will befall us. On last Thursday at Burgess' Mill we had three brigades to oppose six divisions. On our left two divisions to oppose two corps. The inequality is too great. Our cavalry at Burgess' Mill I think saved the day. I came along our whole line yesterday from Chaffin's Bluff to this place. Today I shall visit the lines here & tomorrow go down to the right. I always find something to correct on the lines, but the great necessity I observed yesterday, was the want of men.[16]

If Lee's plight was grim, that of the other great Confederate force east of the Mississippi, the Army of Tennessee, was worse. Atlanta fell to Sherman in early September. Confederate Pollyannas might speculate in the newspapers that from Atlanta, Sherman was "in retreat" through the heart of Georgia, but Jefferson Davis knew better.

This was the tightening noose that inspired him finally to attempt a drastic change of policy, to make a last desperate effort to gain both manpower for the army and recognition of the Confederacy by England and France. If Lincoln could change his policy and adopt emancipation as a means toward preserving the Union, why might not Jefferson Davis, in his own legalistic southern style, urge a beginning at least of emancipation by the Confederacy as the last, best hope of achieving independence?

In the summer of 1864, Davis cautiously began to prepare the way for his new policy. In July he gave an interview to a north-

---

[16] Robert E. Lee to Jefferson Davis, November 2, 1864, in Clifford Dowdey and Louis H. Manarin (eds.), *The Wartime Papers of R. E. Lee* (Boston, 1961), 868.

ern journalist, one James R. Gilmore (who used the pen name of "Edmund Kirke"), and a self-appointed peace envoy, Colonel James F. Jaquess. Davis emphasized that, contrary to Alexander Stephens' famed speech in 1861, the South wanted first and foremost not slavery but national independence:

. . . Mr. Benjamin occupied his previous seat at the table, and at his right sat a spare, thin-featured man, with iron-gray hair and beard, and a clear, gray eye, full of life and vigor. He had a broad, massive forehead, and a mouth and chin denoting great energy and strength of will. His face was emaciated, and much wrinkled, but his features were good, especially his eyes,—though one of them bore a scar, apparently made by some sharp instrument. He wore a suit of grayish-brown, evidently of foreign manufacture, and, as he rose, I saw that he was about five feet ten inches high, with a slight stoop in the shoulders. His manners were simple, easy, and most fascinating; and there was an indescribable charm in his voice, as he extended his hand and said to us:

"I am glad to see you, gentlemen. You are very welcome to Richmond."

And this was the man who was President of the United States [actually Davis was secretary of war], under Franklin Pierce, and who is now the heart, soul, and brains of the Southern Confederacy!

. . . The Colonel replied:

". . . We have asked this interview, in the hope that you may suggest some way by which this war may be stopped. Our people want peace,—your people do, and your Congress has recently said that *you* do. We have come to ask how it can be brought about."

"In a very simple way. Withdraw your armies from our territory, and peace will come of itself. We do not seek to subjugate you. We are not waging an offensive war, except so far as it is offensive-defensive,—that is, so far as we are forced to invade you to prevent your invading us. Let us alone, and peace will come at once."

"But we cannot let you alone so long as you repudiate the Union. That is the one thing the Northern people will not surrender."

"I know. You would deny to us what you exact for yourselves—the right of self-government."

"No, Sir," I remarked. "We would deny you no natural right. But

69

we think Union essential to peace; and, Mr. Davis, *could* two people, with the same language, separated by only an imaginary line, live at peace with each other? Would not disputes constantly arise, and cause almost constant war between them?''

''Undoubtedly,—with this generation. You have sown such bitterness at the South; you have put such an ocean of blood between the two sections, that I despair of seeing any harmony in my time. Our children may forget this war, but *we* cannot.''

''. . . I desire peace as much as you do. I deplore bloodshed as much as you do; but I feel that not one drop of the blood shed in this war is on *my* hands,—I can look up to my God and say this. I tried all in my power to avert this war. I saw it coming, and for twelve years I worked night and day to prevent it, but I could not. The North was mad and blind; it would not let us govern ourselves, and so the war came, and now it must go on till the last man of this generation falls in his tracks, and his children seize his musket and fight our battle, *unless you acknowledge our right to self-government.* We are not fighting for slavery. We are fighting for Independence, and that, or extermination, we *will* have.''

. . . [Gilmore inquired of Davis:] ''And slavery, you say, is no longer an element in the contest?''

''No, it is not. It never was an essential element. It was only a means of bringing other conflicting elements to an earlier culmination. It fired the musket which was already capped and loaded. There are essential differences between the North and the South, that will, however this war may end, make them two nations.''

. . . ''Then the two governments are irreconcilably apart,'' [Gilmore said.] ''They have no alternative but to fight it out. But, it is not so with the people. They are tired of fighting and want peace; and, as they bear all the burden and suffering of the war, is it not right they should have peace, and have it on such terms as they like?''

''I don't understand you; be a little more explicit.''

''Well. Suppose the two governments should agree to something like this: To go to the people with two propositions; say: Peace, with Disunion and Southern Independence, as your proposition; and: Peace, with Union, Emancipation, No Confiscation, and Universal Amnesty as ours. Let the citizens of all the United States (as they existed before the war) vote 'Yes,' or 'No,' on these two propositions, at a special election within sixty days. If a majority vote Disunion, our government to be bound by it, and to let you go in peace. If a majority vote Union, yours to be bound by it, and to stay in peace. The two governments can contract in this way, and the people, though constitutionally unable to decide on peace or war, can elect which of any two propositions shall govern their rulers. Let Lee and Grant, meanwhile, agree to an armistice. This would sheathe the sword; and, if once sheathed, it would never again be drawn by this generation.''

''The plan is altogether impracticable. If the South were only one State, it might work; but, as it is, if one Southern State objected to emancipation, it would nullify the whole thing, for you are aware the people of Virginia cannot vote slavery out of South Carolina, or the people of South Carolina vote it out of Virginia.''

''But three-fourths of the States can amend the Constitution. Let it be done in that way—in *any* way, so that it be done by the people. I am not a statesman or a politician, and I do not know just how such a plan could be carried out; but you get the idea—that the PEOPLE shall decide the question.''

''That the *majority* shall decide it, you mean. We seceded to rid ourselves of the rule of the majority, and this would subject us to it again.''

''But the majority must rule finally, either with bullets or ballots.''

''I am not so sure of that. Neither current events nor history shows that the majority rules, or ever did rule. The contrary, I think, is true. Why, Sir, the man who shall go before the Southern people with such a proposition—with *any* proposition which implied that the North was to have a voice in determining the domestic relations of the South— could not live here a day! He would be hanged to the first tree, without judge or jury.''

. . . As we were leaving the room, he [Davis] added:

''Say to Mr. Lincoln from me, that I shall at any time be pleased to receive proposals for peace on the basis of our Independence. It will be useless to approach me with any other.'' [17]

[17] Edmund Kirke (pseud. J. R. Gilmore), *Down in Tennessee and Back by Way of Richmond* (New York, September, 1864), 269–81. A shorter version of Gilmore's account of the interview appeared in the *Atlantic Monthly* for September, 1864.

☞ On a speaking tour through the Southeast following the fall of Atlanta, Davis attempted to rally the war-weary masses, but also he candidly spoke of the manpower shortage and the massive problem of army desertions. In Augusta, Georgia, on October 5, 1864, he again set forth the priorities that he had declared in the midsummer interview.

. . . Ours is not a revolution. We are a free and independent people, in States that had the right to make a better government when they saw fit. They sought to infringe upon the rights we had; and we only instituted a new government on the basis of those rights. We are not engaged in a Quixotic fight for the rights of man; our struggle is for inherited rights; and who would surrender them? Let every paper guaranty possible be given, and who would submit? From the grave of many a fallen hero the blood of the slain would cry out against such a peace with the murderers. The women of the land driven from their homes; the children lacking food; old age hobbling from the scenes of its youth; the fugitives, forced to give way to the Yankee oppressor, and now hiding in your railroads, all proclaim a sea of blood that free-men cannot afford to bridge. There is but one thing to which we can accede—separate State [national] independence. Some there are who speak of reconstruction with slavery maintained; but are there any who would thus measure rights by property? God forbid. Would you see that boy, with a peach-bloom on his cheek, grow up a serf—never to tread the path of honor unless he light the torch at the funeral pyre of his country? Would you see the fair daughters of the land given over to the brutality of the Yankees?

If any imagine this would not be so, let him look to the declarations of Mr. Lincoln, the terms he offers; let him read the declarations of the Northern press; let him note the tone of the Northern people; and he will see there is nothing left for us but separate independence.

Who now looks for intervention? Who does not know that our friends abroad depend upon our strength at home? That the balance is in our favor with victory, and turns against us with defeat, and that when our victory is unquestioned we will be recognized, and not till then.

We must do our duty, and that duty is this: Every man able to bear arms must go to the front, and all others must devote themselves to the cause at home. There must be no pleading for exemption. We are fighting for existence; and by fighting alone can independence be gained. . . .[18]

☞ Having tried to clarify for the southern people his view that national independence was the one overarching war aim for which all else must be sacrificed, Jefferson Davis, in his message to the Confederate Congress on November 7, 1864, emerged in a role that is not generally associated with him, that of would-be Confederate emancipator.

[18] Richmond *Dispatch*, October 10, 1864, as reprinted in Dunbar Rowland (ed.), *Jefferson Davis, Constitutionalist: His Letters, Papers, and Speeches* (10 vols.; Jackson, Miss., 1923), VI, 357–58.

❧ CHAPTER III ☙
The Great Debate
Begins

🔫 BEFORE PRESIDENT DAVIS made his own bid for a change in southern policy concerning the slaves, various lesser voices clamored in the early fall of 1864 for greater military use of blacks by the Confederacy. One of these voices was that of Governor Henry W. Allen of Louisiana, whose confidential letter to the Confederate secretary of war in September, 1864, was captured by the Federals and published:

The time has come for us to put into the army every able-bodied negro man as a soldier. This should be done immediately. Congress should at the coming session take action on this most important question. The negro knows that he cannot escape conscription if he goes to the enemy. He must play an important part in the war. He caused the fight, and he will have his portion of the burden to bear. We have learned from dear-bought experience that negroes can be taught to fight, and that all who leave us are made to fight against us. I would free all able to bear arms and put them into the field at once. They will make much better soldiers with us than against us and swell the now depleted ranks of our armies. I beg you to give this your earnest attention.[1]

🔫 Allen's and other such proposals created mere ripples, however, as compared to the splash caused by the Richmond *Enquirer* in October, 1864. Described by one historian as "perhaps the finest daily newspaper in the South," the *Enquirer* (October 6, 1864, as reprinted in the Lynchburg *Virginian,* October 8) floated a trial balloon that commanded widespread attention not only

[1] Henry W. Allen to James A. Seddon, September 26, 1864, *O.R.*, Series I, Vol. XLI, Pt. 3, p. 774.

throughout the South but in the North and even in England.[2] The fact that the *Enquirer* usually supported the policies of Jefferson Davis heightened the interest in its views:

. . . We should be glad to see the Confederate Congress provide for the purchase of two hundred and fifty thousand negroes, present them with their freedom and the privilege of remaining in the States, and arm, equip, drill and fight them. We believe that the negroes, identified with us by interest, and fighting for their freedom here, would be faithful and reliable soldiers, and under officers who would drill them, could be depended on for much of the hardest fighting. It is not necessary now to discuss this matter, and may never become so, but neither negroes nor slavery will be permitted to stand in the way of the success of our cause. This war is for national independence on our side, and for the subjugation of white[s] and the emancipation of negroes on the side of the enemy. If we fail the negroes are nominally free and their masters really slaves. We must, therefore, succeed. Other States may decide for themselves, but Virginia, after exhausting her whites, will fight her blacks through to the last man. She will be free at all costs.

The *Enquirer*'s proposal inspired a quickening controversy throughout much of the South, for the five daily newspapers of Richmond, described by one northern journalist as being "in many respects the ablest on the continent," were closely watched and widely quoted by southern as well as northern newspapers.[3] The Lynchburg *Virginian* (October 8, 1864), for example, promptly endorsed the *Enquirer*'s stand:

The *Enquirer* has . . . arrayed itself against the prejudices of a very large majority of the people of the South who, added to a natural distaste of seeing negroes clothed in regimentals with arms in their hands, have no confidence in their prowess as soldiers. It does not follow, however, that the popular instinct in this regard points to right conclusions. Indeed, the Yankees have taught us a lesson to the contrary.

[2] The quotation is from Harrison A. Trexler, "The Davis Administration and the Richmond Press, 1861–1865," *Journal of Southern History,* XVI (May, 1950), 178.
[3] Whitelaw Reid as quoted in J. Cutler Andrews, *The South Reports the Civil War* (Princeton, 1970), 26.

They have stolen our negroes and made soldiers of them; so that the hands which might have been taught to defend, have been turned against us. The late conflicts about Petersburg, and that at Saltville, where negro soldiers were in the van and suffered most, show that they can be disciplined to take the post of danger and fight for the men who prepare them for it. They stopped many a "rebel" bullet that would have struck down their white confederates.

Lincoln has acknowledged that he relies more upon his two hundred thousand negro soldiers, than upon all the whites at his command. Without them, he says, it would strip the North of its white population, to conquer the South and end the war. However this may be, we know that he is making good use of his negro soldiers. When, therefore, we see a Government controlling a population three times greater than ours, buying up European mercenaries and pressing our slaves into its service to save its native population from the ravages of the sword, it becomes a question for us to consider whether our prejudices should longer allow us to condemn the flower of our population, the hope of the country, to be wasted and destroyed, rather than mould to our use and make subsidiary to the great ends of independence, the inferior race that has so long acknowledged our guidance and control! Surely, they are good enough for Yankee bullets, without our demanding that, in every case, the sacrifice we offer to the fierce Moloch of war and the demon of the North—who seeks to depopulate our country of the high-spirited race who inhabit it—shall be the best blood of the nation. Negroes fighting for the soil upon which they were raised; for the homes of those with whom they have grown up; whose children they have nursed and cared for, could surely be made as efficient as the negro soldiers of the invader. *And they could as well be spared to feed the insatiate appetite of war.*

More than a year ago we threw out suggestions similar to those we take from the *Enquirer*; but, with the exception of the Mobile *Register,* we do not remember that another *journal* in the Confederacy favored them. The time had not arrived for the discussion of the subject. But it will come, it is coming, unless an early peace make it unnecessary. We believe that an army of two hundred thousand able-bodied slaves of the better class, could be organized and induced to fight for their freedom on the Southern side of this question. We should agree to give it to them and a home amongst us for themselves and their posterity in all time to come. If they will fight for freedom by the side of strangers from the North, they will fight better for the same boon in the armies where the sons of their former masters contend for the homes of both master and slave.

With respect to the details of organization, that would be a matter for our military authorities to perfect and arrange, with a due regard to the feelings and prejudices of our soldiery and people.

But, the sooner attention is turned to the subject the better it may be. Our armies need to be replenished and if we are to have another campaign, Congress, at its meeting in November, should adopt a policy upon this subject and provide for an auxiliary force to be composed of two hundred thousand negroes to act in conjunction with our armies. Circumstances, we fear, may compel us, the weaker party, to recede from the high ground we have taken and force us to match Yankee negroes with Southern defenders of the same class; putting also, in the matter of exchange, the one against the other, and thus relieve the question of its present embarrassment. We sincerely desire to see a frank and open discussion of this subject by the Press of the Confederacy, so that not only the attention of the Government may be directed to it, but that such indications of the public sentiment may be manifested as will induce Congress to take action in the premises.

☞ Adding to its argument for emancipating slaves who would bear arms for the Confederacy, the Lynchburg *Virginian* (October 20, 1864) set forth historical precedents for such a policy and emphasized the alleged attachment of the blacks to their southern homes:

. . . We once knew a free negro who served under Decatur during the last war with Great Britain. He was at the taking of the Macedonian, and was as proud of the achievements of the great Commodore as any man could have been who ever served under him. This negro was a patriot, and died at last, by an accident, while engaged in firing a salute in honor of Fillmore and a portion of his Cabinet, then on a visit to Harper's [*sic*] Ferry. Many of our citizens will remember the old colored drummer who came with the first troops that reached this city from New Orleans. He had served in the same capacity during the last war, and was as full of martial pride, and expressed himself as anxious to get "Lincoln's head" as any of the gay young men who marched to the music of his drum. These are only isolated cases out of many that could be cited. Negroes can be imbued with martial spirit and converted, by drill and discipline, into that living machine which we denominate a soldier. They gave many individual instances of heroism during the war for our independence of Great Britain. The cases of Gen. Marion's servant, Billy, and of Capt. Snipes' boy, Cudjo, occur to us at this moment. A book has been written about "The Colored Patriots of the Revolution," from which we could extract largely if it were deemed necessary. The British sought to liberate the slaves of the Colonists and to turn them upon their masters. No reader well versed in the history of the country and of this State especially, can be ignorant of Dunmore's proclamation. The Yankees have but followed his infamous example, going a little further however and organizing the stolen slaves into companies, regiments and battalions. Many of them were found faithful to our fathers notwithstanding, and so they will adhere to our fortunes.

This is their home and country. They know no other. If they desire freedom, and can be stimulated to earn it, they will make greater exertions to secure and enjoy that boon *here* than elsewhere. They have grown up amongst us. They have nursed our children and known our care. They have no disposition to migrate. The power of local association is great over them, and they are attached to the soil. Can they not therefore, under the influence of the same stimulus, be made to do all for the people amongst whom they are reared, and upon the soil that has fostered them, that they would do for the enemy? This is a plain proposition and easy of demonstration.

. . . With respect to the moral effect of such a military organization, we think it would be good. Already the world, and especially our enemy, has been greatly deceived in the conduct of the slaves. They thought that the first blast of their bugles would be the signal for revolt and servile insurrection. But they have been disappointed. They stand aghast at the evidence which our colored population give of affection for our people and attachment to our soil. Let them be armed and marshalled for our defence, and the whole world will confess that they have been altogether mistaken in their estimate of Southern slavery and the feelings of the inferior race toward their masters. Let us present to them a grand moral spectacle such as this world has rarely seen. . . .

☞ From the Deep South, the Mobile *Register*, which like the Lynchburg paper had earlier advocated a greater Confederate use of the blacks, urged favorable consideration of the *Enquirer*'s scheme. Paradoxically, the *Register* (as reprinted in the Lynchburg *Virginian*, November 3, 1864) would free some blacks in order to preserve "the freedom of the master race":

If the Yankee Government comes at us again with huge armies in the spring, it will become necessary to tap a yet untouched spring of muscle and bone. The question of the use of our slaves as soldiers is one of simple expediency and necessity. If justification were needed, which it is not, the Yankees have offered it in seizing and arming the servants of the South against their masters. If our slaves are to take part in this unhappy conflict, certainly we have a choice as to the side they shall take. The independence of these States and the freedom of the master race is what we are fighting for. If we lose that in the contest, we lose our slaves as a matter of course. If we can save the first at the expense of the last, the result is so much clear gain. But the proposition does not involve a loss of the last. It is to give freedom to those only who by faithfully fighting for their masters have merited it as a reward. It affects units of the race and not the whole institution. The moral effect of a successful employment of this element of fighting strength would be prodig[i]ous, not only upon the civilized nations of Europe who are watching this great struggle, but it would be staggering to our enemies. It would spike the best guns of the Abolitionists, and greatly enervate the war spirit of the North. We cannot conceive of a more powerful persuasive to peace than to add 150,000 of these men to Gen. Lee's army in Virginia, and officer them with meritorious non-commissioned officers and privates from the armies who have distinguished themselves in battle, and turn the faces of that host towards the Potomac next spring, with Philadelphia as the objective point and the whole line of march to be made the scene of retaliation for the villainous vandalism of Sheridan in the Valley of the Shenandoah. There would be booty enough to excite such an army to warlike deeds. We might empty a town or two of its inhabitants, Atlanta fashion, and establish colonies of Southern contrabands in the places of the forced exiles. By *this* means we can make offensive war, ''carry it into Africa,'' and carry Africa with it and give our philanthropic brothers of the North such a taste of the beloved nigger as would last them for all time. We may have to adopt this policy and the country will have to consider and decide upon it this winter. The only question with us is this—is it necessary to our defense? That decided affirmatively, we should adopt it without a misgiving as to its military results.

The views of private citizens now began increasingly to be heard. The New Orleans *Picayune* (November 3, 1864) carried a story about one slaveholder in the Gulf states who gave enthusiastic support to President Davis' emphasis on independence as the primary war aim:

There is no doubt of a growing disposition within the Confederacy to make soldiers of the negroes. At the same time there is less and less stress laid upon the immutability and inviolability of the institution of slavery. A correspondent of the Mobile Advertiser [and *Register*], of the 27th, whose communication is placed in leaded type in its most conspicuous column, and who says of himself, ''I have made some sacrifices for the Confederacy, and am devoted to its cause; I was raised in the South, and have always been a slaveholder,'' over the signature of ''Corn Bread'' makes these among other observations. Speaking of the danger to the institution of slavery, which, it is feared, will occur from arming them, he says:

Is it in danger now? What becomes of it if we are whipped? What becomes of it even if we are not whipped eventually, and Mr. Sherman, and Mr. Hunter, and Mr. Sheridan, *et id omne genus,* continue to make raids upon us and gather their fighting material from our own doors? Sir, we must look the fact firmly in the face that the institution of slavery is endangered by this war. There are fifteen million of people fighting for its extinction. There are one hundred million applauding them! It is useless to hide our heads under the blanket. We are fighting for national independence, and not for slavery, and so, I think, believes Mr. Jefferson Davis; for the question of slavery, as an object of this war, has never, to my knowledge, obtruded itself in any of his public documents. If we can succeed in this war and maintain our original position, that slavery is a beneficial institution, the only solution of the great problem of the relation of labor to capital; if we can prove the world wrong, and eventually overcome its prejudices, so much the better for us. But let us never forget the great fact that we are fighting for independence, independence! and perish slavery if it stands in its way.

Upon the main question he then observes:

I am firmly convinced that public sentiment is in favor of putting our negroes in the army. I hear it expressed daily by those who own slaves and those who do not. A member of the Mississippi Legislature told me last week that he had seven men he would give to the Government if it would put arms in their hands. A majority of those who are silent on this question speak not their views because they fear being stigmatized as anti-slavery men. I feel sure that before the next meeting of Congress the propriety, expediency, and necessity of arming the negroes will have taken such hold on the public mind, that it will be advocated by a large majority of our representatives. If I am correct, then let every patriotic slaveholder canvass his slaves and find out who among them will volunteer for freedom and his home. Let him prepare the negro's mind for the position he is about to assume, and excite in him that love of country and of home which I believe strongly exists in his breast.

☞ An aspect of the growing controversy that received relatively little attention was the question of whether slaveowners should be compensated for any slaves who might become soldiers. The Mobile *Tribune* (as reprinted in the New Orleans *Picayune*, November 4, 1864) stuck by the view that the slave was property that would have to be paid for by the government:

The question of putting negroes in the army is being discussed somewhat gingerly by some of the papers. One of them (the Charlottesville Chronicle) declares that it might be done, as a last resort, but objects to the Government's giving compensation to the owners; and it gets to this conclusion by showing that the slave is not property in the full sense of the term—that his relation is a mixed one—that he is considered a person by the State and municipal authorities and was also by the constitution of the United States. The article is ingeniously written, but whilst its premises are correct, its conclusions are not true.

A slave, under the law, is a sort of mixed person. He has been represented in the legislation of the country—has the right of trial, as freemen have—is protected within his sphere as carefully as is the owner. All this is true; but he is, nevertheless, nothing but property as regards the rights of the owner. He is bought and sold like other property. He is to the owner worth a given sum paid for him or improved by time, as one pays for a farm or improves it. So that, while in law a person, he is nothing but property to the owner—that is, not a person so far as the law of bargain and sale is concerned.

It follows, of course, that to impress a slave is to impress a certain amount of property—just as much property as is a mule, or a horse, or an amount of corn; and the Government is as much bound to pay for the one as it is for the other.

The question of using the slave for service in the army is not by any means a complex one. It is as easy as an elementary arithmetical problem, and its substance is simply this: The independence of the Confederacy is paramount. Every thing must be sacrificed to that. All the negotiations, whether with Abraham Lincoln or Gen. McClellan, will amount to nothing unless that shall be attained. Less than that is cowardice. Less than that is subjugation by the slow instrumentality of craft. Less than that is putting off the evil day to our posterity. Without independence, and with reconstruction, we shall be subjugated finally, just as much as though Lincoln's army occupied every foot of our country.

There is a difference to be sure. Men of property by this reconstruction might be able to save something of what they possess; but they would hold it only by the sufferance of a section which would have power to rule us by legislation and by individual rapacity; and all that they could leave to their children would be the shame of attempting to establish justice and failing because they lacked the manhood to fight for it. It would not only be eternal disgrace, but it would be flying from a present misery to transmit it to their heirs, on the presumption that the young men of to-day are unfit for anything but a condition of serfdom.

This, however, is foreign to the putting of the slaves into the service. It is not necessary to do that now. The white men are sufficient for the emergency. When they are weakened so much that they cannot hold their position against the enemy, then we can resort to the blacks; and when we do that, as the last resort, then we shall be willing to see slavery sacrificed to the independence of the country. That independence will justify any sacrifice. Everything is well spent that purchases that boon.

🐾 As Southerners debated the question among themselves, they also noted and reacted to northern and European opinions. A "leader" or editorial that was widely reprinted, at least in part, throughout the South appeared in the mighty "Thunderer," the London *Times* (November 7, 1864) :

Nothing in the history of the great struggle which has desolated America is more striking than the gradual dissipation of the illusions with which both parties began this dreadful conflict. The North believed that it was an affair of seventy-five thousand men and ninety days; they thought little of the resistance of the South, which they have found so stubborn and invincible, but worked themselves up into paroxysms of unnecessary fear and anger at the apprehension of a European intervention, of which there was never any chance at all. The South, on the other hand, besides partaking the illusion about intervention, which they believed the want of cotton would very speedily bring to pass, had dreams of their own about the possibility of successfully invading the North and carrying their victorious arms to Philadelphia, or even to New York. Both parties seem to have outlived these illusions; each, from well-founded conviction of the strength and obstinacy of the other, has given up all idea of a speedy peace, and each settles down to the dreary and exterminating conflict with a dogged and unswerving resolution, founded on the realities of the case, stripped of all the gay colouring of hope, and yet unshaken by uncertainty or despondency. No wonder that the war increases in atrocity; no wonder that crimes are every day perpetrated from which in the first months of the struggle both sides would have recoiled with horror. As the tragedy deepens fresh agencies of destruction are brought to bear, the mutual hatred becomes keener, and the abuse of victory more outrageous. From many symptoms, it seems evident that the South are about to add one more element of misery and destruction to those already employed. The North has long broadly admitted that without the 200,000 negroes whom it has in its service it would find it impossible to continue the conflict. These negroes were obtained by the simple process of first manumitting the slaves of disloyal Southern proprietors, and then, by way of a sample of their newly acquired freedom, impressing them into the ranks of the Northern armies. The South has hitherto resisted the far larger population of the Northern States, fed by a continual supply of German and Irish emigration as well as a considerable proportion of their own population, extracted from them by the ingenious device we have just mentioned—the device of making them free in order to plunge them into the very worst of slavery. The peculiar tactics of General Grant, who seems to have derived his notion of war from a game of chess, and is always ready to clear the board by exchanges, giving two or even three pieces for one, has naturally drawn the attention of the South to the fact that they may sink by exhaustion even in the very arms of victory. A campaign in the hands of this new master in the art of war have [*sic*] ceased very much to be a matter of strategy; it is a question of calculation of no very refined kind. The principle of Federal warfare may be thus announced:— Given two numbers, the larger one of which is susceptible of indefinite increase, while the smaller one is constant, to obtain the utmost reduction possible in the smaller one by any reduction, however great, in the larger one. It is an auction of men,—two Federals, five Federals, ten Federals, for a single Confederate life.

We are not therefore surprised to find that the South are seriously taking into consideration the propriety of arming a portion of their population which, though in general bearing towards them very hearty goodwill, has hitherto taken no part in the conflict. The matter is not even yet settled, and the proposal to employ negroes on the Southern side is put forth with obvious uncertainty and trepidation. Nothing can more strikingly illustrate the strongly aristocratic spirit of these slaveholding States, the pride of race, and that unbounded self-reliance which is generated by the constant use of arms, by the habit of absolute command, and the spectacle of implicit obedience, than this reluctance to employ an expedient so obvious in itself and so plainly suggested by the practice of the adversary. The Governor of Louisiana, Mr. Allen, writes to Mr. Seddon, the Confederate Secretary of War, proposing at once to put into the army every able-bodied negro as a soldier. The South, he says, has learnt by bitter experience that the negro can be taught to fight, and that if he is not enlisted on the side of the South he is very likely to find himself forced into the armies of the North. The *Richmond Enquirer* does not presume to say what will be the decision on the question, but it opens its columns to opponents as well as to friends of the proposition, and seems a good deal hampered by the fear of raising certain questions which, doubtless, in other times would have been found exceedingly formidable. It is at much pains to show that the proposition has in it nothing of Abolitionism. The negroes must, indeed, be freed, not as a concession to Northern opinion, but as a reward for the defence of the Southern cause. Nor does the *Enquirer* think the South ought to be revolted by the notion of placing the negro on an equality with themselves. Many of the soldiers in their childhood have been fondled and nursed by faithful negro nurses, and yet no question of equality between the two races has ever been raised. Many a man has manumitted slaves without being suspected of being an Abolitionist. Failure would make slaves of white and black alike. At such a time the rights of property should not be insisted on too strongly. "We have," says the Southern paper, "in our midst half a million of fighting material, which is property. Shall we use that property for the common cause? We make a conscript of the master and every other property, except slaves. The exception of this kind of property ought not to continue."

These arguments are very singular and very noteworthy; they show the difficulties that must be met before Southern opinion can be brought round to the necessity of saving its cause by means of arming the slaves. The argument is very curious, dealing as it does with points which no European community would ever think of raising, and consequently ever think of arguing. The difficulties that would occur to us would be rather of a practical than of a speculative nature; we should not, if we were to be troubled to decide the question for the South, make ourselves at all uneasy about the difference between manumission and abolition, as taught and preached in the great cities of the North, or the right of property involved in taking the help of negroes for the public service. On the question which really appears to us the important one—the safety of putting arms into the hands of the slaves —there really seems to be no difference of opinion. Whatever might be the case if the mob of New York were instructed in military discipline and furnished with weapons of war, whatever danger might result to the Government of Mr. Lincoln from putting arms into the hands of the citizens of Baltimore, the South has no reason to doubt that the negro will fight just as bravely in support of the cause of slavery, which is the cause of his master, as he will in the cause of liberty, and that his fidelity may just as well be relied on in the one case as in the other. We do not expect that this unfortunate race, doomed first to be the cause and afterwards the main instrument of the war, will distinguish itself by prodigies of valour in favour of either side. But we believe there is no reason whatever to think that the negro will be less faithful to those who manumit him as the price of his military service than he is to those who first make him free, and then, as an unforeseen fruit of his freedom, send him forth to die for a boon the sweets of which he has never been allowed to taste. So far from wondering that this thing has been done now, we can only express our surprise that it has never been done before. The objection, we conceive, must have been, after all, not so much to the employment of the negro in itself, as the shock to the rights of property which it involved. On this one kind of possession the South had concentrated all its proprietary feeling, and the man who would submit without a murmur to the impressment of his horses or his crops may very likely shrink back with a species of superstitious horror from the attempt by his own Government to deprive him of those very slaves for whom he has already fought a long and desperate war. But the obvious expediency of recruiting by any means the shrunken battalions of the Southern armies, the advantage of possessing a kind of troops which if not to be trusted in very arduous duty may yet relieve the veteran white battalions from much labour that wears down their strength and thins their numbers, is so manifest that we are convinced the suggestion of Governor Allen will before long be adopted, and that the South will confront the North with an equal number of negroes, thus undoubtedly greatly increasing the horrors of a war which needs no aggravation, but at the same time redressing in a great degree the inequality between the two contending parties.

☞ As interested as educated Southerners were in the views of the London *Times,* the quarrel was essentially among homefolk, that is among and for Southerners themselves. The Richmond *Enquirer* opened its columns to supporters as well as opponents of its proposal and the letters poured in. A Confederate military officer from Halifax County, in south-central Virginia, one of the early army voices in the newspapers, strongly endorsed the plan and emphasized emancipation as vital to it (*Enquirer*, November 4, 1864) :

. . . That the owners of fifteen negroes and upwards would prefer that Congress should conscript ten or even a greater per centum of their negroes for the army rather than the present law exempting *them*, [owners or overseers] should be revoked, there can be not the least question; that the negroes then remaining at home on large plantations would produce, with the attention of their masters, more than the whole number would if the master were conscripted, and they left intact, cannot be denied. Then what are the objections to bringing this power, which has so long been overlooked, to bear upon our enemy, who are using men of every faith, clime and color to subdue us? Some pretend that the army has great aversion to seeing the negro conscripted, that they will not allow themselves thus to be put on an equality with the negro; others that there is a great principle of morality involved in thus forcing the negro to risk his life for the freedom of his master. If the first class would cultivate the society of our intelligent soldiers more, they would discover the real sentiments of the army to be greatly in favor of negro conscription for recruiting the army for the ensuing Spring. As to those who entertain the latter view of "moral objection," etc., their opinions, consciences and moral suasions smack too much of the fanatical and Puritanical love for the negro which the Northman professes when we see them unwilling to allow him to strike a blow against those who would enslave to a worse than Hindustan servitude both master and servant.

That the negro will fight more faithfully for his master than for the Yankee, no one can doubt who has seen the attachment of slaves to their masters in camp, and the reliance and faithfulness with which they discharge sometimes the most dangerous and difficult duties. Then, too, the wonderful change which would be brought upon them by giving such as were enlisted their immediate freedom, with the promise of a grant of land after the war, would cause them to acknowledge and look upon the Yankee as their inferior, whom they now consider as their equal. Let this freedom be given them in due form by their masters, and solemnly confirmed by the seal of the County Court upon their being conscripted, and we would hear no more of negroes running to the enemy to be free. Contented and happy around their camp fires, they, with proper discipline and drill, would make us soldiers superior to any the enemy have yet brought against us.

. . . In other words only the best officers should be selected to command these troops, and, our word for it, we will have in the fourth year of the war a new and powerful reinforcement, a force capable of anything less than the greatest emergency, and an offset to the hirelings and blacks that the enemy are bringing against us which they never dreamed of. Do this now and we will only do what is evidently becoming more apparent we will have to do sooner or later, namely: meet with the same material that class of the enemy's army which, unless counterbalanced thus, will form an important element in our defeat and subjugation. These remarks are dictated by a clear conviction of what is daily becoming more urgent by the great desire of the majority of our people and army for this enactment and by the circumstances around me; for be it noted that I write from a section of Virginia the most prosperous, and that there are ten farmers living adjacent owning more than twenty thousand acres of land between them and from this broad area not one single soldier is furnished to the army. Think, Virginians, of twenty thousand acres of land in Virginia owned by ten different families not furnishing a single representative in the army. If such be the case in Virginia, what must it be in the less populous South, where the extensive cotton lands of the rich planter extend for miles away. Yet these men are willing, yea many of them anxious to contribute their proportion of negroes to the service, and one hundred could be raised in this immediate neighborhood without material detriment to the farming interests of the country. Then can there be any reasonable wish on the part of Congress to delay legislation on this subject when the forces are wanted in the army, the officers are at hand to command them, and the masters are willing to contribute them.

Let Congress take this into consideration at an early day. Let us have prompt and vigorous action on this subject, and not have to lament in the Fall of sixty-five the many reverses which would have been prevented by the organization of such a force.

🖝 In the same column of the *Enquirer* with the army officer's letter, a citizen signing himself "South," and also from Halifax County, expressed his horror at homegrown abolitionism:

. . . Can it be possible that you are serious and earnest in proposing such a step to be taken by our Government? Or were you merely discussing the matter as a something which might be done? An element of power which might be used—meaning thereby to intimidate or threaten our enemy with it as a weapon of offence which they may drive us to use? Can it be possible that a Southern man—editor of a Southern journal—recognizing the right of property in slaves, admitting their inferiority in the scale of being and also their social inferiority, would recommend the passage of a law which at one blow levels all distinctions, deprives the master of a right to his property, and elevates the negro to an equality with the white man?—for, disguise it as you may, those who fight together in a common cause, and by success win the *same* freedom, enjoy equal rights and equal position, and in this case, are distinguished only by color. Are we prepared for this? Is it for this we are contending? Is it for this we would seek the aid of our slaves? To win their freedom with our own independence, to establish in our midst a half or quarter of a million of black freemen, familiar with the arts and discipline of war, and with large military experience! Has the bitter experience of Virginia with regard to free negroes already been forgotten? Has that fixed subject of legislation found its solution and remedy in the wise expedient of arming and training to arms not only her worthless free negro population, but is this class to be multiplied ten-fold by this slave conscription? Will ignorant, thieving, brutal free negroes be rendered less ignorant, less thievish, more humane by this training of the camp? by the campaigns of three or four years? When President Davis said: "We are not fighting for slavery, but independence," he meant that the question and subject of slavery was a matter settled amongst ourselves and one that admitted of no dispute —that he intended to be independent of all foreign influences on this as well as on other matters—free to own slaves if he pleased—free to lay our own taxes—free to govern ourselves. He never intended to ignore the question of slavery or to do aught else but express the determination to be *independent* in this as well as in all other matters. What has embittered the feelings of the two sections of the old Union? What has gradually driven them to the final separation? What is it that has made two nationalities of them, if it is not slavery? It was slavery that caused them to denounce us [as] inferiors; it was slavery that made the difference in our Congressional representatives; it was slavery which made the difference in our pursuits, in our interests, in our feelings, in our social and political life; it is slavery which now makes of us two people, as widely antagonistic and diverse as any two people can be, and it only needs a difference of language to make the Northerner and Southerner as opposite as the Frenchman and the Englishman. You say "the liberty and freedom of ourselves and children; the *nationality* of our country," &c., are involved in this struggle. Yes; and of this *nationality* you would deprive us, for, instead of being as we now are, a nation of freemen holding slaves as our property, you would make us a nation of white men with free negroes for our equals. Messrs. Editors, if you had sought in the political body of the Confederacy for some spot at which to aim and strike one blow which should at once deprive it of life, you could not have found one more vital or had struck with more deadly certainty than you have done by the advocacy of such a scheme; and, if there is any member of Congress so lost to his sense of the duty which he owes to his country and the Constitution which he has sworn to defend; if there is one who is not tired of the scenes of blood and ruin and devastation which have stained and desolated many portions of our beloved land, but yet desires to see more and yet a thousand fold more of the strife and woe and misery, begotten by civil revolution, let him persuade Congress to pass such a law and attempt to carry out such a system, and the things which have been will be nothing to the things which shall be—the revolution and war, born and nurtured and raging in our midst, shall be nothing when compared to that struggle in which we are now engaged, as the wind and desolating tornado, compared to the mild Summer wind—as the angry fury of the ocean waves, when lashed by fierce blasts, to the smooth surface of the mountain lake.

The Yankee *steals* my slave, and makes a soldier and freeman of him to *destroy* me. You *take* my slave, and make a soldier and freeman of him to *defend* me. The difference in your intention is very great; but is not the practice of both equally pernicious to the slave and destruction to the country? And at the expiration of ten years after peace what would be the relative difference between my negro *stolen* and freed by the Yankee and my negro taken and freed by you? Would they not be equally worthless and vicious? How would you distinguish between them? How prevent the return of him whose hand is red with his master's blood, and his enjoyment of those privileges which you so lavishly bestow upon the faithful freedman?

Have you thought of the influence to be exerted by these half or quarter million of free negroes in the midst of slaves as you propose to leave them at the end of the war; these men constitute the bone and sinew of our slaves, the able-bodied between 18 and 45. They will be men who know the value and power of combination; they will be well disciplined, trained to the use of arms, with the power and ability of command; at the same time they will be grossly and miserably ignorant, without any fixed principle of life or the ability of acquiring one. The camp and the battle are not considered the best school of virtue. With habits of idleness learned in camp, with no fixed calling or business in which to engage, a class by color and circumstances proscribed and unable to rise. Then, again, these men must have their wives and children slaves, subject to all the restrictions of slavery, whilst they are to enjoy all the privileges of freedom. Will not this necessarily make them discontented? or if, as you ought in *gratitude* and perhaps in policy, to free their wives and children. This will give you, instead of a half a million, a million and a half or two million free negroes in your midst. That is more than one half of the present slave population of the Confederate States.

How long would slavery last under this strain? Is not your proposition *abolitionism* in disguise? No, Messrs. Editors, we could not live in a country inhabited by such a class. Either they or we would be forced to leave. Which would it be, and where and how would they go? Abra[ha]m Lincoln emancipates all he can steal. You would take and emancipate one-half at a word, or at all events you would take and emancipate that portion without whom the other portion would be valueless and a charge upon the country. No, our cause is not so desperate, nor its condition so low, as to need the aid of an army of free negroes. There are stout arms and brave hearts enough amongst the white men of the Confederacy to win and secure its freedom, and he who would call upon the poor ignorant slave to fight his battles for the boon of a worthless freedom must not only be deeply despondent. But [he is also] regardless of the duties he owes to his country, to his negro and to himself. It is not for the slave, either, to win freedom for the white man, as you would have him; or to take the yoke of subjugation

91

upon him, as would the Yankee. But it is for the Southern white man
to achieve his own independence, to secure himself in the possession
of his slave, and to secure the slave the secure possession of a good
master.

🖎 In Montgomery, Alabama, where the peripatetic Memphis *Appeal* was now refugeeing, after a spell in Atlanta before Sherman arrived, a Confederate soldier also expressed his opposition to the idea of black comrades and his doubt that white resources of the South were truly exhausted (*Appeal*, November 3, 1864):

It is with regret that I notice some of the papers of this city, Augusta
and Mobile, advocating the policy of placing negroes in our armies,
"armed and equipped as the law directs." It is well known to every
intelligent man in the country that it would not only affect the social
community in the future, but would be a most ruinous step to our
armies in the field. Were it the last resort, I don't think there would
be much objection to the plan; but until all the men are brought out
who are now in the Confederacy able to bear arms, I think it premature and untimely.

The Yankees for eighteen months have had negroes in their armies;
and from what they say, got very little good fighting out of them.
Would it be any better if they were in our armies? I think not, and if
it is ever tried disaster and defeat will follow in its train.

I think the advocates of the move hear the low mutterings in the
President's speech here, pretending a storm that will shake them from
their "soft places," and place a musket in their hands.

One correspondent, "Now's the Hour," went so far as to say, "I
have no idea the niggers will desert worse than the white soldiers."
Quite a compliment, indeed, to the troops who have for nearly four
years, defended his splendid fortune from the enemy!

I hope such a proposition may not come before our Congress, though
should it be brought up they will deal with it as men regardless of
favor. But should such a measure meet with success before the Congress our Chief Executive knows too well how to keep the armies together to let it pass from under his hand.

🖎 Much of the powerful journalistics opposition to any Confederate tampering with the "cornerstone" lay low, especially in Richmond, as the controversy began. One exception was a newspaper in Lynchburg, Virginia, the *Republican* (November 2, 1864) :

The proposition is so strange—so unconstitutional—so directly in conflict with all of our former practices and teachings—so entirely subversive of our social and political institutions—and so completely destructive of our liberties, that we stand completely appalled [and] dumfounded at its promulgation. When Lincoln first armed the negroes against us, we all remember what just indignation it excited throughout the world, and how revolting it appeared to the minds of our people; and when insult was added to injury, by requiring us to exchange negroes for white men, the base proposition was indignantly rejected as worthy only of such a brutal nature as Beast Butler's. To this day, thousands of our soldiers are languishing in Northern prisons, because neither they nor we will consent to acknowledge Lincoln's negroes as their equals. But those just and refined sentiments of gentlemanly warfare seem no longer to be regarded by a portion of the Southern press as matters of any consequence at all, and they not only virtually declare that Lincoln and Butler's theory of amalgamated warfare is right, but that the South should improve upon their example and elevate the slave to full political and civil equality with his master! In short it is abolition. This is the naked proposition of these journals when stripped in all its deformity.

They propose that Congress shall conscribe two hundred and fifty thousand slaves, arm, equip and fight them in the field. As an inducement of them to be faithful, it is proposed that, at the end of the war, they shall have their freedom and live amongst us. "The conscription of negroes," says the *Enquirer*, "should be accompanied with freedom and the privilege of remaining in the States." This is the monstrous proposition. The South went to war to defeat the designs of the abolitionists, and behold! in the midst of the war, we turn abolitionists ourselves! We went to war because the Federal Congress kept eternally meddling with our domestic institutions, with which we contended they had nothing to do, and now we propose to end the war by asking the Confederate Congress to do precisely what Lincoln proposes to do —free our negroes and make them the equals of the white man! We have always been taught to believe that slaves are property, and under the *exclusive* control of the States and the courts. This new doctrine teaches us that Congress has a right to free our negroes and make them the equals of their masters.

Now, we are free to say that if the South is to be abolitionized in the end, it would have been far better for us to have been abolitionized in the beginning, and that, if such a terrible calamity is to befall us at all, we infinitely prefer that Lincoln shall be the instrument of our disaster and degradation, than that we ourselves should strike the cowardly and suicidal blow. Lincoln steals our negroes and burdens his people with keeping them; the *Enquirer* proposes to free our negroes and make them a perpetual burden to the Confederacy, a standing insult to the manhood of our people!

But this is not the most hateful aspect of this question. "Justice and sound policy," says the *Enquirer*, "demand that we make freemen of those who fight for freedom." This is the beast in all its frightful deformity. Lincoln and Butler declare that the negroes who they make fight for "freedom," are entitled to it, and therefore should be treated and exchanged as the equals of Southern gentlemen. If the wild doctrines of the *Enquirer* be sanctioned by our people or Government, then President Davis cannot gainsay the propositions of Butler and Lincoln, and must consent to the exchange of negroes for white men. But this is not all.

If "those who fight for freedom" are entitled to it then they are "entitled" to it equally. If the negro is made to fight our battles of "freedom" then he must be governed by the same laws of war, and he must stand upon the same footing of the white man after the war. What will be the consequences? Why, if 250,000 negro men are entitled to their freedom because they fight for it, then their wives, children and families are also entitled to the same boon, just as the wives, children and families of the white man who fight the same battle. In other words, the South is to be converted by this war into an abolitionized colony of free negroes, instead of a land of white freemen, knowing their rights and daring to maintain them. If the negroes are to be free, they must be equally free with the master. If they are to be armed like the master, then they *are in fact* equal to the master. What is the result? Why, they never can be slaves again, and must be treated as the master, politically, civilly and socially. "Those who fight for freedom are entitled to freedom," says the *Enquirer*, and we say so too. If the white men of the South are willing to make the shameful confession that they have accepted a war which they cannot fight to a successful issue, and that they claim rights in slaves which they are incapable of maintaining by force of arms, then we say we deserve no other fate than to be leveled to the equality of our negroes. . . .

☺ Joining the Lynchburg *Republican* in its horror at the heresy suggested by the *Enquirer* was the *North Carolina Standard*, published at Raleigh by William W. Holden. One of the most enigmatic and controversial figures in Tarheel history, Holden by 1864, after various convolutions, spoke for the powerful peace movement in the Old North State. In the terms of a later generation of wartime Americans, Holden had become a Southern "dove," but, at the same time, he and his *Standard* (October 18, 1864) made a strong appeal to Tarheel friends of slavery and of the racial status quo:

. . . Do we dream, or is this sad reality? Do we indeed live in a Gospel land, under the sun of the nineteenth century? What people is this? Are these the descendants of Washington, and Jefferson, and Gaston, and Lowndes, and Moultrie, and Prentiss, and Jackson, and Polk, and Harrison, and Clay? The people—no, the government of the North—with a refinement of cruelty to which language can give no adequate expression, has armed hundreds of thousands of these poor creatures, huddled them in camps, and hurled their bodies against our breast-works and through storms of grape, and canister, and minnie [*sic*] balls, and thus sent them to their death in their efforts to overcome us; and now it is proposed that *we* should do the same thing—should "lay aside our scruples," and commit this great sin against our slaves, against ourselves, against humanity, and against God. Is our government going to do it? If it does, it will proclaim by such an act that the white men of the Confederate States are not able to achieve their own liberties, and will thus in reality give up a contest which it will seek to prolong by the cowardly sacrifice of an unwarlike and comparatively innocent race.

The proposition is to free two or three hundred thousand slaves, and then order them to fight for us. Will they do it? Would they not, with arms in their hands, either desert to the enemy or turn their weapons against us? And what would our soldiers say to a proposition which would place negro troops on the same footing with themselves?

We have a right to speak freely, and we intend to do so, so far as the Conservatives [wartime party of opponents of the Davis administration] of this State are concerned. They, the Conservatives, have done more than their duty in this war. There are fewer deserters among them, and there are fewer of them at home than the original secessionists. They are willing to continue the war *by* white men, and *between* white men, as long as there is ground to hope that the South can succeed, provided every honorable effort is made meanwhile to obtain peace; but they are not willing to remain in the ranks and fight side by [side] with the negroes, against negroes and abolitionists, while originals are skulking from service, or making the employment of negroes as soldiers a pretext for not going to the war themselves. The abolitionists of the North are thrusting the poor negro between themselves and danger; and now the secessionists of the South are suggesting the same thing, and proposing to arm our slaves, in the hope that some of them may escape the bullets they ought long since to have dared on the field of battle.

This proposition to arm our slaves is not only inexpressibly wrong in itself, but it is calculated to demoralize our slave population, and thus increase the chances that the institution will be destroyed by the war. Every intelligent slaveholder and non-slaveholder, and every citizen who has a spark of Conservatism or humanity in his bosom, should set his face against it like a flint. The prayer which, in the very nature of things, would be put up for the success in battle of *our* share of these poor creatures, as against the share or interest in similar creatures on the federal side with which they would contend, would cause the blood to run cold and the hair to stand on end. Our secession readers may imagine such a prayer, but we must be spared the effort to conceive it and commit it to paper. . . .

☞ While Holden played on the hopes of those who clung to slavery, the *Southern Presbyterian* (as reprinted in the Raleigh *Confederate,* October 26, 1864) seemed to be in a sentimental mood as it ignored certain messages that were writ large on the wartime wall:

OUR SABLE DEPENDENTS.—We were gratified recently by hearing from a highly intelligent, influential citizen of Charleston, the expression of some views which had often occurred to our own minds on a very inter-

esting and important subject. The subject of the remarks which gratified us were [*sic*] the negro. The precise point which gave us pleasure
was the earnest and eloquent expression of the idea that one result of
this dreadful war will be, by God's blessing, a kindlier feeling than
ever on the part of the master to his slaves. They have proved themselves for the most part so faithful, so docile, so true to their only
friends on earth, the masters God has given to them, that there is not
a Southern heart that will not beat more tenderly towards these affectionate dependents than ever before. We look confidently to see slavery
shorn of all its abuses, so far as may be in any way practicable, within
a very short time after the close of this war. . . .

🖙 South Carolina produced even fewer supporters for the *Enquirer*'s proposal than did North Carolina. Emerging early as a
vehement foe of any Confederate move against slavery was the
Charleston *Mercury*. Edited by Robert Barnwell Rhett, Jr., and
long since made famous as the vehicle for the views of his fire-
eating secessionist father, the newspaper's fury would vastly increase after Jefferson Davis himself became involved in the matter. But even in this initial phase the Rhetts warned through the
Mercury (November 3, 1864) that the stage was being set for
what they regarded as the third great usurpation of power by the
Confederate government:

Usurpation is ever prolific. When the Confederacy, by the Confederate
Congress, claimed omnipotence over the States and its citizens, including the officers of the States in its military resources, by the Conscription Law, any one conversant with human nature must have
known that this might not be the end of its usurpations. A Constitution is like a dyke keeping out the sea. Cut it and the influx of waters
must be endless. This usurpation was soon followed by the Direct Tax
Act, by which the Confederate Government claimed to be omnipotent
and consolidated, in its taxing, as it was, by the Conscription Law, in
its military powers. We are now at a third stage of its usurpations,
soon to [be] accomplished, if not promptly met by the States—*the
power to emancipate our slaves.*

 . . . Now, if there was any single proposition that we thought was
unquestionable in the Confederacy it was this—that the States, and
the States alone, have the *exclusive* jurisdiction and mastery over

their slaves. To suppose that any slaveholding country [*i.e.*, state] would voluntarily leave it to any other power than its own, to emancipate its slaves, is such an absurdity, that we did not believe a single intelligent man in the Confederacy could entertain it. Still less could we believe that after what had taken place under the United States, with respect to slavery in the Southern States, it was possible that any pretension to emancipate slaves could be set up for the Confederate States. It was because the exclusion of slaves from our Territories by the Government of the United States, *looked to their emancipation,* that we resisted it. The power to exercise it was never claimed by that Government. The mere agitation in the Northern States to effect the emancipation of our slaves largely contributed to our separation from them. And now, before a Confederacy which we established to put at rest forever all such agitation is four years old, we find the proposition gravely submitted that the Confederate Government should emancipate slaves in the States. South Carolina, acting upon the principle that she and she alone had the power to emancipate her slaves, has passed laws prohibiting their emancipation by any of her citizens, unless they are sent out of the State; and no free person of color already free, who leaves the State, shall ever afterwards enter it. She has laws now in force, prohibiting free negroes, belonging either to the Northern States, or to European powers, from entering the State, and by the most rigid provisions, they are seized and put into prison should they enter it. These were her rights, under the Union of the United States, recognized and protected by the Government of the United States, and acquiesced in by all foreign nations. And, now, here, it is proposed that the Government of the Confederate States, not only has the right to seize our slaves and to make them soldiers, but to emancipate them in South Carolina, and compel us to give them a home amongst us. We confess, that our indignation at such pretensions is so great, that we are at a loss to know how to treat them. To argue against them, is self-stultification. They are as monstrous as they are insulting.

The pretext for this policy is, that we want soldiers in our armies. This pretext is set up by the *Enquirer* in the face of the fact disclosed by the President of the Confederate States, that two-thirds of our soldiers, now in the army, are absentees from its ranks. The *Enquirer* is a devout upholder of President Davis and the Administration. It does not arraign the Government for such a state of things. It passes over the gross mismangement which has produced them; and cries out, that negroes are wanted to fill the ranks of our armies. . . . It is vain to attempt to blink the truth. The freemen of the Confederate States must work out their own redemption, or they must be the slaves of their own slaves. The statesmanship, which looks to any other source for success, is contemptible charlatanry. It is worse—it is treachery to our cause itself. Assert the right in the Confederate Government to emancipate slaves, and it is stone dead. . . .

🖙   The *Mercury*'s apprehensions arose not only from the Richmond *Enquirer*'s proposal but also from certain resolutions passed by a group of southern governors who met at Augusta, Georgia, in October, 1864. With Governor William Smith of Virginia presiding, the state leaders called generally for renewed zeal in waging war so that peace based on the independence of the Confederacy might be established. But the particular resolution that roused the suspicious ire of the *Mercury* touched on the matter of an increased military role for the slaves:

Resolved, That there is nothing in the present aspect of affairs to cause any abatement of our zeal in the prosecution of the war to the accomplishment of a peace, based on the independence of the Confederate States. And to give encouragement to our brave soldiers in the field, and to strengthen the Confederate authorities in the pursuit of this desirable end, we will use our best exertions to increase the effective force of our armies.

. . . And whereas, the public enemy having proclaimed the freedom of our slaves, are forcing into their armies the able-bodied portion thereof, the more effectually to wage their cruel and bloody war against us; therefore, be it

Resolved, That it is the true policy and obvious duty of all slave owners timely to remove their slaves from the line of the enemy's approach, and especially those able to bear arms; and when they shall fail to do so, that it should be made the duty of the proper authorities to enforce the performance of this duty and to give to such owners all necessary assistance as far as practicable.

Resolved, That the course of the enemy in appropriating our slaves who happen to fall into their hands to purposes of war, seems to justify a change of policy on our part, and whilst owners of slaves, under the circumstances, should freely yield them to their country, we recommend to our authorities, under proper regulations, to appropriate such of them to the public service as may be required.

. . . And, lastly, we deem it not inappropriate to declare our firm and unalterable purpose, as we believe it to be that of our fellow citizens, to maintain our right of self-government, to establish our independence, and to uphold the rights and sovereignty of the States, or to perish in the attempt.

Resolved, That the Chairman be requested to send a copy of these resolutions to his Excellency, President Davis, and also one each to the President of the Senate and the Speaker of the House of Representatives, to be laid before their respective bodies.[4]

> The southern governors, it should be noted, spoke cautiously and vaguely only about "a change of policy" that might be justified and about appropriating such part of the slaves "to the public service as may be required." In the wake of the stormy outcry that greeted Jefferson Davis' proposal, most of the governors, save Smith of Virginia, hastened to deny that they had ever meant to urge anything remotely resembling emancipation. But in October, 1864, even such stalwart spokesmen for states' rights as Governors Vance of North Carolina and Brown of Georgia had unwittingly helped to set the stage for the Confederate President's careful yet crucial bid for a change of policy as the war dragged into the last half of its fourth year.

[4] Adopted on October 18, 1864, by the governors of Virginia, North Carolina, South Carolina, Georgia, Alabama, and Mississippi; in Augusta *Chronicle and Sentinel,* as reprinted in New Orleans *Picayune,* November 2, 1864.

◆§ *CHAPTER IV* §◆
Jefferson Davis
Proposes Emancipation

WRACKED THOUGH THE SOUTHERNERS WERE with the agony of a war they were losing, most Confederates, contrary to those persons who prefer to read history backward, did not know in November, 1864, that they were beaten. Indeed the very duration and magnitude of the war made defeat seem all the more unimaginable and unacceptable to them. Of no one was this apparently truer than of Jefferson Davis.

By November 7, 1864, when he sent his presidential message to the Confederate Congress, Davis had clearly decided, so far as slavery was concerned, that the time had come to cross the Rubicon. He had, obviously in conjunction with his close associate Secretary of State Benjamin, hit upon a scheme that was both modest in its immediate impact and far-reaching in its implications; one that might hold diplomatic as well as military hope for the South; and, above all, one that he believed could be reconciled with a constitution that so elaborately left slavery in the sole hands of the states.

Naturally Jefferson Davis, whom many Southerners were now making the scapegoat for their miseries, broached the subject gingerly and in the most cautious language. A basic feature of his proposal was the distinction, long established in law even if often blurred in practice, between the slave as property and the slave as person, the peculiar characteristic, in other words, of the slave who was at one and the same time both a chattel and a human being. This was the legal pivot on which swung the "radical modification in the theory of the law" for which the Confederate President asked.

After reviewing the military, foreign, and financial situations,

Davis turned to the matter of several proposals for adding "to the number and efficiency of the Army." Then he came to the matter of the slaves:

The employment of slaves for service with the Army as teamsters or cooks, or in the way of work upon the fortifications, or in the Government workshops, or in hospitals and other similar duties, was authorized by the act of 17th of February last, and provision was made for their impressment to a number not exceeding 20,000, if it should be found impracticable to obtain them by contract with the owners. The law contemplated the hiring only of the labor of these slaves and imposed on the Government the liability to pay for the value of such as might be lost to the owners from casualties resulting from their employment in the service.

This act has produced less result than was anticipated, and further provision is required to render it efficacious; but my present purpose is to invite your consideration to the propriety of a radical modification in the theory of the law.

Viewed merely as property, and therefore as the subject of impressment, the service or labor of the slave has been frequently claimed for short periods in the construction of defensive works. The slave, however, bears another relation to the State—that of a person. The law of last February contemplates only the relation of the slave to the master and limits the impressment to a certain term of service.

But for the purposes enumerated in the act, instruction in the manner of encamping, marching, and parking trains is needful; so that even in this limited employment length of service adds greatly to the value of the negro's labor. Hazard is also encountered in all the positions to which negroes can be assigned for service with the Army, and the duties required of them demand loyalty and zeal. In this respect the relation of person predominates so far as to render it doubtful whether the private right of property can consistently and beneficially be continued, and it would seem proper to acquire for the public service the entire property in the labor of the slave, and to pay therefor due compensation rather than to impress his labor for short terms; and this the more especially as the effect of the present law would vest this entire property in all cases where the slave might be recaptured after compensation for his loss had been paid to the private owner. Whenever the entire property in the service of a slave is thus acquired by the Government, the question is presented by what tenure he should be held. Should he be retained in servitude, or should his emancipation be held out to him as a reward for faithful service, or should it be granted at once on the promise of such service; and if emancipated, what action should be taken to secure for the freedman the permission of the State from which he was drawn to reside within its limits after the close of his public service?[1] The permission would doubtless be more readily accorded as a reward for past faithful service, and a double motive for a zealous discharge of duty would thus be offered to those employed by the Government—their freedom and the gratification of the local attachment which is so marked a characteristic of the negro, and forms so powerful an incentive to his action. The policy of engaging to liberate the negro on his discharge after service faithfully rendered seems to me preferable to that of granting immediate manumission, or that of retaining him in servitude. If this policy should recommend itself to the judgment of Congress, it is suggested that, in addition to the duties heretofore performed by the slave, he might be advantageously employed as pioneer and engineer laborer, and in that event that the number should be augmented to 40,000.[2]

To summarize the above portion of the President's message, Davis had indeed proposed a "radical modification." The Confederate employment of as many as forty thousand rather than twenty thousand blacks for noncombatant military service would certainly occasion no great shock. But to have found a way partially to circumvent the hopelessness of any kind of emancipation by the southern states themselves and to have the Confederate government commit itself, and thus the South, to the principle of compensated, gradual emancipation was indeed radical. Davis and his closest allies would continue for some months to pin their hopes on such a scheme; and, as will be explained below, Davis and Benjamin would shortly make a daring diplomatic gamble

[1] Davis referred here to the fact that, just as a number of northern states had laws barring the entrance of Negroes, the southern states not only made emancipation by a slaveowner, for whatever reason, quite difficult but also prohibited the freed slave from remaining within the state.

[2] *O.R.*, Series IV, Vol. III, pp. 797–99. Despite the shortage of paper and space, most southern newspapers carried the full text of the message, as they did important documents from the North.

that was intimately related to Davis' proposal—even if, for understandable reasons, they could never publicly acknowledge either the gamble or the relationship. Events in the six grim months ahead would reveal that Jefferson Davis had overestimated the capacity of the Confederate Congress, but ultimately one suspects of the southern people, for voluntary change in the matter of the peculiar institution and the racial relationships that were intertwined with it.

Once past his "radical modification," the President next made the statements that have, strangely enough, received so much attention that they have, at least for later generations, largely obscured what preceded them. He expressed his opposition, strictly for the time being, to making arms-bearing soldiers of the blacks. Why? Davis did not put it this way, but he clearly thought, altogether apart from the diplomatic impact of emancipation, that before the South considered putting guns into the hands of large numbers of Negro men, it would be psychologically sound from the standpoint of the blacks and prudent from the standpoint of the whites to consider first the matter of emancipating them. This is how he proceeded after his proposal concerning the forty thousand slaves:

Beyond these limits and these employments it does not seem to me desirable, under existing circumstances, to go. A broad moral distinction exists between the use of slaves as soldiers in defence of their homes and the incitement of the same persons to insurrection against their masters. The one is justifiable if necessary, the other is iniquitous and unworthy of a civilized people; and such is the judgment of all writers on public law, as well as that expressed and insisted on by our enemies in all wars prior to that now waged against us. By none have the practices of which they are now guilty been denounced with greater severity than by themselves in the two wars with Great Britain, in the last and in the present century; and in the Declaration of Independence of 1776, when enumeration was made of the wrong which justified the revolt from Great Britain, the climax of atrocity was deemed to be reached only when the English Monarch was denounced as having "excited domestic insurrections amongst us."

The subject is to be viewed by us, therefore, solely in the light of policy and our social economy. When so regarded, I must dissent from those who advise a general levy and arming of the slaves for the duty of soldiers. Until our white population shall prove insufficient for the armies we require and can afford to keep in the field, to employ as a soldier the negro, who has merely been trained to labor, and as a laborer the white man, accustomed from his youth to the use of fire-arms, would scarcely be deemed wise or advantageous by any; and this is the question now before us. But should the alternative ever be presented of subjugation or of the employment of the slave as a soldier, there seems no reason to doubt what should then be our decision. Whether our view embraces what would, in so extreme a case, be the sum of misery entailed by the dominion of the enemy, or be restricted solely to the effect upon the welfare and happiness of the negro population themselves, the result would be the same. The appalling demoralization, suffering, disease, and death which have been caused by partially substituting the invader's system of police for the kind relation previously subsisting between the master and slave have been a sufficient demonstration that external interference with our institution of domestic slavery is productive of evil only. If the subject involved no other consideration than the mere right of property, the sacrifices heretofore made by our people have been such as to permit no doubt of their readiness to surrender every possession in order to secure their independence. But the social and political question, which is exclusively under the control of the several States, has a far wider and more enduring importance than that of pecuniary interest. In its manifold phases it embraces the stability of our republican institutions, resting on the actual political equality of all its citizens, and includes the fulfillment of the task which has been so happily begun—that of Christianizing and improving the condition of the Africans who have, by the will of Providence, been placed in our charge. Comparing the results of our own experience with those of the experiments of others who have borne similar relation to the African race, the people of the several States of the Confederacy have abundant reason to be satisfied with the past, and to use the greatest circumspection in determining their course. These considerations, however, are rather applicable to the improbable contingency of our need of resorting to this element of resistance than to our present condition. If the recommendation above made, for the training of 40,000 negroes for the service indicated, shall meet your approval, it is certain that even this limited number, by their preparatory training in intermediate duties, would form a more valuable reserve force in case of urgency than threefold their number suddenly called from field labor, while a fresh levy could, to a certain extent, supply their places in the special service for which they are now employed.[3]

Undoubtedly, Jefferson Davis knew all too well that his proposal would face rough sledding in the Congress, particularly in the Senate. The elections of 1863 had increased the number of Whigs at the expense of Davis' old party, the Democrats. While prewar party ties were supposedly submerged for the duration of the war and for the sake of the Confederate cause, partisanship actually continued to run strongly.[4] And, as mentioned above, war weariness and the sheer frustration of a proud, free people as they suffered one painful defeat after another made Davis and any measure that he might propose attractive, even irresistible targets for many men in and out of Congress.

What may have surprised the Confederate leader was the vehemence and extent of the journalistic opposition to his plan. In Richmond the brilliantly edited *Examiner,* one of the most powerful critics of the Davis administration (despite the editor's clinging to eccentric, antiquated spelling), broke its silence on November 8, 1864 upon what it declared to be a provocative, impractical subject:

The writer of the [President's] Message intended to be cautious, but has in several points written an indiscreet paper. That part which will attract most attention is the passage relating to a suggested conscription of negro soldiers. This project originated with those who had not fully reflected on its character, and has been made a matter of some publicity by others who delight in all things which make a sensation. The proposition has, in fact, made a considerable sensation both in Northern and the Southern States. It has not hitherto been mentioned

---

[3] *Ibid.* This latter portion of Davis' message was foreshadowed by the report to the President a few days earlier from Secretary of War Seddon, *ibid.*, 761–62.
[4] The most helpful study concerning these matters is W. Buck Yearns, *The Confederate Congress* (Athens, Ga., 1960), especially chap. four; chap. seven, 95–99, deals briefly with the question of arming the slaves.

in these columns, because there was no possibility that it would become a practical measure of policy, and because it was a matter to provoke violent discord of feeling and speech at a period when such discussion was most undesirable. Both from its delicacy and from the fact it has never been a subject of official deliberation, we are surprised to see it treated in the President's Message. But since the question has been so introduced, its consideration can no longer be avoided.

It is a proposition which can be supported only on the ground that good soldiers can be made of the negroes. Now what is the real value of the negro as a soldier? The enemy's actual experiment is not the only test which has been applied to the race. Since the conquest of Algiers the French army has contained a considerable force of negroes. They constitute nearly the whole of the troops popularly called "Turcos." It is generally supposed that these Turcos are Moors. There are some Moors among them—but most, even of these, are of the mixed blood. The mass of these troops are negroes, blacker than any of our slaves. They were employed in the Italian war of 1859, or at least they constituted a part of that army which NAPOLEON III marched into Italy five years ago, and which gained the famous victories of Magenta and Solferino. Great expectations were entertained of the negro soldiers by the uninformed. Their appearance among the European troops was a novelty,—and the people amused themselves with apochryphal tales of their ferocious valour in Africa, about to be newly illustrated on the Austrians. But in none of the Italian battles which followed were the negroes prominent; and they were only heard of occasionally as the guards of Lombard regiments, who had thrown down their arms and surrendered [as] soon as they got an opportunity. These negro legions were of course commanded by white officers and kept under severe discipline. The writer of this made enquiries of many among said officers as to their military worth. When any of them would give a definite reply it was always to this effect—that they were good sometimes for a rush but they could not be made to stand grape. *Ils vont bien a la bayonette [sic]—mais il ne valent rien pour la mitraille.*

This answer is the truth, and the whole truth on the subject. The Yankees have taken great pains and persevered in the effort, to make soldiers out of negroes. They have given them the best of everything. Nothing has been left undone to create a martial spirit. Their courage has been carefully nursed. They have been kept near to many battles without being exposed to the fire, so that they might become accustomed to the sights and sounds of war without being unnerved by their own slaughter. But what has the enemy gained by them after two years trial? They got them to make "a rush" at Port Hudson and Battery Gilmer—but they took neither. Those who know the negro never expected less, and will never look for more. That race is capable of blind, brute, contagious excitement, and while in that state it can make, not a charge, but a rush on points where the intelligence of a trained white soldier would show to him only death without the possibility of success. By such wild and senseless onslaught batteries are not taken, nor victories won; for their mob-like rush is not fighting, nor is the excitation, which destroys the sense of danger by a frenzied bewilderment, the courage which directs the aim of the rifle and the point of the sword.

It is sometimes said that negroes would make better soldiers for us than for the Yankees, because they would fight under the eyes of their masters and friends. Such sentimental suppositions show a great ignorance of the negro's character; and even if they were founded on some truth, attachment to his master would be no balance to his native fickleness and the strong incentives to desertion which the enemy would hold out to him. The fact is, the negro soldier costs far more than he is worth to Frenchman and Yankee, and to us he would be more troublesome than to either of the others.

Our enemy has raised its negro army, not as a military, but a political measure—to have the cant of the world on its side—to procure the full and consistent support of the Abolitionist party. With his views and purposes, the creation of the negro soldier is consistent and natural.

But the existence of a negro soldier is totally inconsistent with our political aim and with our social as well as political system. We surrender our position whenever we introduce the negro to arms. If a negro is fit to be a soldier he is not fit to be a slave, and if any large portion of the race is fit for free labour—fit to live and to be useful under the competitive system of labour—then the whole race is fit for it. The employment of negroes as soldiers in our armies, either with or without prospective emancipation, would be the first step, but a step which would involve all the rest, to universal abolition. It would be so understood and regarded by all the world. Our enemy would perceive that he had succeeded in his design to the point of moral subjugation, and would not doubt that our absolute submission was far removed. To our own hearts it would be a confession, not only of weakness, but of absolute inability to secure the object for which we undertook the war. It would be felt by all as a compromise to the abolitionism of the world, incompatible with that independence of action for which the South strives.

But the objections to this project are so manifest that it is unnecessary at present even to suggest them. The President opposed the introduction of negroes into the army as soldiers, but desires a corps of forty thousand to be used in labour on fortifications as engineers, as teamsters and as sappers and miners. To a proposition of that sort, no one could have the least objection, if he had not concluded with an obscure passage, which, if it means anything, means that the forty thousand slaves so employed shall be set free at the end of the war as a reward for their service. Here, while refusing to employ the slaves under arms, he adopts the fatal principle of the original proposition to its fullest extent and puts forth an idea which, if admitted by the Southern people as a truth, renders their position on the matter of slavery utterly untenable. We hold that the negro is in his proper situation—that is to say, in the condition which is the best for him; where he reaches his highest moral, intellectual and physical development and can enjoy the full sum of his natural happiness; in a word, that while living with the white man in the relation of slave he is in a state superior and better for him than that of freedom. But the negro's freedom is to be given him as a reward for his service to the country; his freedom, therefore, is a boon—it is a better state—a natural good of which our laws deprive him and keep him from. Now, that is the whole theory of the abolitionist, and we have the sorrow to think that if one portion of this Presidential message means anything it means that. . . .

🖙 The Richmond *Whig*, another influential foe of President Davis and his policies, expressed its glee that the *Examiner* had spoken out with such "a tremendous crack of its cat-o'-nine-tails." The position of the *Whig* (November 9, 1864) is suggested by its argument that if the slave had to fight, "he should fight for the blessings he enjoys as a slave, and not for the miseries that would attend him if freed'':

Two propositions are plainly deducible from the President's Message, which we cannot for a moment believe he would deliberately give his sanction to. The first is that the condition of freedom is so much better for the slave than that of servitude, that it may be bestowed upon him as a reward and boon. The second is that the Confederate Government has the right to acquire possession of slaves by purchase, or impressment with compensation, and then emancipate them, without the consent of the States, or, in the case of impressment even without the consent of the masters.

The first proposition is a repudiation of the opinion held by the whole South and by a large portion of mankind in other countries, that servitude is a divinely appointed condition for the highest good of the slave, is that condition in which the negro race especially may attain the highest moral and intellectual advancement of which they are capable, and may enjoy most largely such comforts and blessings of life as are suited to them. Of this, we have no doubt, and we hold it to be an act of cruelty to deprive the slave of the care and guardianship of a master. If the slave must fight, he should fight for the blessings he enjoys as a slave, and not for the miseries that would attend him if freed.

This second proposition is still more startling. It is a concession that the Confederate Government has the power and the right to exterminate slavery, by the simple process of impressing or purchasing all the slaves, and then emancipating them. Lincoln has never gone so far as this, for in his plan for ''compensated emancipation,'' he expressly referred the question to the States, acknowledging that they only could determine it.

It is unnecessary to dwell on this subject. We are perfectly sure that the President could never have designed to give his assent to so monstrous a proposition as this. The multiplicity and magnitude of the subjects that claim his attention will suggest a sufficient excuse for the inadvertence of expressions and immaturity of views from which theories so out of place in a communication from the President of these slaveholding States are deducible.

🖙   The Richmond *Dispatch* (November 9, 1864) confessed that it had hoped to avoid the discussion of the painful subject altogether. Then it proceeded to muddy the waters by attacking the suggestion of arming the slaves. Davis himself, of course, had rejected that idea for the time being, and it was not the issue upon which he was attempting to focus attention.

We have forborne to take any part in the discussions relative to the making soldiers of our slaves because it had not yet been formally proposed as a practical question, and we had hoped that it would be passed over. We did not wish to create a breach at a time when harmony is so desirable. As the discussion is to be forced upon us, however, we wish to express our opposition, and the grounds thereof in as few words as we can.

The proposition, in the first place, is totally unconstitutional. We parted from the Old Government because of its determined purpose to interfere in the domestic affairs of the States. Were we still under that Government, engaged in a war with all Europe, and invaded by a million of men, surely nobody will contend that the General Government would possess the power, under the pretext of necessity, to abolish slavery in the States by making soldiers of the slaves; for such is the undoubted effect of that measure. Now, we are not aware that the Confederate Government has any powers which the Federal Government had not.

Second. Let it be conceded that the constitutional power exists. The exercise of it is, nevertheless, a confession of weakness, or rather a *profession* of a weakness which does not exist. We have no occasion to resort to any such extreme measure. Our affairs are in a better condition, and our prospects brighter, than they ever have been since the commencement of the war.

Third. Armies must be fed, and in order to feed them crops must be made. The negroes are our agricultural laborers. Take them from farm-work, and you destroy the army more effectually than Grant can do it with a million of men to back those he has in the field.

Fourth. It would be a powerful stimulant to recruiting for the Yankees. There can be no doubt that a vast number would resort to them who are restrained at present by the apprehension of being forced into the ranks. They stay at home because they are in no danger. Let them see that it is as dangerous to stay as to go, and they will be pretty certain to go. For, with the Yankees, they get a high bounty for enlisting, and liberty and equality into the bargain. The services are set before them which of the two to choose, and there will, we fancy, be little hesitation as to the choice.

Fifth. We give up the whole question when we adopt this measure. Whatever we may be fighting for, the Yankees are fighting for "the nigger"; that is, to abolitionize the South. We are not disposed to gratify them if we can avoid it. Henry Ward Beecher, in one of his speeches, made about a year ago, boasted that slavery had received a mortal blow, and that this war would be the means of spreading "New England ideas," that is, abolitionism, Fourierism, free-loveism, and the whole brood of Yankeeisms, throughout the continent. These ideas, he concluded, would make a surer conquest than the sword.

The Numantians of old won immortal renown by burning up their city, their wives and children, and themselves, rather than be subjugated. If we are reduced to the same extremity, perhaps it will be well to make soldiers of our negroes; for it seems to us that the one is about as much an act of desperation as the other. But we deny that we have come to that point, or are likely to come to it.

The proposition of the Confederate Executive to introduce a larger number of blacks into the public service, as teamsters and laborers, cannot be reasonably objected to. There will be some division on the subject of setting free after the war such as are purchased by the Government for these purposes. It is to be hoped that the discussion of the matter will not be indulged to an unnecessary length, and that the action of the Government will be at once prudent and practical.

☞ With three of the five Richmond newspapers expressing such views, no one could have been surprised that there were cries of outrage and shock from various newspapers in the states to the south of Virginia. The temperature, and with it the rhetoric, of the Charleston *Mercury* (November 12, 1864) began to soar:

The African is of an inferior race, whose normal condition is slavery. Prone to barbarism, and incapable of any other state than that of pupilage, he is at his best estate as the slave of the enlightened white man of this country. All history, experience, and the closest observation and research for the truth have brought the people of these States to this conclusion; and it constitutes, in a moral point of view, the rock of their defence. But if the slavery of the Confederate States be not the best condition for the negroes amongst us—if they are fit for freedom, and manumission be a desirable improvement in their political *status* —an improvement which they may obtain as a reward for service— then the justification heretofore set up for holding them as slaves is false and unfounded. Then is the base of our institution but shifting sand, and the superstructure, unable to support the beating of the winds and waves, must fall.

We would owe an apology to our readers for these stale remarks, but for the extraordinary suggestion in the President's message to which these remarks are pertinent. The purchase of forty thousand male slaves by the Confederate Government . . . might possibly be judicious if properly managed, but to emancipate them afterwards, would not merely disturb the *status* of our negro population, but would go a great way to justify the arguments and views of the abolitionists, while it would give the lie to our professions and surrender the strength and power of our position. We cannot believe that a policy so inconsistent, unsound and suicidal can meet the sanction of any respectable body of Southern men. The liberation of slaves is against the laws of South Carolina, and we believe of most of the other Confederate States. It [liberation] dooms them [Negroes] to ruin, as it does in the United States.

🖙 In a public letter to William Aiken, a former governor of South Carolina, the senior Rhett wailed that nothing since the war began had alarmed him as had the proposal made by Jefferson Davis. Wearing his constitutional blinders in the best Calhounian fashion, South Carolina's most famous secessionist used phrases that harked back to Alexander Stephens' cornerstone speech.

We are in political retirement, and therefore, perhaps, better able than those who control our affairs and shape our destinies, to judge of the wisdom of their measures—the soundness of their policy. . . .

I do not know how it has impressed you or others, but nothing since the war commenced, has struck me with such alarm and despondency, as the late message of the President of the Confederate States, claiming for the Confederate Government the power to emancipate our slaves. . . .

When the people of South Carolina, in Convention assembled, seceded from the Union of the United States, they put forth in justification of their course, as its proximate or *immediate cause,* the various acts of the people of the Northern States, interfering with their institution of slavery. . . .

We did not choose to live in political association with a people who would not leave us at peace with our institutions; but faithlessly sought to destroy them by *indirect* and hostile agitations; and, therefore, we cast off our political association with them. It would be the most extraordinary instance of inconsistent self-stultification the world ever saw, if, under such circumstances, South Carolina should have adopted a Constitution, by which she established the very evil over her people she seceded from the Union of the United States to avoid—if she gave to the Congress of the Confederate States the direct power to emancipate her slaves. I am satisfied that not a single man in the General Convention of the Confederate States which framed the Constitution of the Confederacy, and not a single man in the Convention of South Carolina which adopted it for the State, if conscious that it contained such a power, would have voted for it. If the power exists in the Constitution, it is there contrary to the intention of every statesman who had anything to do with the creation or adoption of the Constitution.

The power, I undersand, is claimed for the Confederate Government from the clause of the Constitution which gives to Congress the power "to raise and support armies." It is contended that, under this clause, the power of Congress is limitless: It has the right to pass laws conscribing into the army every freeman and every slave in the Confederacy. There is not a word in the Constitution directly giving this power. It is claimed by inference—by construction—the very instrumentality which destroyed the Constitution of the United States. A power by which the States may be annihilated and our slaves emancipated, if granted at all, would surely never have been left to inference. It would have been plainly expressed.

. . . Nor is it consistent with the right interpretation of any instrument, to give it the power by inference to destroy that which it was created to protect and perpetuate. The Confederate States had seceded [*sic*] from the Union of the United States—and as separate and independent sovereignties, they set up the Confederacy. To infer from any general power that they parted with the power of self-existence, and gave to their agency, established to perpetuate it, the power to destroy it, is manifestly absurd. Yet if the grant "to raise and support armies" is unlimited, this must be the consequence. The conscription of all the officers of the States, by which the Government of the States is carried on, into the army of the Confederacy, annihilates them, for a State without a Government is dead. The same pretensions with respect to slaves is equally untenable. Slavery is recognized and protected by the Constitution, but contains not a word giving Congress the power to destroy it. . . . There is ample power to protect and perpetuate slavery, but not one word exists in the Constitution that gives to Congress the power to emancipate a slave. The true view of the Constitution seems clearly to be, that it establishes a Confederacy *of freemen*. Freemen constitute the militia of the States. Freemen made—freemen own—and freemen, who made and own the Confederate Government, alone can be called on by that Government to defend it. The power "to raise and support armies," means armies *of freemen*. Over the slaves in the States, the Confederate Government has no power whatever. They are a part of the domesticity of the States, exclusively under their jurisdiction and their control.

The President proposes that Congress shall appropriate money from the Confederate States Treasury to buy and emancipate slaves. Where is the authority for any such appropriation? The purposes for which money may be appropriated from the Treasury of the Confederate States are carefully enumerated in the 8th section of the 1st article of the Constitution. . . . The States may consider such proposition if they think proper. South Carolina as one of the co-sovereigns, forming the Confederacy, claims the right *exclusively* to emancipate slaves within her sovereign jurisdiction, and to exclude from her Territory all Africans, slave or free, from contiguous States or from foreign nations, and I trust in God, she will surrender this right, only with her existence.

The truth is, my dear sir, few of us, I fear, realized the difficulty of mantaining a free Government in War. All free Governments have been destroyed by the Executive absorbing the other departments of Government. Dangerous at all times, from the immense power and patronage always at its disposition—in war, this patronage and power is [*sic*] immensely increased. In waging the gigantic war in which we are engaged, true statesmanship, it appears to me, required that all the great principles which originated it, should have been most sacredly observed. The one great principle, which produced our secession from the United States—was *constitutional liberty—liberty protracted* [sic] *by law.* For this, we have fought; for this, our people have died. To preserve and cherish this sacred principle, constituting as it did, the very soul of independence itself, was the clear dictate of all honest—all wise statesmanship. If any policy was expedient to carry on the war, beyond the power of the Confederate Government to accomplish, there stood the States, ready and willing to cooperate with all their powers, and the appeal was to them. But unfortunately, I think, a different course prevailed, at Richmond. To ignore the States, and to usurp any power deemed expedient to carry on the war, has been the policy pursued. By this course, the high motives—the grand enthusiasm, which lifted us up, to meet our foes, has been chilled and wasted. The Confederate Government threatens to put upon us all the evils we threw off the dominion of our Yankee enemies to avoid. This desperate policy is one of the causes of proposed reconstruction, and also of absenteeism in our armies. Take away from our people the high motive of Constitutional liberty to fight for, and what remains? Set up at Richmond, as our practical Government—an authority usurping, by the single power of conscription, to abolish the State Governments—overthrow the freedom of the Press—and emancipate our slaves—and what becomes of our cause? At a time when union amongst ourselves is so essential to meet the assaults of our foes—is it prudent—is it wise to put forth such despotic pretensions for the Confederate Government?

Will our soldiery fight beside slaves? Emancipation, once begun, soon extends, or must be eradicated. Who would live in such a country as ours without slaves to cultivate it? and who but slaves will live in any country with four millions of emancipated slaves? The hideous ruin consequent upon such a policy the mind revolts in contemplating. Our slaves have acted well throughout the war. They have been an immense source of strength, in furnishing, by their labor, the means for supporting our people and armies. Generally not of their own accord, but by compulsion, those who have been captured have been forced to take up arms against us. They are in their normal condition as slaves, by the decree of God himself. The benefit of emancipation which President Davis would confer upon them, all experience has proved will be the greatest curse. Yet I will dispute neither his ethics nor his wisdom, if he has the power to carry out his policy. I deny his power.

It is not too late for the Government of the Confederate States to reverse its whole policy, and to come back to an honest administration of the Government, within the limits of the Confederate States Constitution. Let the war it has steadily carried on against the Constitution, cease. Let the rights of the States be respected, and their co-operation be evoked. Above all, let us not imitate our Yankee enemies, in their usurpations and oppressions, but faithfully and fearlessly strive to work out our redemption, in humble dependence upon God, through the legitimate means he has placed in our hands. With our affairs thus administered, I have not a doubt of our success.[5]

☞ Much more succinctly than Rhett, the Macon, Georgia, *Telegraph and Confederate* (November 14, 1864) expressed its disapprobation of Davis' proposal in measured words:

. . . The employment of negroes is the most important topic treated in the Message. . . . There can be but little doubt that this portion of the Message will greatly please our enemies, and furnish them with an additional argument in favor of the abolition of slavery. It is an admission that slavery is a state, the release from which is a blessing and a boon.

. . . Negroes can be used to advantage in the army and hospitals, but there is no reason why they cannot successfully be employed and liberally rewarded—not by freedom, which would prove a curse to them and a danger to us; but by such wise enactments as might improve their condition, without changing their *status*. As slaves they should be used and as slaves returned to their masters. If it be necessary to secure their services for the Government, to purchase the negroes required for the army, let them be bought, and, at the expiration of their term of service, let them, as a reward for duties faithfully done, be permitted to select the State in which they will reside and the

[5] Charleston *Mercury*, November 19, 1864. The more sedate Charleston *Courier* (November 12, 1864) expressed its satisfaction with the message as a whole but warned: ''The relations of the white man to the negro are and must be subjects of the States, not of the Federal agency—had we adhered to and insisted on this, the true original and constitutional and political doctrine, we could have prevented this war.''

master whom they will serve. The negro, like the child, is little influenced by promises of reward in the future, and while our enemies would soon find means to make him distrust our promise of freeing him, he could easily be induced to believe that for faithful service rendered, he would be permitted to choose his own home and master. . . .

🕏 A letter-writer ("Q.") in the Macon *Telegraph* (January 6, 1865) used striking language to argue that the preservation of slavery was indeed the central purpose of the war—and threw in, for good measure, some dire threats about possible slave risings:

Amid the storm of revolution, governments are apt to forget the principles to secure which they were instituted, and by which they should be controlled. All history admonishes us of this truth. . . .

It should be constantly kept in view, through all the bloody phases and terrible epochs of this relentless war, that slavery was the *casus belli*—that the principle of State Sovereignty, and its sequence, the right of secession, were important to the South principally, or solely, as the armor that encased her peculiar institution—and that every life that has been lost in this struggle was an offering upon the altar of African Slavery. In the light of this great and solemn truth, is it not a matter of wonder and astonishment, that Southern men should gravely propose to arm, and as a necessary consequence, emancipate all the able-bodied slaves in the Confederacy, or a large portion of them, thereby striking an irretrievable and fatal blow at the institution. The adoption of this policy would be foul wrong to our departed heroes who have fallen in its defense. The compulsory adoption of such a policy would be tantamount to defeat; for what else is the forced assimilation of our institutions to those of the North but the abandonment of the whole object of the war?

. . . The advocates of this measure surely have not considered well the consequences likely to result from arming our slaves. Evidences are not wanting to illustrate the ill-suppressed discontent of many of our slaves in the past. The people seem to have grown over secure because of the unexpected subordination of our slaves during the war. They should remember that the whole white population being under arms, any uprising of the negroes was more than ever impracticable. How different might be the state of things, if they too were armed. They would be equal, perhaps superior, in numbers to our effective white force. What horrors might result from a general revolt? Yankees without and negroes within! At best it is not to be expected that they would be more true than our white veterans, and if two-thirds of them should desert and disperse themselves over the country, co-operating with and led by bad men and deserters of long standing, how appalling would be our condition!

Upon the whole, the proposition under consideration seems to be opposed by principle, consistency, self-respect, honor and safety.

☞ Even in faraway Texas, which had been relatively lucky in escaping the full impact of Federal armies and where news from Richmond now took about a month to arrive, many persons apparently regarded as inexcusable even the discussion of a Confederate policy that might tamper with slavery. The Galveston *Tri-Weekly News* (December 12, 1864; refugeeing in Houston), for example, apologized for having to mention the subject:

. . . It is difficult to imagine any act of the Confederate States Government more unauthorized and more dangerous than to assume the ground that negro slaves may become entitled to their freedom by meritorious services; but if there can be a greater assumption of power, of a more dangerous exercise of it, it is an act of the Confederate States Government, by which it is declared that slaves who have been in the military service shall be free; that the freedom of negroes is to be won by their fighting for it.

We purposely avoid discussion of this subject at this time in all its various aspects and relations, but present the foregoing as our reasons, in part, for hoping that the recommendation of Mr. Davis in his late message, in regard to the employment of slaves in the military service, may not be adopted by Congress.

We think it is a matter of regret that any suggestion should ever have been made in high official quarters, that any emergency can arise to compel the South to an abandonment of the foundation principle upon which the institution of slavery rests; that is, the principle that slavery is the best possible condition for the slave himself, and the only one he can occupy consistent with the welfare of the white race among whom their lot is cast, not by any agency of the present owners, but rather by the ancestors of those now clamoring for their emancipation. . . .

🖙 Given the angry reception that the President's proposal met, no wonder that the Richmond *Sentinel,* one of the more consistent but by no means sycophantic supporters of the Davis administration, had earlier suggested (November 2, 1864) that to enter into a discussion of freeing and arming the slaves would be "premature and hurtful" and could only arouse "prejudice and passions and pride of opinion, which will be bad counsellors." Subsequently, even though it praised the "admirable style" of the President's message and thought that his views had been so "clearly and happily presented as to need no elucidation," the *Sentinel* (November 8, 1864) persisted in the suggestion that it would be "injudicious" to debate the "delicate question."

When the question, delicate or not, obviously was not cooling but growing hotter by the day, the *Sentinel* (November 24, 1864) finally flailed into those who loudly professed a desire to prosecute the war for independence with any and all resources but who then attacked the President's proposal as one that gave up the cause:

The Congress and people of the Confederate States have entered into firm and unanimous resolve, to prosecute the war of independence with all the weapons and resources at our command. The defeat of the enemy is the one great end and aim, to which all others are subordinate, because all others depend upon success in this. Whatever is necessary to secure victory to our arms, must, for that reason, be adopted and employed, however inconvenient it may prove in other respects. We cannot hesitate between a greater and a lesser misery; between the supreme calamity of subjugation which includes all other evils, and any one of the evils thus included. We must have military success; and the means indispensable to effect this, must be unhesitatingly yielded and freely applied.

In those views we all concur; but we do not equally concur in their application. Abstractly, we are ready to yield everything; practically, we say "anything but *that.*" Whatever proposition is made is discussed, not as to the imperative *necessity* of adopting it, but the inconveniences that would result, the sacrifice of our old notions, the damage to our cherished theories, and the like. This is the kind of argument, for example, which is relied on by those who oppose the employment of slaves as soldiers under all circumstances. It is not sound reasoning. It is wide of the real point. The true question is, does *necessity* require it? If it does, or if it shall, that fact answers a thousand objections. It is the great argument that silences opposition, and puts an end to all questions. Necessity is said to know no law. In our case it is at least paramount law; for we have resolved that at every hazard and every cost, we will maintain our independence, and that "*never*, on any terms," will we again associate with our enemies. If it be *necessary* to employ the aid we have referred to, in order to secure our independence, every note of opposition ought to be at once hushed, every voice should be heard in assent. Nothing can be plainer.

Strange arguments, however, we are daily forced to hear in reference to this possible measure. When the President proposes to employ forty thousand domestics in positions for which they are acknowledged to be fit, and in order to secure greater zeal and efficiency, suggests the tender of freedom as a condition of faithful service, we are told by some horrified individual that this is "giving up the cause." What cause? We thought that *independence* was, just now, the great question. Is it giving up *that?* No; but it is giving up the *slavery* question. To this an obvious answer is, that if it be *necessary* to give up slavery in order to secure independence, we ought to give it up. Every thing for independence! But it is idle to say that the proposition gives up slavery. If the emancipation of a part is the means of saving the rest, then this partial emancipation is eminently a pro-slavery measure. If the liberation of forty thousand adds such strength to our military service as to secure the defeat of the enemy, it will save the four millions who remain. Give up the question—it is the very means to gain it!

Citizens cannot too vividly realize that subjugation means the loss of our liberties *and emancipation too*. Nothing is better established than that. The very proclamation is already over us, and nothing remains but the military success of the enemy to put it in complete effect. If, to save our liberties, we find it necessary to emancipate, we shall have, therefore, lost nothing, while we shall have gained the supreme issue—our independence.

There is nothing (outside of adequate authority in the Government) to restrain us from the largest liberality in our dealing with this policy, if exercised as military necessity and expediency shall dictate. The whole question lies just there. If this war presented the issue of Submission and Slavery *vs.* Independence and Emancipation, then there might be some room for argument for those who weigh slavery against independence. But there is no such issue. It is Submission and Emancipation complete, oppressive, ruinous *vs.* Independence with Slavery complete, if possible, or as much of it as may be. Such alternatives leave no room for a hesitating choice. When pirates are pursuing, it is better to sacrifice the cargo, if need be, in order to facilitate escape, rather than to lose both ship and cargo; for capture implies the loss of both.

We are of those who believe that slavery is the natural condition of the African; that for which the Creator designed and fitted him, and that in which he is most happy. But we perceive nothing in the tender of freedom in testimonial of faithful military service, to justify the adverse criticisms in which it is somewhat fashionable to indulge. Military rewards are always of a sort to please the fancy and stir the ambition, rather than to confer any solid advantage. A furlough, an inscription on a flag, a bit of ribbon in the button-hole, a badge or a medal, are employed to inspire the enthusiasm of the soldier, and to stir him to deeds of uncommon toil and peril. Liberty is to the slave like one long furlough. It excites his interests and hopes, pleases him, and tends to instigate him to a zealous discharge of what is otherwise his duty. Nor is it unusual, or in the opinion of the world reprehensible, to encourage laudable conduct by rewarding it with indulgences, even though these may be abstractly considered, of questionable advantage. A wise teacher sometimes gratifies his pupils with an extra holiday, for unusual merit; rewards diligence by idleness. The Virginia Legislature in the Revolution, considered it a duty to confer personal freedom on the slaves who had assisted in gaining the freedom of the country. The slave who saves his master's life, is generally considered to have earned his freedom, and the giving of it is regarded as encouraging others to a like devotion. It is not probable that the popular instincts are astray in these concurrent testimonies. Agreeing in the general judgment, we believe that it is allowable to stimulate the zeal of our slaves in a good and laudable work, by that which is pleasing to him, although in a cold business view, it may not be, in our judgment, the best for him. . . .

⌦ The Richmond *Sentinel,* like the *Enquirer,* opened its columns to writers of clashing shades of opinion. On November 28, 1864, the *Sentinel* commenced a long series of articles by "a distinguished and popular citizen of Virginia" identified only by the pen name "Bland." The articles were presented as "an exposition of the reasons which imperatively forbid the thought of reconstruction; and will make plain the unspeakable folly of attempting to join together those whom God hath put asunder."

While the *Sentinel* emphatically and consistently shared "Bland's" aversion to all talk of reconstruction—that is, peace without southern independence—in his third article (December 1, 1864) "Bland" expressed views about "a partial emancipation" that were at odds with those of the *Sentinel*:

. . . The constitution of Southern society is wholly different. The Southron finds his chief happiness in his calm and quiet pursuits, and in his social life, where hospitality shares with the friends it unites in genial intercourse the products of his industry, or bestows without ostentation the fruits of toil upon the humble laborer, to the promotion of whose comfort his life is in a great degree devoted.

But their sentiments differ radically upon the relation which should exist between the two races which Providence has cast into one society on this continent.

The North hates the negro, and repels him from association with the white man; but insists upon their equality in the South, where they are associated. It repels association to avoid that equality which its philanthropy would enforce in the South. Its *moral* principle is, "all men are equal"; but it evades the application of that principle to itself, by seeking to apply it to others, whose aversion it decides to ignore; and thus idolizes as a dogma what it never practices, and satisfies its conscience by making others practice its own cardinal principles!

The South does not hate, but loves the negro. It associates with him as the inferior of the white man. Its principle and its practice are to take care of the African, whom God has subjected to its control and committed to its guardianship. It does not abhor the negro, but refuses amalgamation and equality with his race, as contrary to the laws of nature and the clear will of God.

Thus on this fundamental point in our social polity, the sentiments of North and South are in fierce opposition.

. . . It is our solemn duty, as our highest policy, to maintain slavery as a system of labor, and abjure the mongrel policy of a partial emancipation. The negro must be held as a slave, as best for the white man as it is for himself; and the relation of superiority of the white to the negro, as an axiom in our social policy. To admit the negro to an *independent* sphere of action as an equal partner in the struggle for our rights, would be fatal to the idea which underlies our whole system, and would lead first to partial, then to total emancipation, and then to civil and political equality between the races. To avoid these evils separation is essential. We certainly entail them upon us by reconstruction. . . .

☞ A nonslaveholder in Georgia, writing as "Sydney," differed from "Bland" about arming the Negroes but avoided the question of emancipation (Macon *Telegraph and Confederate,* November 19, 1864) :

. . . Now there is [*sic*] in the Confederacy one or two hundred thousand able bodied negroes not engaged in agriculture. Many of them [are] refugees from the country overrun, and they consume just as much as if they were in the army and can be very well spared. While thousands of poor white men that have nothing but their country to defend, have bled and died, their families are left to the cold charities of the world. The rich planters can stay at home undisturbed, and if it is hinted [that] cuffey [the Negro] is wanted to help defend his country and property we see a great howl set up about it, and more fuss made than if 1000 white men were sacrificed. Try to hide it as much as we may, yet the question of negro slavery was the great leading cause of this war, and but for it we would have been recognized long ago by foreign powers, but in that particular the world is against us, and so we will remain until this war shall have placed it upon a basis too firm to be questioned.

Then why may not the negro help to establish the only government that looks to the Christianizing of the African and placing him in a condition far above his fellow countrymen in any part of the world, if the exigency demands men to the extent above referred to, in God's name, do not sacrifice every white man in the Confederacy in preference to taking a few negroes from their fondling masters. . . .

🖙 Amid the raging controversy, relatively few editors stood unflinchingly behind President Davis in the matter of the emancipation of slaves by the Confederate government itself rather than the states. One newspaper that did, and refused to be stampeded on constitutional grounds, was the Wilmington, North Carolina, *Journal*:

. . . Another matter in the President's Message, namely in reference to engaging in a certain way the services of forty thousand negroes as military workers, has, we think, given rise to more passionate animadversion than the occasion calls for, or the language of the Message would justify. The *policy* of acquiring for the public service the entire property in the labor of the slave, and holding out to him the prospect of eventual emancipation as the reward of faithful service, may admit of question; but we do not see wherein the principle of State rights is infringed by any part of the President's recommendation. The rights of private proprietors to surrender their proprietary right in the labor of their slaves, and deport them to any point consistent with the *status* which they wished to confer upon them, has never been denied. The granting of permission to reside here or in any other slaveholding State has always been reserved by the States, and President Davis submits for the consideration of Congress what action should be taken to secure for the freedman the permission of the State from which he was drawn to reside within its limits after the close of his public service.

President Davis is no neophyte in political science—he is no new convert to the doctrine of State Rights, and it will be difficult for mere declaimers, who make their zeal for State Rights the cloak for personal opposition, to find him really at fault.[6]

🖙 Perhaps the most powerful of the journalistic supporters of Jefferson Davis and his policies was, after all, the Richmond *Enquirer*. Davis had asked for something far less bold and sweeping

[6] As reprinted in the Richmond *Sentinel*, December 14, 1864. The Raleigh, North Carolina, *Confederate* (November 16, 1864) also calmly analyzed the President's proposal and supported it.

than the paper had urged in early October; but the *Enquirer* (November 11, 1864) boldly confronted the question of the South's ultimate purpose in the war and the related question of the European world's reaction to how the South now faced the issue:

The employment of slaves as soldiers was never suggested as a proposition preferable to any other, but solely as a remedy to which dire necessity might eventually drive the Confederate Government. Considerations of a double character are involved in this measure. There is the moral influence which the conscription of a quarter of [a] million of slaves to fight for their freedom, and our freedom from Yankee masters, would have upon our enemies and the world at large; and there is the physical influence of such an augmentation of our army, upon that army, our people, our enemy, and our cause. Nor should these two considerations be separated in the discussions of this proposition.

The war has been slanderously called the slaveholders' war; undertaken for slavery, and maintained and supported solely for the perpetuation of negro slavery. Our enemies have charged, and much of the world believes the charge, that we have sacrificed the best and noblest of our land, heartlessly and cruelly, to maintain the negro property of some three hundred thousand slaveholders. The unparalleled suffering of this inhuman war has been slanderously misrepresented as detailed [? word is semilegible] upon the poor and rich of these States by the selfish slaveholder for the security of his "human chattels." The people of these States know the infamous falsity of these charges, but that public sentiment of the world, which influences the action and opinions of men and nations, will not understand the base mendacity of these charges if the people of this country shall decide this question by *its ultimate effect upon negro slavery.* Whether or not slaves shall be conscripted must be decided upon some higher and nobler principle than the evils of free-negroism; the people of these States could have escaped these dangers by submitting to Mr. Lincoln.

The President, in that Jacques[*sic*]-Gilmore interview, indignantly repudiated the charge that this war was for slavery, and the sentiment of the country approved and applauded his declaration. If it shall appear that the necessities of the army demand more men than the white population of the country can supply, and the people of this country exhibit an unwillingness to make soldiers of their slaves, does it not give color to the charge that the war is for slavery, and that we prefer our negroes to our liberties?

If the necessity exists, then, we say not forty thousand only, but any number that the necessity may require; for negro slavery was the mere occasion, and is not the object or end of this war. We would show to the world the lesson that, for national independence and freedom from Yankee domination, in addition to sacrifices already made, the people of these States are ready and willing, when the necessity arises, to sacrifice any number or all of the slaves to the cause of national freedom. And we would teach the enemy that "emancipation" has but merely brought to our attention the fighting resources of four millions of slaves, and that the Spring campaign shall open with an army of a quarter of million of negroes, besides our noble veterans, and that the scene of operations shall be the country of the enemy. We would respond to General Grant's "cradle and grave" assertion with the battle shout of an army of half a million.

We would encourage our own gallant soldiers, by adding to their number every man that a negro could relieve, whether as teamsters, cooks, hospital attendants, garrison of subordinate forts, as well as "pioneer and engineer laborer."

But the discussion has been clouded by the proposition of freedom after the war, and some say if freedom is recognized as a boon to be given as the reward for fidelity, a blow is struck at slavery. We believe that but one State in the Confederacy forbids manumission. In Virginia, "any person may emancipate any of his slaves, by last will in writing, or by deed recorded in the Courts of his county or corporation." Is this statutory boon a denial that slavery is the best condition for the negro? Unquestionably not; and yet fidelity to the master is here permitted to be rewarded with emancipation. Now, cannot fidelity to the national cause, attested by endurance of hardship, by gallantry in action, and exposure to death, be rewarded with freedom without any compromise to the relation in which those are still held who have given no assurance of such fidelity? We cannot see that reward for faithful services in the least conflicts with the reasons and arguments which support and sustain negro slavery. We hold the belief that the negro is best off, is in "the right place," when he has a good master;

but the negro may think otherwise, and the *salus populi* which induces his employment as a soldier demands sacrifices that shall secure his fidelity. This sacrifice is made in offering him his freedom for faithfulness. Nothing is yielded to the ignorant prejudices of the world; a simple bargain is struck. The negro wants his freedom; whether a boon or a curse, he wants it, and for it may be willing faithfully to serve in the army of his country. That country stands in need of those services; one is offered for the other. It has no touch of philanthropy about it—no sympathy or connection with Abolitionism.

But who shall give this freedom? The master, the State or the Confederate Government?

The master, if he will; but if not, then the State or the Confederate States Government. We are wholly opposed to compensation for the negro. What! conscript a son, a husband, a father, and pay for the slave! ! The negro pays for himself when he fights for his former master, just as the son reaps the reward of his services in the freedom of his country. But these are minor points. The great question is, does the necessity exist? This Congress should first ascertain, and then the question is properly debateable.

🖙 When the New York *Herald* jeered that southern slaveholders, having used up all the available "poor whites," would never yield their slave property to Jeff Davis, the *Enquirer* (November 15, 1864) roared back its answer to "dollar-worshipping Yankees":

No people ever misunderstood another so much as the Yankees do the people of this Confederacy. With the enemy, every feeling, every motive, every principle, has its pecuniary price, its weight in greenbacks, its measure in gold and silver. As there is not vice without its price, so there is no virtue without its market value. So entirely utilitarian have our enemy become in their tastes, ambition and motives, that they cannot conceive or understand how any people can "sacrifice *three or four cotton crops*" unless for the protection of some other property. They can understand how all the bloodshed, misery and want of this war might have been thrown away by the "slaveholders" for their negro property; but, after destroying "three or four cotton crops," they will not believe that the *slaveholders* are such fools as to use their negro slaves, throwing away such valuable property upon a principle! They cannot understand the use of so costly a principle; they see no virtue in such an expensive nationality. No Yankee ever understood or appreciated the Sermon on the Mount, or would have given a wooden nutmeg for all the Beatitudes. "The Kingdom of Heaven" may do for the "poor in spirit," but Hell is the proper place for the Yankee, "poor" in greenbacks. Their philosophy, their morality, their religion, are summed up in the word philanthropy, which, with them, means such a love for the Southern man's negro as shall make him the Northern man's slave.

With such ideas it is impossible for that nation to understand or appreciate how a people can reduce themselves to absolute poverty, sacrifice their sons and brothers and fathers, endure the want and misery of a long war, for a principle. . . . Hence, the New York "Herald" expects to find "the main difficulty in this business" of conscripting slaves among the "slaveholders." The men who own slaves will, the "Herald" thinks, rather submit to Lincoln than give up their slaves. Notwithstanding all classes, all professions, all trades have vied with each other in supporting and sustaining the war, our enemy still persists in believing that this is the "slaveholders' war." It has become necessary to teach the enemy another lesson. For three years they persisted in believing that there existed a strong Union sentiment among the non-slaveholders of these States, which was suppressed and kept down by the dominant slaveholders; the enemy have learned the fallacy of this hope. They have yet to learn that the slaveholder prefers nationality and free government to negroes and negro property. That men who have freely given their sons and brothers to the cause of their country, will not withhold their negroes. We must teach the enemy that there are blessings and happiness, for the attainment of which, the people, slaveholders and non-slaveholders, are willing to sacrifice, not only three or four crops of cotton, but all the negroes that once grew that cotton.

We are all "poor whites" in this Confederacy; but thank God we are not so poor, as we should be, if we owned all the negroes and cotton that ever was [sic] in the Confederacy, and submitted to the Yankees. Gen. Cobb, in a late speech, after depicting, in vivid colors, the meanness of the Yankees, said that there were meaner people even than the enemy, and they were those who would submit to them. Of all the reptiles that crawl the earth, the Southern submissionist is the meanest and most loathsome.

It is to be seen whether the "Enquirer" or the "Herald" best understands the people of these States. If we are right in our opinion on them, they will only ask: Is the sacrifice necessary, and will the negroes make soldiers? and let the Government decide for them. If the "Herald" has correctly judged them, there will be opposition and cavilling and delay and defeat, and the world will believe that the war is a "slaveholder's war," and all our noble sacrifices degraded into a shameful holocaust to the "peculiar institution."

We are unable to affirm that the negroes will make soldiers. The President's recommendation is an experiment that will decide that question. But the spirit that should actuate our people in sacrificing their negroes to the cause is of more importance even than the strength our negroes may bring to our army. We must exhibit to the world an unselfish patriotism, a spirit that will not balance property against liberty; a Heaven-born love of freedom that knows no price it is not willing to pay for its attainment. It cost the enemy four years of war to learn that Unionism was dead in these States; and, however expensive the lesson was to us, it has not been without its value to our cause. We must dispel this other delusion—that slavery is preferred to nationality—negroes to liberty—cotton to freedom. When this last cloud is dispelled, the day star of peace will have arisen, and the dawn of nationality will cast its light over our cause, and gild in glory all our sacrifice.

That our readers may understand the low estimate of our resolution and purpose entertained by the enemy, we append the conclusion of the "Herald" article on negro conscription:

"The main difficulty in this business still remains to be considered—how will this scheme for arming their slaves be received by the slaveholders of 'the Confederacy?' This is their rebellion, their Southern Confederacy, contrived, inaugurated and controlled by them for the protection of their slave property, and for the perpetuation and expansion of their 'peculiar institution.' It is the corner-stone of their political and social fabric; it is 'the alpha and omega, the beginning and the end' of their hopes and designs. They have managed to use up all the poor whites of their Confederacy; they have sacrificed three or four cotton crops; they have bled freely in many other ways to sustain their dictator, Davis; vast numbers of their brethren have been completely stripped of their slaves by 'the Yankees'; but there is still a considerable remnant of this Southern ruling class of rebel slaveholders, whose 'negro quarters' remain intact; and the question is, what will these men do when called upon to try the game of abolition against Lincoln to secure Southern independence?

"They will tell Master Davis that this thing is impossible, and they will abandon him in the attempt to enforce it. They will tell him that Southern men who have lost their slaves, and Southern politicians and the 'poor white trash' who never had any slaves, are raising this clamor, but let him beware of the consequences of yielding to it. If the issue, they will say, is to be reduced to this disgusting game of abolition between Abe Lincoln and Jeff. Davis, the Southern slaveholder, who has sacrificed everything but his negroes for the cause of slavery, will throw up his hand. Why should he protract this war and continue to play the fool if all the Southern Confederacy promised him is to be abolished, as it will be, with the abolition of slavery? This is the rock upon which Davis will split in attempting to arm the slaves of the rebellious States on the basis of emancipation and a free negro Southern Confederacy. Whatever 'arrangements,' therefore, may be making at Richmond to this end 'for the spring campaign,' we predict that Davis will not attempt to put them into practice. Against the Southern 'poor white' and the non-slaveholding politician the Southern slaveholder is still the master. Finally, 'the spring campaign,' from all present appearances, will find Jeff. Davis either dead in his 'last ditch,' or a fugitive from justice and his rebel confederacy defunct."

☞ Newspaper readers in central Georgia noted that the New York *Times* (as reprinted in the Macon *Telegraph,* November 18, 1864) did not question the possibility of the Confederacy's arming its slaves, as the New York *Herald* had so scornfully doubted; but the *Times* saw the development as merely an additional reason for the North to persevere in the struggle:

. . . What the South is now fighting for, therefore, is the establishment of the Confederacy not as a slave society but as a free one; in other words, to detach half this continent from the jurisdiction of the United States Government without reference to the form of political or social organization which is to exist on it afterward; and as its white population has been too much weakened to effect this object it proposes to accomplish it by the aid of an army of negroes, dragged against their will from the plantation to the field of battle. To this complexion it has come at last.

What the North has now between it and peace is an army of negro slaves, bought like cattle for service, and fighting under the lash. We think the news ought to send a thrill of joy through the whole country. After having done and dared so much, after having met and frustrated a most desperate attempt, made by one of the most warlike races in the world, to found a slave empire on our soil, we are hardly likely to lay down our arms, now that the integrity of the Union is threatened by an army of purchased blacks. What the masters have tried in vain the slaves shall certainly not accomplish. "We have despised Catiline's sword; we shall certainly not quail before yours." If there were any shrinking now, the dead who perished in the fiercest of the struggle would mock us from their graves.

☞ Horace Greeley's New York *Tribune* (as reprinted in the Richmond *Sentinel,* December 28, 1864) picked up an item of recent history that had more than passing interest for the southern readers who saw it:

If we are not misinformed, it will in due time be suffered to transpire that we were saved from a formal European recognition of the Southern Confederacy by the timely issue of President Lincoln's initial Proclamation of Freedom. At the close of McClellan's Peninsula campaign, the Governments of France and England professed to have become satisfied that the independence of the Confederacy was a fixed fact, and were concerting measures for according an early admission of the new power into the family of nations. We believe, but are not sure, that our Government was confidentially apprised of this determination so early as September, if not in August, 1862, and that the more conservative members of the Cabinet, if not impelled to advise, were fully reconciled to the issue of the aforesaid Proclamation by their knowledge of that purpose.

That issue gave pause to the Maritime Powers; and when it had been followed by the proclamation of Jan. 1st, 1863, it was found that the public opinion of the more intelligent middle class throughout

Western Europe would be shocked by a recognition which would be a virtual alliance with the Slave Power. The Confederate envoys were confidentially apprised of the serious obstacle which had been interposed to a compliance with their desires, and advised to promote its removal through some form of Emancipation; but they did not—or rather, could not—achieve what was desired, so matters went on as we have seen.

These items of hitherto unpublished history derive a present consequence from the probability that the rebel authorities are about to decree some sort of emancipation, in the hope of thus retrieving their bankrupt fortunes. Should they do so satisfactorily, and thereupon be favored with any gleam of military success, we may look for indications from Europe of an unequivocal desire that they should achieve their independence.

Hope, desperate though it was, that Britain and France might yet come to their rescue had not died in the hearts of many Southerners. The Macon *Telegraph and Confederate* (December 29, 1864) carried an editorial from the London *Telegraph* that took a cold view but one that was not unencouraging to Southerners:

. . . Such a measure [as arming the slaves] would be depreciated by all friends of humanity, although no one can deny to the South a belligerent right which has been most unscrupulously used by the North. It would infinitely add to the horrors of the war; it would, in a word, be a sign of desperation. Mr. Lincoln never dreamt of calling the negroes to arms until his white soldiers had been soundly beaten; and if Mr. Davis was also to summon the slaves to the field, it would be for the obvious reason that he was horribly in want of recruits.

The Confederacy is by no means so exhausted as [its] adversaries believe; it has not yet been driven to employ means of warfare generally condemned by civilized nations; but plain and ominous is the President's fierce declaration that, rather than submit, every slave in the land shall be armed. Whether this would be safe for the Confederates themselves is a point which we have not sufficient data to determine; but, if dangerous to the South, it would be terrible for the North. So long as the Secessionists can keep the aggressive armies at bay, while often in their turn, menacing Washington, Philadelphia and Baltimore

themselves, the time has hardly come for putting muskets into the
hands of every negro. Still, if ever the danger of subjugation seems
imminent, the President will at once resort to that last fearful weapon
which he now holds in reserve. Meanwhile he allows the North the exclusive use of this agency, and trusts his own cause to the bright sword
of Robert E. Lee.

☞ "The bright sword of Robert E. Lee!" The London newspaper
had indeed correctly assessed one vital point: the gallant, enigmatic Virginian had captured the imagination and admiration of
a war-weary people as had no one else. The Richmond *Sentinel*
(November 24, 1864) urged that the whole troublesome question
should ultimately be left to Lee:

. . . In short, we look upon the whole subject of the employment of
slaves in the public defence, and the mode and degree in which such
use of them ought to be made, as a practical question for the judgment
of military men, rather than a theme for the closet speculation of
scholars and theorists. Gen. Lee knows better what the necessity is
than we. The full extent of that necessity, however imperative it
might be, it would not be proper for him to disclose. He and his council
of officers know better, too, than civilians can, whether such recruits
would be available, and what motives and discipline would best develop
their usefulness. We are disposed, therefore, to be very much guided
in this matter by the opinions of the military men. We would not discuss the question too much in the press or on the rostrum. There is an
obvious impropriety in it. We would simply declare, and we would do
so meaning what we said in all its extent, that there is no sacrifice
which we would not make, sooner than be subjugated. . . .

☞ Lee, however, carefully stayed in what he regarded as his proper
military sphere. The Charlottesville, Virginia, *Chronicle* (as reprinted in the *Sentinel*, November 25, 1864) best expressed the
growing hunger for Lee's leadership:

General Lee never speaks. What does he think about? None of us can
read the thoughts of that impenetrable bosom. He works in silence like
some powerful engine. . . .

. . . When will he speak? Has he nothing to say? What does he think of our affairs? Should he speak, how the country would hang upon every word that fell from him!

🕮 One important example of Lee's early involvement in the matter is furnished by certain correspondence that he had with William Porcher Miles of South Carolina, the chairman of the military affairs committee of the Confederate House of Representatives. In late October, 1864, Miles wrote to General Lee:

Congress meets on the 7th of next month and the increase of our Army and the improvement of its organization, discipline and efficiency are questions which will immediately and largely occupy our time and attention. As Chairman of the Military Committee of the House I would be very glad to have your opinion on various points. I am aware that any suggestions or recommendations which you might desire legislation upon would, officially, be addressed to the War Department, but I have thought a free interchange of views and opinions on Army matters (so far as they may depend upon or be affected by the action of Congress) and the eliciting of *your* opinions touching sundry mooted points, would be of the greatest service to my Committee. I state the simple truth when I say—as our experience on several occasions has abundantly proved—that in urging any measure upon the House the strongest argument we can offer in its support is that "Gen'l. Lee thinks it very desirable."

I would like to have your opinion on the three following points particularly—

1st. The arming of a portion of our negroes and making a regular military organization of them.

. . . Should you not feel disposed *formally* to express yourself upon all, or any of these matters, I should still be greatly obliged to you for any views which you might think proper to communicate to me, under such restrictions, (as *to quoting you as authority in the premises*), as might be most agreeable to yourself.

The time has come when we must all work together frankly, heartily and harmoniously to insure the success of the great cause in which we are all engaged, and in everything affecting the interests of the Army all eyes naturally turn to you with anxious inquiry and earnest con-

fidence. Should you prefer communicating with me personally I shall
be happy to wait upon you at any time that you will indicate.[7]

🖙   Lee's prompt response to Miles's letter has not been found, but he
clearly endorsed the general proposal for freeing and arming the
slaves. That is made clear by the next letter that Miles addressed
to Lee on November 3, 1864:

Accept my thanks for your very full and interesting letter in response
to mine asking your views touching sundry matters of Army organization. I confess I have considerable misgiving as to the question of
Negro troops, both as to their efficiency and the effect of such a measure upon our political and social system. Of course anything is better
than our subjugation by such a people as this war has revealed the
people of the Northern States to be, and to avert such calamity and
degradation I would be willing to sacrifice all the wealth of the Confederate States, including Slavery which is its chief element. It is not
however as I have already intimated merely a question of wealth and
property. But I do not propose to discuss the subject generally. Looking at it in a purely military point of view can the negro in our armies
effectually aid us in our struggle? And has the time arrived when our
entire arms-bearing white population can no longer resist the tide of
invasion? These are the two present and pressing questions, and I feel
that upon both of them you speak with a weight of authority second to
no one in the Confederacy. Your opinion seems mature and decided.
In deference however to the sensitiveness of our people on so delicate a
subject—and the violent opposition which the proposition for arming
our slaves will excite in many quarters—would it not be well even if
Congress should concur in yr. opinion to proceed guardedly and gradually? For instance suppose Congress were to authorize the organization
of large bodies of sappers & miners, composed of negroes, say fifty or
sixty thousand in all, and see how that will work, between now and the
next session. They certainly would be very useful, as much so perhaps
as they could be in any capacity. This and the exclusive employment of
negroes as cooks, teamsters, Artillery drivers &c &c would constitute

[7] Copy of William Porcher Miles to Robert E. Lee, October 24, 1864, in William
Porcher Miles Papers, Southern Historical Collection, University of North Carolina
Library, Chapel Hill.

practically an addition of perhaps one hundred thousand men to our armies. With more stringent legislation on the subject of Exemptions and Details we ought to put from fifty to seventy-five thousand men in the field. Would not this suffice for the next campaign? With my acknowledgments for your willingness to respond to any inquiries I may desire to make concerning subjects connected with the Army. . . .[8]

☞ It should be noted that these private letters between Lee and Miles were exchanged before President Davis made his own bid for Confederate emancipation. Lee's public support for the "radical modification" proposed by Jefferson Davis, if in fact Lee approved of the idea, might or might not have made a difference. At any rate, the support never came, and given the proud and always correct punctiliousness of both Lee and Davis, it may never have been sought.

Lee's views became increasingly crucial in the controversy, but the public at large could hear about them only secondhand, through various officials who claimed to know his opinions. Moreover Congressman Miles was not persuaded by Lee any more than by Davis and would become a powerful opponent of the President's proposal.

Breaking a long and strict policy of public silence on key political questions, Lee would eventually speak out directly and dramatically in favor of freeing and arming the slaves, as will be discussed subsequently. But he did not do so until February, 1865, after hope was almost gone for the plan advanced by President Davis in November.[9]

Not even in Virginia, however, where the Lee cult first flourished, was everyone ready to let the general decide the great issue. The Richmond *Whig* (November 25, 1864), for example, scorned the rising inclination to look to "military men" for sole guidance about the question of freeing and arming the slaves:

[8] Miles to Lee, November 3, 1864, *ibid.*
[9] N. W. Stephenson's important article of 1913 (see note 1 of the introduction) remains the best analysis of Lee's crucial intervention in the final phase of the controversy; but Stephenson, as has been stated, ignored Davis' earlier plan. Apparently the whole subject was not a matter that interested Douglas Southall Freeman, for in his massive *R. E. Lee* (New York, 1935) he devotes less than a page (p. 544) of the third volume to it.

Will the *Sentinel* inform anybody in virtue of what law, in accordance with what traditions, the "military men" have become the constitutional expounders of the land? Surely the *Sentinel*, so zealous in finding out mares' nests, will not be less so in explaining what to us looks like some wonderful discovery on its part.

☞ With only certain newspapers scattered around the South left to protest, the majority of Confederate congressmen hastened to bury and try to forget the heretical notions that had been put forth by the President. Of course Jefferson Davis had some loyal supporters in both houses of Congress. But on his proposal relating to emancipation they clearly were a hopeless minority. Senators Robert M. T. Hunter of Virginia, William A. Graham of North Carolina, and Louis T. Wigfall of Texas, to name only three of the more prominent opposition leaders in the upper house, possessed and used the necessary votes to stifle any hint of emancipation.[10]

While the opposition to Davis' proposal was actually more powerful in the Senate than in the House, various representatives were bolder and quicker to take public stands than were the more secretive senators. Even before the President's message was read on the opening day of the session, Representative William G. Swan of Tennessee introduced a resolution declaring that "no exigency exists or is likely to occur . . . which demands that negroes shall be placed in service as soldiers in the field." And Henry S. Foote of Tennessee, in response to the President's message, demanded that the Congress should declare "that no important movement looking to the emancipation of the slaves of the South . . . should be taken by this Government without the

[10] Bills to amend the Impressment Act of February 17, 1864, were introduced in the Senate in November, 1864, but they contained no mention of Davis' proposal. After countless postponements, amendments, disagreements with the House-passed amendments, and a conference committee, S. 129, which was reported from the Senate's committee on military affairs on December 6, 1864, was finally passed on February 28 and signed by the President, although it was drastically less than and different from what he had wanted, on March 2, 1865. The tedious course through the Senate of this legislation may be followed, albeit in the skeletal record that is the only one available, from the entries under "Slaves" on p. 788 of the *Journal of the Congress of the Confederate States of America, 1861–1865: Senate* (Washington, 1904), IV. The entire act is printed in *O.R.*, Series IV, Vol. III, 1,114–1,117.

unanimous consent of the people of [the] States in convention assembled.'' [11]

A good example of the sort of bitter resistance that the majority of Confederate congressmen felt toward Confederate emancipation is afforded by a long speech, fortunately available in pamphlet form, that Representative Henry C. Chambers of Mississippi delivered in the House on November 10, 1864, three days after the President's message. This is the portion most directly concerned with the question of Negro soldiers for the Confederacy:

. . . No man of observation can be unaware of the present anxious and unsettled condition of public sentiment. The popular mind is groping in a labyrinth of perplexity, seeking solutions for great questions, to some of which allusion has been made. How to increase our armies, how to bring about peace and independence, and in some quarters, let it be confessed, whether it might not be prudent to entertain even the project of reconstruction; these, Sir, are some of the enquiries that are arresting the attention of the country. It cannot be denied that at least one proposition of a startling character is forced upon our consideration. I allude to the employment of negro troops. Undoubtedly, as I think, if this question was not raised with evil design, it must have originated with timid or despairing patriots, who, ignorant of the relative numbers of the contending armies and the statistics of their loss and increase, imagine the worst. But, however or by whomsoever brought forward, it presents itself now with imposing sponsors, and must be met. The President in his message has not disdained to notice it, and distinguished gentlemen on this floor have pronounced it worthy of grave consideration. I shall barely allude to distinguished and influential personages currently reported as advocates of the measure, fearful, if I were to name them, of doing injustice to their views, or of smothering myself at once under the weight of their authority.

. . . But, sir, if all these calculations fail—if, as our despairing friends declare, we have approximated to final exhaustion, and must find some extraordinary source of re-inforcements—will negro troops answer the purpose—will the African save us? There is no moral, no

[11] *Journal of the Congress . . . : House of Representatives* (Washington, 1905), VII, 247, 261–62.

pecuniary objection to employing them, if they can be made to serve the occasion. The question is not whether they have not been known to fight, but whether they can be relied on to fight successfully for us now in the present death grapple with our enemies. In what form of organization is it proposed to use them? It can hardly be designed to intermingle them in the same companies with our citizens soldiers; no one has yet had the audacity to propose that. Would it be safe to confide to negro troops so much of the line of battle as would be occupied by a regiment or a brigade—much less a division or a corps? And an entire line so composed might by sudden flight or wholesale surrender involve the whole army in confusion and disaster. To surrender to them the duty of defending forts or outposts would be to place the keys of the situation in their hands. Then, but one alternative remains; it is to form them into companies and place these in alternation with white companies in the same regiments. The electric current of mutual confidence and devotion—the triumphant glance, the answering smile, the sympathetic cheer—no longer passes from company to company. The silence of distrust now broods along the line, which hesitates, halts, wavers, breaks, and the black troops fly—perhaps to the embrace of the enemy. Even victory itself would be robbed of its glory if shared with slaves. God grant that our noble army of martyrs may never have to drink of this cup!

. . . This argument proceeds upon the presumption that the negro, whether slave or free, cannot be made a good soldier. The law of his race forbids it. Of all others the best adapted to slavery, he is therefore of all others, the least adapted for military service. Of great simplicity of disposition, tractable, prone to obedience, and highly imitative, he is easily drilled; but timid, averse to effort, without ambition, he has none of the higher qualities of the soldier. It is difficult to conceive a being less fit for plucking honor from the cannon's mouth. At the beginning of this war, he fled to the enemy to avoid work; his local attachment was not sufficient to retain him; now he remains to avoid military service in the Yankee army—his aversion to work being greater than his aversion to slavery, and only less than his aversion to war. Such is his character as it appears in history. It is not denied that, under the influence of revenge, of a desire for plunder, or other maddening or special excitement, he has been known to surrender himself to slaughter and to wade deep in blood; so in his native Africa, he surrenders himself a sacrifice to his gods; but history will be searched in vain to prove him a good soldier. . . . Sir, on what motive is he to fight our battles? He is after all a human being, and acts upon motives. Will you offer him his freedom? The enemy will offer him his freedom, and also as a deserter, immunity from military service. Will you offer him the privilege of return home to his family, a freeman, after the war? That you dare not do, remembering it was the free negroes of St. Domingo, who had been trained to arms, that excited the insurrection of the slaves. And the enemy would meet even that offer with the promise of a return free to his Southern home and the right of property in it. The amount of it all is, that in despair of achieving our independence with our own right arms, we turn for succor to the slave and implore him to establish our freedom and fix slavery upon himself, or at least upon his family and his race, forever. He, at least, after the expiration of his term of service, is to be banished to Liberia or other inhospitable shore, for the States could never permit an army of negroes to be returned home, either free or slave.

Sir, if the employment of negro troops should be attempted successfully, our army would soon contain only slaves. . . . Sir, this war is to be fought solely by white soldiers and black laborers, or white laborers and black soldiers: try to intermingle the two when you may, the attempt will fail; the strands will separate; when the negro enters the army the white soldier will leave it. He becomes the laborer—not reposing as a veteran upon his laurels—enjoying the repose of home after his long services; but the natural laborer of the country being absent in the military service, he supplies the place left void in the field; his labor must support himself, his family and the negro soldier. Sir, this scheme, if attempted, will end in rapid emancipation and colonization—colonization in the North by bringing up the slaves by regiments and brigades to the opportunity of escape to the enemy; emancipation and colonization abroad to those who render service to us for a specified period. I argue on the presumption that nothing of the kind will be attempted without the consent of the States, whether as to employing them on the promise of freedom, or as to returning them free and disciplined to their old homes. By means of the power of impressment or purchase, this Government could not safely be permitted, without the consent of the States, to inaugurate a system of emancipation that might end in the abolition of the institution, nor do

I suppose that the President designed the contrary. In suggesting freedom as the motive to be offered to the slave, he performed a simple official duty, leaving to Congress if it adopted the suggestion, to provide by law all the conditions it might be proper to impose.

In any aspect of the case, this is a proposition to subvert the labour system, the social system and the political system of our country. Better, far, to employ mercenaries from abroad, if dangerous and impracticable expedients are to be attempted, and preserve that institution which is not only the foundation of our wealth but the palladium of our liberties. Make the experiment, of course, with negro troops as the last means to prevent subjugation; but when we shall be reduced to the extremity of exclaiming to the slave, "help us, or we sink," it will already have become quite immaterial what course we pursue!

But if the experiment must be made, let him be used still as a slave, without promise of special reward. Let him be made to fight as he has been made to work, as a duty exacted under the authority of his owner. So he has been accustomed to live and move and have his being, and so he will continue to render any service with less reluctance and with less inquiry. . . .[12]

☞ Thus did the nay-sayers both in Congress and in the newspapers largely hold the floor in the immediate aftermath of the shocking proposal made by Jefferson Davis.

[12] "Policy of Employing Negro Troops. Speech of Hon. H. C. Chambers . . . ," Pamphlet in Flowers Collection, Perkins Library, Duke University, Durham, N.C.

CHAPTER V

Hope for Action
by Virginia—and the
Kenner Mission

THE CONFEDERATE PRESIDENT had made his own careful bid for a "radical modification" not only in the law concerning slavery but, in fact, in the whole Confederate stance toward the institution. Facing the storm of opposition that his proposal encountered, Davis may well have despaired of securing any change in the one area where the South had for some forty years passionately denied both the possibility and the desirability of any change.

Yet there came a ray of hope for Davis. Governor William Smith of Virginia, almost alone among the Confederate state governors save for Allen in distant Louisiana, lined up behind the President. In his message to the Virginia legislature on December 7, 1864, Smith boldly stated his position:

. . . When this war began it was confidently believed by our enemy that it would be of short duration. Relying upon his vast superiority in numbers and material of war, he expected to overrun us with facility and ease. But the result of a single year's operations corrected this expectation and impressed him with the conclusion that he had on hand a contest of great magnitude, full of danger and difficulty. Having soon exhausted his floating population, he openly recruited his armies on the continent of Europe. Not satisfied with this, he seized our slaves and, in violation of all civilized war, armed them against us. Under every disadvantage the war has been protracted deep into its fourth year, and we find ourselves looking around for material to enlarge our armies. Whence is it to come? The laws of natural accretion will not furnish a sufficient supply of men. Foreign countries are in effect closed against us. Recruiting from the prisoners we capture will not, except to a limited extent, supply our wants, and the public attention naturally turns to our own slaves as a ready and abundant stock from which to draw. This policy, however, has given rise to great diversity of opinion. Some consider it as giving up the institution of slavery. Others declare that to put our slaves in the ranks will drive our fellow-citizens from them and diffuse dissatisfaction throughout the country. In reply, it is said that this policy will effectually silence the clamor of the poor man about this being the rich man's war; that there is no purpose to mingle the two races in the same ranks, and that there cannot be a reasonable objection to fighting the enemy's negroes with our own; that as to the abandonment of slavery, it is already proclaimed to be at an end by the enemy, and will undoubtedly be so if we are subjugated, and that by making it aid in our defense it will improve the chance of preserving it.

This is a grave and important question and full of difficulty. All agree in the propriety of using our slaves in the various menial employments of the Army, and as sappers and miners and pioneers, but much diversity of opinion exists as to the propriety of using them as soldiers now. All agree that when the question becomes one of liberty and independence on the one hand or subjugation on the other, that every means within our reach should be used to aid in our struggle and to baffle and thwart our enemy. I say every man will agree to this; no man would hesitate. Even if the result were to emancipate our slaves, there is not a man that would not cheerfully put the negro into the Army rather than become a slave himself to our hated and vindictive foe. It is, then, simply a question of time. Has the time arrived when this issue is fairly before us? Is it indeed liberty and independence or subjugation which is presented to us? A man must be blind to current events, to the gigantic proportions of this war, to the proclamations of the enemy, who does not see that the issue above referred to is presented now. And, I repeat, the only question is, Has the time arrived? Are we able beyond a question to wage successful war against a power three times our own in numbers, with all Europe from which to recruit, and who unhesitatingly put arms in the hands of our own negroes for our destruction? I will not say that under the providence of God we may not be able to triumph, but I do say that we should not from any mawkish sensibility refuse any means within our reach which will tend to enable us to work out our deliverance. For my part, standing before God and my country, I do not hesitate to say that I would arm such portion of our able-bodied slave population as may be necessary, and put them in the field, so as to have them ready for the spring campaign, even if it resulted in the freedom of those thus organized. Will I not employ them to fight the negro force of the enemy? aye, the Yankees themselves, who already boast that they have 200,000 of our slaves in arms against us. Can we hesitate, can we doubt, when the question is, whether our enemy shall use our slaves against us or we use them against him; when the question may be between liberty and independence on the one hand, or our subjugation and utter ruin on the other?[1]

🖙 The other southern governors who had joined with Smith in the conference in October, 1864, denied that the governors' vague resolution calling for a "change in policy" concerning slavery had looked toward emancipating and arming the slaves. Smith, however, stood his ground in the matter:

The object of these resolutions, as understood by me, was to call public attention to the consideration of the policy of bringing our slaves into this war. It seems that a change of policy on our part was contemplated; and we determined, in reference to our slaves, to recommend to our authorities, under proper regulations, to appropriate such part of them to the public service as may be required. I am aware that a clamor has been raised against the policy of putting the negroes into the Army by good and loyal men, because, they say, "the end is not yet"; that our Army of citizen soldiers is still competent to make good our defense. No one would advocate the policy of thus appropriating our slaves except as a matter of urgent necessity; but as public opinion is widely divided on this subject, does not common prudence require us to fear that those opposed to this extreme measure may be mistaken? Suppose it should so turn out, how deep would be their responsibility to the country, to freedom and independence everywhere! I know it is the opinion of some of the highest military authorities that the time has come when we should call our slaves to our assistance; and I hold it to be clearly the duty of every citizen, however much he may doubt the wisdom and necessity of the policy, to co-operate in strengthening by every means our armies. I repeat, I know this policy is looked

[1] *O.R.*, Series IV, Vol. III, 914–15.

to with anxiety by some of the ablest military men of the age, who believe that it is of the last importance that it should be adopted without delay. I therefore earnestly recommend to the Legislature that they should give this subject early consideration, and enact such measures as their wisdom may approve. . . .[2]

🐎 The salty and independent-minded editor of the Charlottesville *Chronicle* (as reprinted in the Richmond *Sentinel*, December 21, 1864) made some interesting comments about Governor Smith and his forthright message:

The Message of Gov. Smith takes the bull by the horns. He is not for any mincing experiments. Governor Smith may be surpassed in a certain kind of talent by some of the school that formerly controlled the old Democratic party, and now control the destinies of this country; but he is essentially a practical man, and used to act with the great practical rank and file of the Democratic party. Very sublimated political philosophy he did not pretend to; he knew little of subtle theories and the nicer disputes about States Rights; but he devoted himself to carrying elections, and fighting the battles of the party he belonged to. He has exhibited greater command over the people, and greater political vitality than any other man in Virginia. After his career was supposed to be closed, he came back from California, and wrested his Congressional district from all competitors and all combinations, and held it until the dismemberment of the country. He then —seventy years of age—put himself at the head of a regiment, and plunged into the active operations of the war. Soon he was a brigadier —and just as bad a one as the rest of our political generals. Then he had himself returned for the Confederate Congress—a general in the army and a member of Congress; and on this he became Governor of Virginia—the second time Governor of Virginia—by the popular suffrage and when there was a conservative feeling prevailing, and we were in the midst of a revolution. . . .

When such a man winds a new note on the bugle, people may well prick up their ears—he has never missed the temper of the popular heart yet—even when he wavered on the Know Nothing question, he

[2] *Ibid.*, 916. For a good study of Smith, see Alvin A. Fahrner, ''William 'Extra Billy' Smith, Governor of Virginia, 1864–1865: A Pillar of the Confederacy,'' *Virginia Magazine of History and Biography*, LXXV (January, 1966), 68–87.

was the reflex of the popular feeling, which also wavered—but he missed those shoals, on which that ship stranded. Governor Smith has now taken the boldest step of his life; he has lifted his voice above all his associate leaders; and the key which he has struck will ultimately find its echoes throughout the length and breadth of the land. It is not one measure—novel and startling in its character—that he proposes; but he propounds three grand theses, each one calculated to produce the liveliest sensation, at once: he is for arming the negroes; for calling in the Confederate currency; for a law of maximum prices. One scratches his head.

The maximum is an absurdity. . . .

The recommendation about the slaves is also prophetic. They will go in the army, if the war goes on through next year. They will be needed next spring. There will be a storm of opposition; a thousand good reasons will be urged against it; but one imperious consideration will weigh down them all—we shall want men, if the war continues, and it is just simply ridiculous to assert the contrary, without pointing out precisely the grounds for the assertion. Our Southern people have not gotten over the vicious habit of not believing what they don't wish to believe. Shall we go through another eight months campaign, next year, without meeting the new drafts of the enemy? We certainly have no special fancy for the measure, but just now we are speaking of what is to be—not of our own preferences and objections. Gov. Smith snuffs [?sniffs] it in the wind. He will be followed by other Governors, and by Legislative bodies. We shrewdly suspect the Confederate Government is behind Gov. Smith.

. . . On the whole, we like the message, though dissenting to the extent we have signified. We despise the wishy washy way of doing things one observes in Congress. They seem utterly bewildered. Gov. Smith is at least in favor of something, and he does not shrink. No movement like this can be steered by any timid helmsman. Men are trying to grasp at the future and cling to the past at the same moment. We must elect. If we want to keep the negroes out of the army and avoid other extreme resorts—*peace* will do it.

☞ Perhaps it was the hope of joint action by Virginia and the Confederate government that inspired Jefferson Davis and Secretary of State Benjamin to make their last great effort to secure recognition and assistance from Britain and France. The Confederate leaders were obviously taking a desperate gamble of dubious constitutionality, and they proceeded with cautious secrecy and with a minimum of documentation. Nevertheless, the mission of Duncan F. Kenner as secret envoy empowered to discuss Confederate emancipation, among other things, in exchange for Anglo-French recognition has long been known.

Concerning Kenner and his mission to France and Britain, one of the principal sources of information is a memorandum of a conversation that occurred many years after the Civil War at one of the famed summer resorts of the South:

A few years before the death of Mr. [Duncan F.] Kenner of Louisiana, Dr. J. L. M. Curry and myself spent some time at the Greenbrier, White Sulphur Springs, West Virginia, with him, and he gave us a detailed account of his mission to England and France in the winter of 1864–5, as special envoy from President Jefferson Davis. Mr. Kenner was a large slave owner, and a prominent member of the Confederate Congress; I believe the chairman of the Finance Committee. He said that on the fall of New Orleans, which he heard of on his way home from Richmond, he became convinced that the Southern Confederacy could not succeed if it held to slavery, as the prejudice of the civilized world was against it, and to succeed the South needed the countenance and support of England and France. I would say here that Mr. Kenner was then very wealthy and probably owned more slaves than any man in the Southern Confederacy. He said that on his return to Richmond to attend Congress, he informed Mr. Davis of his conclusion, and of his determination to move in Congress that a commission be sent to Europe to propose to the courts of England and France that if they would acknowledge the Southern Confederacy it would abolish slavery. Mr. Davis did not approve of the proposal, and said that the affairs of the Confederacy were not so desperate as to warrant it, and he begged Mr. Kenner not to make the move at that time. Mr. Kenner did as Mr. Davis requested, but some time afterwards Mr. Davis sent for him and said that he was convinced that the proposed mission should be undertaken, and that he desired him to be the commissioner. Upon his consenting, Mr. Davis gave him in cipher his credentials and directions. Mr. Kenner then went to Wilmington,

N. C., in order to run the blockade, but while he was waiting for a ship to go out, Fort Fisher fell in the middle of January, 1865, and he thereupon returned, by night, to Richmond, where he found provisions had gotten very scarce. He next determined to try to get to London, by way of New York, and under an assumed name he was put in charge of a man whose business it was to run the blockade across the Potomac, and bring back goods of various sorts. . . .

Mr. Kenner found that Mr. Mason was in Paris. He thereupon went to Paris and sought an interview with him and Mr. Slidell. When they came together in a room he found Mr. W. W. Corcoran was present. He thereupon said[,] "I was directed to show my instructions to Mr. Mason and Mr. Slidell and to no one else." But these gentlemen told him that he could safely proceed in the presence of Mr. Corcoran, as he was their confident[ial] adviser. He then had his instructions translated by the clerk of Mr. Slidell who had the key. The two Confederate Commissioners were greatly astonished, and Mr. Mason at first declared he would not obey instructions. But he yielded upon finding that if he did not, he would be suspended.

The French Emperor was communicated with through some one connected with Mr. Slidell, and he replied that he would recognize the Confederacy if England would do so; Mr. Kenner and Mr. Mason then returned to London, and the Prime Minister was indirectly sounded. He replied that under no circumstances would her Majesty's government recognize the Southern Confederacy. This of course put an end to all hope of Mr. Kenner's mission being successful, and in a few weeks he learned of General Lee's surrender.[3]

☞   Kenner, as the above indicates, sailed for Europe in disguise from New York in January, 1865. Secretary of State Benjamin's cautiously worded dispatch to the Confederate envoy in Paris, John Slidell, dances around the subject of Kenner's supersecret mission, for some Confederate dispatches had already been captured and published by Federal authorities:

[3] "Mem[orandum]: for I. M. Callahan Esq. of Johns Hopkins Uni[versity]. Sent 24 March, 1899, by W. W. Henry," in *William and Mary College Quarterly*, Series 1, XXV (July, 1916), 9–13. The standard secondary account of the Kenner mission is in Frank L. Owsley, *King Cotton Diplomacy* (1931; repr. ed., 1959), 532. Robert D. Meade, *Judah P. Benjamin: Confederate Statesman* (New York, 1943), 263–67, is enlightening.

. . . While unshaken in the determination never again to unite ourselves under a common Government with a people by whom we have been so deeply wronged, the enquiry daily becomes more pressing, what is the policy and what are the purposes of the western powers of Europe in relation to this contest? Are they determined never to recognize the Southern Confederacy until the United States assent to such action on their part? Do they propose under any circumstances to give other and more direct aid to the Northern people in attempting to enforce our submission to a hateful Union? If so, it is but just that we be apprised of their purposes, to the end that we may then deliberately consider the terms, if any[,] upon which we can secure peace from the foes to whom the question is thus surrendered and who have the countenance and encouragement of all mankind in the invasion of our country, the destruction of our homes, the extermination of our people. If on the other hand there be objections not made known to us, which have for four years prevented the recognition of our independence notwithstanding the demonstration of our right to assert and our ability to maintain it, justice equally demands that an opportunity be afforded us for meeting and overcoming those objections, if in our power to do so. We have given ample evidence that we are not a people to be appalled by danger or to shrink from sacrifice in the attainment of our object. That object, the sole object for which we would ever have consented to commit our all to the hazards of this war, is the vindication of our right to self-government and independence. For that end no sacrifice is too great, save that of honor.

If then the purpose of France and Great Britain have been, or be now, to exact terms or conditions before conceding the rights we claim, a frank exposition of that purpose is due to humanity. It is due now, for it may enable us to save many lives most precious to our country by consenting to such terms in advance of another year's campaign.

This dispatch will be handed to you by the Hon. Duncan F. Kenner, a gentleman whose position in the Confederate Congress and whose title to the entire confidence of all Departments of our Government are too well known to you to need any assurances from me that you may place implicit reliance on his statements. It is proper, however, that I should authorize you officially to consider any communication that he may make to you verbally on the subject embraced in this dispatch as emanating from this Department under the instruction of the President.[4]

🕿 Despite the careful efforts of Davis and Benjamin to keep secret Duncan Kenner's mission, gossip and speculation about something of the sort filled the Confederate newspapers. The Richmond *Sentinel* (December 28, 1864) issued a frantic call for just such a desperate move, if not something even more drastic:

It becomes us coolly and calmly to look into all the circumstances of our condition, and to adopt with firmness and energy such policy as wisdom may point out or necessity constrain. It is childish to whine under misfortune; it is cowardly to sink under it; it is absurd to be enfeebled by it. A brave man struggling with adversity is worthy of special admiration—"a spectacle for gods and men."

We think that our late adverses have done much towards preparing the minds of our people for the most extreme sacrifices if they shall be adjudged necessary to the success of our cause. And in truth they are not sacrifices at all when compared with our situation if subjugated. It is a question simply whether we shall give for our own uses or whether the Yankees shall take for *theirs*. Subjugation means emancipation and confiscation. All our servants and all our property yielded up to assist in defence of our country, would mean no more. But it would be far more glorious to devote our means to our success than to lose them as spoils to the enemy. Our situation, too, stripped of our property, but master of the government, would be infinitely better than if despoiled by the enemy, and wearing his bonds.

These views have long received the theoretical assent of our people. They are now our practical, realizing conviction. A thousand prejudices, a thousand consecrated dogmas, are now ready to be yielded at the bidding of necessity. *Any* sacrifice of opinion, *any* sacrifice of property, *any* surrender of prejudice—if necessary to defeat our enemies—is now the watchword and reply. Subjugation is a horror that embraces all other horrors and adds enormous calamities of its own. The people see this. They have a vivid perception of it. They are ready on their part for the duties which it implies.

[4] Judah P. Benjamin to John Slidell, December 27, 1864, *O.R.N.*, Series II, Vol. III, 1,255–1,256.

Let now our authorities, State and Confederate, rise to the level of the great occasion. Troublous times are upon us. Great exigencies surround us. We need all our strength, and all our wisdom. Let there be a conference of all our wise men. Let there be a calm investigation of our wants, and a catalogue of our resources. Then, by common consent, let all obstacles, to the employment of these resources, be removed. So long as we have a man or a dollar, and the man or dollar be needed, let the call be honored. We must not raise difficulties—it is no time for that! Shall we withhold our sons, and thus reserve them as servants for the Yankees? Shall we send our sons, and deny our negroes? Shall we spend our blood and refuse our money? Shall we withhold anything from our country when we should be but saving it for our foe? It is a disgrace to a garrison to surrender before its ammunition is exhausted. It would be adding disgrace to our misery if we were overcome without having first exhausted every resource of defense. It would be doubly infamous to us, because with contributions to our defence equal to the spoilations we should suffer if conquered, our success would be assured. We should come out of the contest at least with that which would be worth more than all the rest—our liberties and our country. If we had thrown overboard the cargo, we should thereby have saved the ship.

Let Government determine what it needs, and what it can use; and if it be our lands, our houses, our negroes, our horses, our money, or ourselves, it must have them. Strange that we should cling most tenaciously to what is of least moment! Strange that we should give ourselves and grudge our property! Our patriotism must lay aside such selfishness. It must be generous as well as brave.

Our authorities must do more: They must take care, whatever befall us, to save us from the Yankees. If adverse gales and devouring billows should constrain our storm-tost ship into some port, let it be no *Yankee* port. If an unpropitious Providence should condemn us to a master, let it not be a *Yankee* master. Of all the people on earth, we should have most reason to loathe and to dread them. *Any* terms with *any* other, would be preferable to subjugation to them. This is the sentiment of our people. This is their conviction; and it is a wise conviction. Let our rulers remember it and heed it. Our constitution was made as the development of our national life. It may not provide for all the various exigencies of war. Questions of state may arise in our experience, as they have arisen in the experience of almost every other nation, when our best welfare will require of our rulers the exercise of a bold responsibility. The acquisition of Louisiana in 1803, was justified only as a question of state—something over and above the constitution. If in times of peace statesmen have sometimes thus to throw themselves upon the intelligence of their countrymen, and seek their advantage by irregular methods, such occasions may well be presumed more likely to arise during a struggle for life with a powerful, unscrupulous and ferocious enemy.

The clouds that have thickened over us admonish us of the possibility that the time may come when statesmanship, if it cannot deliver us, must at least secure to us the utmost palliation of our misery; if it cannot save us, must at least save us from the Yankees. We lately published from a thoughtful correspondent a "suggestion," that in the event of being unable to sustain our independence, we should surrender it into the hands of those from whom we wrested or purchased it; into the hands of Britain, France and Spain, rather than yield it to the Yankees. From the favor with which this suggestion has been received, we are sure that in the dread event which it contemplates our people would infinitely prefer an alliance with the European nations on terms as favorable as they could desire, in preference to the dominion of the Yankees.

. . . Providence *will not* suffer us to go down, if we show a proper devotion, a proper wisdom, and a proper courage. Let our wise men plan, let our brave men fight, and let our good men pray. God will open up a way of escape for us, and will disappoint our enemies. Let our faith fail not.

🖙 Less frightened and also unimpressed by the *Sentinel*'s logic, the powerful Richmond *Examiner* (December 30, 1864) scornfully attacked the opinions of such newspapers as the *Sentinel* and the *Enquirer* that would tamper with the South's "labour system" in order to try to secure foreign aid:

When in any crisis of a nation's fate men are seen to lose their heads, and to look all around them in wild alarm, it is a proof that *they* at least are subdued: if the mass of their countrymen had not more presence of mind than they have the doom of all would be near at hand. We seem to have some such frightened counsellors in the Confederacy at this moment, and their wild outcries grate and jar dreadfully upon the generally calm and resolute tone of the country. They do not help, but hinder. They resemble the shrieking passengers in the "Tempest," to whom the Boatswain had to say, "You mar our labour: keep your cabins: you do assist the storm." One publick journal exhorts these Confederate States to throw themselves back into the arms of England, France and Spain, the Powers which first planted colonies here—to go back like the prodigal son; to acknowledge that we were young birds that had broke the shell too soon; to recant all those high words we have had in our mouths for two or three generations, about liberty, rights of man and democracy, and promise not to do so any more. To be sure the poor frightened creature tells us to take this course, *if* we should prove unable to maintain our own cause against our enemies: but to utter the suggestion, above all to utter it now, is to say too plainly, not if we should, but when we shall, or rather inasmuch as we have, proved unable to sustain ourselves; that is, seeing we are beaten, overmatched, overwhelmed and ready to sink, come all ye good Christians and rescue us and take us to yourselves as your vassels and liege-subjects forever! The blind panick of the writer makes him even unable to see that neither England nor France, nor Spain, nor the three combined, would touch us with the end of the longest pole if we once made so helpless an exhibition of ourselves. Nations are not good Samaritans: if they see a weaker brother fallen among thieves, wounded and lying half dead, they do not trouble themselves about his hard fate; do not even pass by on the other side; but explore his pockets, if peradventure there be somewhat left to take away from him. If neither England nor France will so much as recognise us, not even know of our existence, while we are vigorously baffling and beating back gigantick invasions, year after year, in haughty reliance on our own prowess and a good cause, and able also to offer them advantageous alliances and reciprocal benefits, how would they receive such an invitation as this, now that we are sinking and perishing under the mighty power of the Yankee nation, now that we are beaten and beggared, we pray you to go to war with that nation for our redemption; and having rescued us—as we have nothing else to offer—take ourselves and our children for vassals to you and your children: take this land that once was ours, and portion it amongst you. This will not do.

The alternative is not offered us, as the panick-stricken mortal imagines—to be colonists under England or France,—or subjects of the

Yankees. We have not the choice: the very proposal suggested to be made to those Powers would prove that we were already subjugated— would be an admission that we had set up a pretension we could not support, and provoked an enemy we could not fight; and they would coldly bid us creep back into the "Union," and stay there. They would understand that the United States, (this Confederacy once subdued) must be the ruling Power of the West; they would be glad to cement their friendship with our enemies by treating us with contumely; and would so endeavour to make a general treaty settling the affairs of all America, and giving guaranties both to Mexico and Canada.

One is ashamed even to refute and rebuke this mean suggestion begotten by terrour upon ignorance. It would be pleasing to think we should never hear more of it. But then there is another; and not very dissimilar in kind, or in origin. Another counsellor (who also, of course, takes for granted that we are virtually conquered) advises us to make known to European nations that we are ready to abolish slavery: "that slavery shall not be permitted to prejudice our recognition as a nation"; and we are assured that this "would secure recognition, and *perhaps* intervention." It is not alleged that England or France, or the Government of either, has ever said or hinted that they would make this bargain: but if they would, then we are exhorted to say that we would. Now this also, however the idea may be muffled up, amounts exactly to an invitation to England and France, or one of them, to make war upon the United States, in order to save us from Yankee domination; and in return we are to offer them, what?—the destruction of our labour power, which would leave us of no use to them, to ourselves, or to anybody else. It is said, indeed, that this would be a great concession to the "opinion of mankind, which is anti-slavery," and that the evil consequences "would fall upon the unfortunate negro," whom we should thus basely abandon. Very well, then it would be a most humiliating confession of defeat, and would also by them be taken as a confession that we had deserved defeat. We must not deceive ourselves; it signifies nothing to say, we would *rather* give up slavery than be subject to the Yankees. So we should of course: but here, once more, this is not the alternative. To give up slavery would not save us from being subject to the Yankees: on the contrary, when we should have made this graceful concession to the publick opinion of Europe, then Europe would very certainly cheat us; and seeing that we were whipped, and the pluck taken out of us, would make friends of our enemy at our expense.

What does our brave army think of these wretched outcries of alarm and self-abasement? They sound as if we were shipwrecked already, and drifting on a raft, waving a white flag to every point of the compass, anxiously scanning the distant horizon, and one crying Lo, here! and another Lo, there! The matter does not so stand with us; and if it did, we should be already lost. Our help and hope never were, and are not now, in Europe, Asia or Africa. Here, on our own ground, we have the powers and materials both to vindicate our independence and destroy our enemies. If our affairs are now somewhat gloomy, it is for want, not of sympathy or aid abroad, but of energy and wisdom at home. It is for want of confidence in the efficient administration of our military affairs, which are the only affairs. Neither can this confidence be restored by always crying Confidence! Only let us have Confidence! Have trust in one another; and slang of that sort. On the contrary, matters are made worse; for mankind naturally abhors your confidence man. Our affairs can be restored only by placing the military affairs of the country in a really capable hand; in the hand of one who will not need to keep piteously appealing for confidence, or feelingly depreciating misconstruction; and by giving to him *carte blanche*—yes and *carte noire* too; and saying, Now lead on and we will follow thee.

Then we will have no need to be looking anxiously across the Atlantick to see whether Freedom is about to dawn upon us from the East. National independence is not carried over the sea in ships; where it grows, there it stands, like an oak. If we have not here, within ourselves, the whole of the elements of it, the materials and the spirit, the body and the soul, then we shall never see it, never.

🖙 Although with less style and vigor perhaps, and generally with a time lag, the newspapers of the other southern states that remained unconquered echoed the controversy raging in the Confederate capital. The Atlanta *Southern Confederacy* (January 20, 1865; refugeeing in Macon) doubted that the Negroes would fight for the Confederacy:

We perceive the public journals continue to urge the measure of putting negroes into the army, and we hear people talking on the street corners in favor of the measure. Put arms in the hands of the slaves, and make them fight for us, they say. We have heretofore expressed our opinion in opposition to this measure, and shall not now repeat what we then said. In continuation of our formerly expressed views, we may add a few additional suggestions now.

One speedy practical result of putting negroes in the army would be the peopling of all the swamps of the South with runaway negro deserters. Trained to the use of fire arms, they would deprecate everywhere on cattle, hogs, etc., and would soon be forced to resort to robbery and plunder to gain subsistence. Attempts to arrest them would be resisted, and the horrors of a servile war would be realized. Very large numbers would desert and pursue this sort of life. If they did not do this, they would desert to the enemy. With the enemy they know they would get freedom *at once*. With us, they would get freedom *after the war*, taking our promises as true. There would exist an immediate certainty of freedom on one side; an *uncertainty* on the other. A well disposed, faithful, and intelligent slave in this region was recently asked by his master some questions on this very point. The view I have taken of the subject in the above remarks, are simply the views of the slave referred to, and constitutes the substance of his reply to his master. Put, said the negro, the slave into any other position in the service you choose—let him dig, drive teams, build roads, do any other duty, but do not call on him to fight.

. . . The negro is willing to *work* for us, but not to *fight* for us. We were passing into the Car-shed of this city two days since. Some idle and vicious looking boys were directing some saucy conversation to a negro man of stalwart frame who stood near them. One of the boys said to the negro, "Uncle, why don't you go and fight?" "What I fight for?" asked the Ebon. "For your country," replied the boy. The negro scowled and said instantly, "I have no country to fight for." Now we think the negro was mistaken. We think his lot an enviable one, and that they constitute a privileged class in the community. As the toil of brain and muscle is daily renewed, amid uncertainties, for the procurement of bread for our wife and little ones, we often feel how happy we should be were we the slave of some good and provident owner. Then simple daily toil would fill the measure of duty, and comfortable food and clothing would be the assured reward. While, therefore, we think the negro was mistaken—that the South is emphatically *his country* while slavery exists—yet we have no idea he can be convinced of the fact sufficiently to take up arms and fight bravely for our cause as his cause, for our country as his country.

But waiving all this, and supposing them to fight, and to so greatly aid us that we win our independence, what then? The fighting negroes are to be freed. What are we to do with them? Let them remain among us? If so, those who remain slaves may be so in name, but they will not be so in reality. Shall the free slaves then be sent out of the country? out of the country whose independence they fought to obtain? Certainly no such reward as *perpetual exile* would be either honorable to us, or just to them. Such an act on our part, would be a stigma on the imperishable pages of history, of which all future generations of Southrons would be ashamed. These are some of the additional considerations which have suggested themselves to us. Let us put the negro to *work*, but not to *fight*.

🖙 The Wilmington, North Carolina, *Journal* (February 10, 1865) reasoned much as had the *Southern Confederacy* and questioned whether the South could really outbid the North for the support of the blacks:

As a general rule our negroes prove faithful, and will probably continue to do so, so long as the enemy puts them in the army and we do not. In this difference we have our main guarantee for their fidelity. Remove this guarantee and what other have we?

. . . It is true that with freedom, we may offer the negro the privilege of a continued residence in the country and upon the soil of his birth, with the climate that suits his temperament and constitution, but will not the Yankees promise the same and more by way of an offset to any inducements we may hold out to secure the fidelity of the negro? It will cost the Yankee government nothing to promise lands and other confiscated property of Southern people, and it is probable that the negroes will be fools enough to believe them.

Desertions are now the bane of our armies and threaten to work the ruin of our country. Deserters are not simply guilty of sins of omission by being absent from the ranks that defend the country, but they are almost always guilty of sins of commission in preventing cultivation and committing acts of robbery and destruction, and men cannot be spared to repress these outrages and compel the return of these men to their commands. How much will the list of desertion be swelled if two hundred thousand reluctant negroes are to be armed and placed in the ranks to contribute their quota? Is it not to be feared that every swamp will be a lair—a lurking place of deserters of every hue? What safety will there be for property? What chance for cultivation when the most able-bodied laborers are taken away from the ranks of the producers to whom they will be liable to become a terror[?]

We do not include in our calculation the mere question of property *as* property. Where the lives of the best and bravest are daily and hourly exposed, we do not see what extra sanctity can hedge in any mere question of property. The question takes in simply the practicability of the scheme—the probability of its success, and the consequences likely to flow from [and] to accompany it. . . .

☞ The Wilmington *Journal* doubted that the Negroes would fight for rather than merely help to feed the Confederacy. But another newspaper published in that threatened seaport, the *Carolinian* (as reprinted in the Raleigh *Confederate*, January 12, 1865), urged that the Confederacy could indeed motivate the blacks to fight—and reward them with land:

The question of putting negroes in the field is one which has lately assumed an importance which few expected. There is but little doubt that Gen. Lee favors the measure, and indeed has recommended it. One thing is evident, that more men must be had or the cause will suffer. . . .

Something must be done, and we propose to consider what is best to do. This incessant drain upon our white population since 1861, has reduced that class to a mere moity, while the black have increased in a ratio commensurate to the decrease of the former. The white race in the Confederacy is, day by day, becoming numerically weaker. And if the policy which has been adopted since 1861, be continued the relative preponderance of the two classes will become alarming. To avoid this alone, something is necessary. If we expect to have a country when the war ends, let us have a few white men saved, who can call it "our country."

It is objected that negroes will become an element of weakness, rather than strength to the army; so we all predicted when the cunning

Yankee took it into his head to make soldiers of them. They have proven the reverse. It is also said that it would give more men to the enemy than the Confederacy. If that be so it will be by desertion; they now recruit from our very doors this class of soldiers, and when we capture them we are compelled to avoid retaliation and to treat them as prisoners of war. When they desert their colors and go to the enemy, they will be deserters, and the penalty of desertion is death. In this respect, therefore, it is better that they be in the field. The objection is also raised that it will be still further depleting the country of its labor, and we will then become less able to feed our armies. This objection is easily met by a provision that when the new levies are placed in the field and sufficiently drilled and disciplined, let our *citizen* soldiery—persons who can do infinitely more good at home than in the army, be discharged, and they, with the labor exempt from military service, can produce much more than all the unsystematized labor now at home can possibly do. One strong recommendation is this: It will make some of these strong war men who own millions of property and who are loud-mouthed for war, bloody, relentless and unsparing war, and who have accursed soft places for their precious heirs, give a little substantial assistance in this struggle.

Another strong recommendation for the measure is, that the soldiers are nearly all in favor of it, and when this is so we, of course, have no right to demur.

It may be argued that the negro will not fight. Upon this point, though not having any very great amount of experience, the little we have had, has convinced us that *discipline* will teach any man to fight, we care not who or what he is. All that is needed is brave officers who have had experience.

But the question will be aske . what will you do with the negro after he becomes unsuited, by reason of his military training, for servitude? Upon this point, we would not say what would be *best* to do with [them], but we will give our views upon what might be *well* to do with them. We admit that after his training and discipline as a soldier, he would become unsuited for his former condition. Would we give him freedom as a *reward?* As soon would we give a child poison. One could use the gift with about as much intelligence and benefit to itself as the other. We would not give him freedom *"as a reward for meri-*

torious service," but we would give him something more substantial. We would have each State provide a homestead for the black soldier on his return home—*this as a reward.* And then we would give him freedom as a means of enjoying the property given him. We would give him the *right to hold any species of property* which a white man could hold. It is all nonsense to talk of the sacredness of the rights of property. Bone, sinew and blood are required in this contest. We have material for hundreds of thousands of able-bodied soldiers in her [? our] midst, and it is high time it should be used, before our armies are depleted. Let Congress act and that quickly. We have work to do. Let us be up and doing. Place these men in the field and you will see gold in New York go up to three or four hundred immediately, while the Northern people will heap their invective upon Lincoln for inaugurating a movement that will prove more disastrous to them than to the rebels. We can place ten soldiers of this class in the field for one of theirs. We trust the views of General Lee may be early adopted, giving to the country additional evidence that we are in earnest.

☞ Supporting its case for following the lead of President Davis, the Raleigh *Confederate* (January 25, 1865) picked up from the northern press an interesting item about Frederick Douglass, the most famous Negro abolitionist:

. . . Fred. Douglas[s]—a runaway negro, who left Maryland some years ago, and has been a pet of certain strong-minded abolition women of the North—made a speech the other day, in New York, which, we are bound to say, was a very sensible speech; and in the course of it he said—"I am of [the] opinion that such is the confidence which the master can inspire over his slave, if Jeff. Davis goes about in earnest to raise a black army, making them suitable promises, they can be made very effective in the war for Southern independence. If Jeff. Davis will hold out to the blacks of the South their freedom—guarantee their freedom—the possession of a piece of land—the negroes of the South will fight, and fight valiantly for this boon." We believe that this negro speaks truly the sentiment of his people; and we are satisfied that, if Congress and the States, had taken steps early last fall to have given Gen. Lee two hundred thousand negroes, we should scarce to-day have had a Yankee foot print on Southern soil.

All to their conviction, say we. These are ours—they are honest. In the perils of this hour, a nation must be inventive, quick to discern, quick to reach, and quick to use its resources.

🖙 Part of the argument in favor of the Confederacy's turning to its black population for military help rested on the knowledge that the relatively few Negroes in the North were generally ill treated. The Raleigh *Confederate* (February 11, 1865) borrowed a story from a Philadelphia newspaper to make that point:

HOW THE YANKEE TREATS THE NEGRO.

Negro Privileges in Philadelphia.—The patrons of the city passenger railways in Philadelphia voted on the question—"Shall colored people ride in the cars?" The [Philadelphia] *Inquirer* of the 31st says:

The vote up to the hour of closing the trips last night was largely in favor of white persons riding inside the cars and the exclusion of the blacks. The vote on one of the lines at noon yesterday stood four thousand opposed and one hundred and sixty in favor of the question. Votes will continue to be deposited during the present week, that all may have an opportunity of depositing their vote as their feelings may dictate.

Thus the poor blacks in Philadelphia are denied even the privilege of riding in the cars, while their brethren are forced into the Yankee armies, and rushed on fortifications with bayonets behind them.

In what Southern State are negroes forbidden to ride in the cars?

🖙 It was obvious that southern opinion was agonizingly divided on the question of freeing and arming the slaves. Although the crisis produced perhaps the fullest and freest discussion of the peculiar institution in the South's history, it was not surprising in the nineteenth century, especially in the South, that few women participated publicly in the debate.

Professor Anne Firor Scott, a leading historian of southern women, has accumulated a number of striking comments from the private diaries and letters of women like the aristocratic Mary Boykin Chesnut to show how they disdained slavery.[5] Yet one suspects that in the case of most southern white women who were

---

[5] Anne Firor Scott, *The Southern Lady: From Pedestal to Politics, 1830–1930* (Chicago, 1970), 46–53.

unhappy about slavery, the situation was much like that with the miserable weather of January and February: one could only suffer and wish that it would somehow go away.

The crisis of 1864–1865, however, inspired one woman ("Celestia") in Georgia to be "unladylike" and to speak out in print (Macon *Telegraph and Confederate,* January 11, 1865):

Water Bend, S. W. Ga., Jan. 6, '65.

Mr. Editor: A lady's opinion may not be worth much in such an hour as this, but I cannot resist the temptation of expressing my approbation of "The crisis—the Remedy," copied from the Mobile Register. Would to God our Government would act upon its suggestions at once. The women of the South are not so in love with their negro property, as to wish to see husbands, fathers, sons, brothers, slain to protect it; nor would they submit to Yankee rule, could it secure to them a thousand waiting maids, whence now they possess one. We cannot believe that a loss of one fifth of the negro men would seriously damage our prospects for provisions. For four years, one fifth or more of the negro women on plantations, have been engaged in making clothes. Will not the ladies and misses of our land undertake a part of this necessary labor, and send the negro women to the field, to take the places of the negro men who go to the army. Yes, let every lady and little girl in our land, go to spinning and weaving with all their might; and let the little boys cultivate the gardens. If the city ladies do not wish to spin, or weave, let them send their surplus house servants to the country, to assist in raising provisions, (hire them out if they own no farm) and do more of their house work themselves—better this, than serving a Yankee woman. Some thoughtless women may laugh at this suggestion. I pray God they may never repent not having aided in this struggle for their independence. I pity my countrymen, when I see them dressed in Yankee fashions, and hear them talking of parties, balls, and theatres—yes, I pity them, pity their ignorance of their country's condition. I cannot believe that God will hold that person guiltless, who stands indifferent to their country's fate. Arise ye, my countrywomen! and once more set to work for your liberty! You have been accused of growing neglect; and it has been asked, where are the Southern women of the two first years of the war? Let not this be asked in vain. Show by words and works where you are. Listen no longer to the croakings of the skulkers at home, who in the absence of the brave have, alas, done too much towards cooling the patriotism of our noble women.

All legislative and military authority has failed and will doubtless continue to fail in bringing out the "home guards" to their duty. There seems to be but one remedy—the negro—and if our brave and good soldiers are willing to call him to their aid, why not let it be done before it is too late. We hear from all sides that S. W. Georgia is threatened by Sherman's thieves and incendiaries. We ask the white men here what they intend doing—the reply of all except a few old men is, "we can do nothing—and the government seems determined to do nothing." Of course the government is not formed of men like themselves! Some of our negroes have been questioned upon the subject of resistance, and very many have said, "If the yankees make us fight for them, I don't see why our masters can't make us fight on our own side." It has been suggested by a few of our old men that companies of negroes be made up of those willing to serve, and let them be officered by white men selected for the purpose, and drilled thoroughly in view of the certainty of yankee raids through this section. Yes, let us try the experiment for the government if necessary. Intelligent men say that a small body of determined guerrillas could successfully defend the swampy country against raiding parties. But, will anything be done, and when? Shame upon Georgia—no longer can she be called "the Empire State"—that Sherman can boast of not having met with any guerrillas from Atlanta to Savannah. The people at home seem to think it a very small matter for "the army" to hurry to their assistance whenever their ill gotten wealth is in danger. When will our people be perfectly united in an effort for Independence!

🔫 "Celestia" strove to arouse Georgians, although Sherman had already marched victoriously through the state. Virginia, despite the fact that it had long been the scene of many bloody battles, had still not known such defeat and humiliation. Yet even in the face of Governor Smith's call and the threat of Grant's ever-swelling army, the Virginia legislature proved almost as dilatory and resistant to change where slavery was concerned as did the Confederate Congress. The following preamble and resolution, introduced in the senate of Virginia on January 11, 1865, illustrate the preoccupations of many of the legislators:

Mr. Collier offered the following preamble and resolutions on the subject of negro slavery, which lie over under the rules:

The general assembly of Virginia doth hereby declare that negroes in slavery in this state and in the whole South, (who are withal in a higher condition of civilization than any of their race has ever been elsewhere,) having been a property in their masters for two hundred and fifty years, by use and custom at first, and ever since by recognitions of the public law in various forms, ought not to be and cannot justly be interfered with in that relation of property by the state, neither by the people in convention assembled to alter an existing constitution or to form one for admission into the Confederacy, nor by the representatives of the people in the state or confederate legislature, nor by any means or mode which the popular majority might adopt; and that the state, whilst remaining republican in the structure of its government, can be lawfully deprived of that species of property, if ever, only by the free consent of the individual owners; it being true as the general assembly doth further declare, that for the state, without the free consent of the owner, to deprive him of his identical property, by compelling him to accept a substituted value therefor, no matter how ascertained, or by the *post nati* policy, or in any other way, not for the public use, but with a view to rid the state of such property already resident therein, and so to destroy the right of property in the subject or to constrain the owner to send his slaves out of the state, or else to expatriate himself and carry them with him, would contravene and frustrate the indispensable principles of free government: and whereas these Confederate States being now all slaveholding, may be disturbed by some act of the majority, in any one of them, in derogation of the rights of the minority, unless this doctrine above declared be interposed: and whereas a question of the propriety of putting negroes as soldiers into the military service of the Confederate States, is at this time, in agitation and perplexing the public councils:

Be it resolved by the general assembly, and proclaimed as the solemn judgment thereof, confirmed, as it is, by an intimate knowledge of the negro's nature, and fortified by the doctrines hereinbefore declared, that it would be as disadvantageous to the negroes, as it would be unjust to the owners, that negro laborers shall be converted into soldiers, by state legislation consenting thereto, and moreover that any attempt by the confederate government to that end by offered freedom to the slaves or by any inducement to the owners would transcend the delegated authority of the congress, and be a direct disregard of the constitutional provision that "congress shall not pass any law impairing the right of property in negro slaves"; whilst if the authority subsisted in the congress of the state or in the state legislatures to make soldiers of the slaves, it would be in bad faith to constrain them to do battle in support of their bondage, if freedom is a boon to them, and inhuman to make them do battle for their freedom, if bondage is their better condition.

Resolved by the general assembly of Virginia, That the governor of Virginia be and he is hereby requested to communicate this proceeding to the several governors of the Confederate States and request them to lay the same before their respective legislatures, and to request their concurrence therein in such way as they may severally deem best calculated to secure stability to the fundamental doctrine of southern civilization, which is hereby declared and proposed to be advanced.[6]

☞ A speech delivered by another Virginian, Thomas S. Gholson, in the Confederate House of Representatives (February 1, 1865) is a full rehearsal of many of the arguments used by Virginians, as well as other Southerners, who were enamored of the status quo concerning slavery—shaky though that status quo was in fact. Printed and distributed in pamphlet form, Gholson's speech, considerably condensed here, was one of the fullest statements of the objections advanced by southern politicians:

Upon the introduction of resolutions to the effect that while we should be ready to treat for peace, we should prepare to prosecute the war with vigor, by placing every man liable to service in the field, and ceasing to agitate the policy of employing negro troops as soldiers, Mr. Gholson rose and said: Mr. Speaker:

No question of more serious import has been agitated, since the commencement of the present war, than the proposition to arm and employ

[6] *Journal of the Senate of the Commonwealth of Virginia . . . Extra Session* (Richmond, 1864), 69–70. Photostatic facsimile in the Virginia State Library. Thomas Preisser, doctoral candidate in history at the College of William and Mary, wrote a helpful paper on Virginia's role in this matter and kindly shared the above *Journal* with me. Since the Virginia legislature, like the Confederate Congress (and both bodies met in the famed Jeffersonian capitol building), was often in secret session, the records are skimpy.

our slaves as soldiers in the field. That they may be judiciously used in building fortifications, and as teamsters, cooks, &c., will not be controverted—indeed, it is to be regretted, that they have not already been more extensively so employed. They are accustomed to such service, and could be kept under the proper discipline and control. Every slave, who takes the place of a soldier engaged in driving wagons, cooking, &c., adds another musket to our number. It is obviously not only proper, but our duty to permit no "able bodied man" to remain in any position, the duties of which may be as well performed by a slave. Let our authorities therefore see to it, that all such positions are at once filled by slaves, and that the legion of strong, athletic men, who are even now, to be found all over the country, filling unimportant offices, the duties of which could be just as well discharged by the "halt or lame," or by men above the military age, are immediately sent to the field, and our armies would be able to drive the enemy from our borders.

But, it is proposed to go further—to put arms in the hands of our slaves, and fight them as soldiers. It is declared, that leading individuals in various sections of the Confederacy, favour the proposition, while several of our prominent newspapers openly advocate the policy. We are to raise a vast army of slaves—from two hundred to two hundred and fifty thousand—arm and equip them, and march them forth to meet our enemies. The advocates of the proposition seem filled with enthusiasm on the subject, and promise themselves and the country the most happy results.

It is assumed, that slaves will make good and reliable soldiers—that some slaves would, need not be denied, but that our slaves generally will make reliable soldiers, the advocates of the measure, are not warranted in assuming. I regard the whole scheme with deep concern, and have the strongest convictions, that no matter in what aspect it may be considered, it is unwise, and should be promptly rejected.

First. It is an *experiment* on a grand scale, and would virtually stake our success in this great struggle, on the capacity and fidelity of negro soldiers. . . . *The experiment is hazardous.*

Nature seems to have fitted our slaves, as a race, above others, for servants. They are loyal, obedient, submissive and grateful, but timid and unstable as children. Kept at home, and subjected to proper discipline, they are useful and happy. Freed from restraint, and exposed to evil influences, they become licentious and fanatical. They are credulous, and may be easily deceived. Let the facts of this war be consulted for confirmation of this. Our enemies hoped, and all Europe expected, that the commencement of hostilities would be followed by the insurrection of our slaves, and deeds too black and horrible to be named. Our slaves were to rise up and conquer us, if our enemies could not. War, with its varying fortunes, has now existed for nearly four years, and yet, although we have among us, more than three millions of slaves, there has been no insurrection or attempt at insurrection, while life and property have been more secure—infinitely more secure with us, than with our enemies. Our wives and children have been left on our plantations—frequently with no other protection, than that afforded by our slaves. These slaves have taken care of our property, cultivated our fields, and gathered our crops. Their loyalty was never more conspicuous, their obedience never more childlike. These are facts —indisputable facts. Let the world ponder them.

. . . But, suppose you make them brave—firm in their courage—you have not yet removed their credulity—their liability to be deceived and deluded by our enemies. If each man could have, in the day of battle, his slave by his side, he could protect him from their fraud and deception, but this would be impossible. The spies and secret emissaries of the enemy, would be continually among them, producing mischief before we apprehended it—encouraging them to infidelity and desertion—and when they fell into their hands as prisoners of war, who can believe, that they would be able to resist Yankee fraud and cunning? They are averse to fighting. Our enemies know this, and would promise all deserters not only their freedom, but exemption from military duty. . . . It seems to me, that they know little of the negro character, who would expect them to remain firm under such circumstances. They would desert by hundreds and thousands. They would go to avoid danger, if for nothing else. But more would be promised—full rations, fine clothes, and no work. Gentlemen may delude themselves, but whenever the experiment is made, it will prove to be a ''recruiting service'' for our enemies. It will weaken our own army. . . .

Second. The introduction of slaves into our army, would not only be hazardous for the reasons stated, but it would be offensive to many of the brave men, who constitute our veteran army. . . .

. . . Let it not be said, it is a mere prejudice, and will soon be overcome. It is a prejudice, which has "grown with their growth, and strengthened with their strength." They feel their superiority, and you can not eradicate the "prejudice." This sense of superiority makes them more manly in their conduct, braver in the field. You should not eradicate it, if you could. It is part and parcel of their character.

Third. To the slaves introduced into our army, and who prove faithful, the boon of freedom is to be given at the termination of the war. What is this but abolition? . . .

If we have been in error heretofore—if liberty to our slaves be really a boon—if they really be fit and qualified for liberty, and should receive it as a merited reward for military service, then we surrender the whole question, and should forthwith emancipate them. . . .

And suppose the war ended—our independence achieved—that the slaves carried into the war have proved faithful; that they have remained with us and fought for prospective freedom, rather than deserted to our enemies and received present freedom, what then is to become of these freed men? We surely will not deny them a home, in the land they have defended—so, we should have a large number of free negroes scattered over the several States. . . . What shall become of their wives and children? Shall they remain slaves, while their husbands and fathers, who have fought for our liberties and their homes, are permitted to become wandering vagabonds, and finally die of starvation—having by their valour, earned the glorious "liberty to starve?" Or shall we give liberty to their wives and children, and thus make our black population part free and part slave? What then would be the condition of our country? Who would consent to live in it? What would become of slavery? What would be the character of the returned negro-soldiers, made familiar with the use of fire-arms, and taught by us, that freedom was worth fighting for? In many sections of the country, the two races could not continue together. According to the census of 1860, the white population of the counties, composing my Congressional District [just to the west and south of Richmond], was 13,792, the black population 31,228. I allude to the counties of Prince George, Nottoway, Amelia, Powhatan and Cumberland. There would be near 6000 male slaves, between the ages of 18 and 45. If 150 or 200,000 slaves were put into the army, it would require, as I will show hereafter, at least half between those ages—so, that from the five counties named, there would be taken about 3000 male slaves. Suppose only 2000 of this number are returned, after having fought as well and bravely, as the friends of the scheme promise themselves, we should then have some 400 free negro soldiers, in each of these counties. We shall have taught them, as already stated, the use of fire-arms, and that liberty is worth fighting for. They will have learned the power of combination, and have their minds set on mustering and guns. Naturally averse to labour, they will have become indolent and mischievous. They will be without restraint, and ready for all excesses. Here let the curtain drop. Objections multiply as we advance, and I can do but little more, than suggest them.

Fourth. By the conscription of slaves, we shall surrender every ground, assumed by us on the subject, at the commencement of the war. . . .

Fifth. It would be a confession of weakness on our part, which would inspire the enemy with renewed confidence, and induce greater exertions. . . .

Sixth. And there is another objection to the experiment—one which ordinary prudence will not permit us to overlook, or lightly to consider. I allude to the effect, which the abstraction of so large a number of able-bodied slaves would have on the production of supplies. . . .

And there is yet another difficulty, and that, too, of a grave and delicate nature. The Confederate Government has no authority over the institution of slavery in the States. Each State manages and controls it, in its own way. The Confederate Government has not a foot of land upon which to bury a slave, much less to settle him, after he is liberated. Surely it would not rush blindly into the employment of negro troops, engaging to liberate them at the termination of the war, without having first made some arrangement with the several States on the subject? Is it certain that necessary terms could be made with all the States? . . .

. . . Nothing, therefore, short of united and harmonious action on the part of the several States, could give efficacy and success to the experiment.

I do not treat this as a question of property. It is not that men are unwilling to surrender their property, it is because they are convinced that the use proposed to be made of it is fearfully dangerous. . . .

. . . With these grave objections to the measure, and these obstacles in the way of its execution, it seems to me, the agitation of the subject was unfortunate. For, it cannot be denied, that it has had a most depressing influence upon the popular mind in many sections of the country. It has been regarded as an admission by our authorities, that we were reduced to an extremity; and the conviction (more general than is supposed) that the proposed measure, so far from affording relief, would only increase our difficulties and embarrassments, has produced a painful despondency. Men's hearts failed them, when it was seriously proposed to employ negro troops, who had never desponded before. I regret to be compelled thus to speak, but I am dealing with a question of great magnitude, and the truth, though painful, must be spoken.

. . . But, we are told, that distinguished Generals favour the employment of slaves as soldiers. Were our Generals to recommend a particular military movement, it would be immodest—presumptuous[—] in mere civilians to criticise such movement; but the propriety of taking slaves from the field, and putting arms into their hands, may be discussed and decided as well by civilians as military men. . . . Surely no General can speak on the subject, with such authority, as to make it my duty, to give up my conviction, that by the employment of negro troops, we should add no strength to our army, while we would jeopard our supplies, and inaugurate a policy which would shake, if not destroy the very foundations of our social system.

We are told, if we do not take the slaves and put them in the army, the enemy will. This proves too much, for if it be true, then we should take every slave capable of bearing arms. If we left half, they would take them.

. . . We hear gentlemen declare on this floor that our Government is a despotism and Mr. Davis a tyrant. Now, Mr. Speaker, is this fair or just to the Executive? If our Government be a despotism, as gentlemen would have us believe, who made it so? The Conscript law gives control over the persons of all from 17 to 50—the Impressment and Tax laws over the property of the country. . . .

No one dreamed, when hostilities commenced, that we should, at the expiration of near four years, be still involved in one of the bloodiest and most gigantic wars that ever shook the earth. We began without an organized government—without the munitions of war—without friends and without money. We have had unnumbered difficulties and obstacles to encounter—all the forms of government for the civil and military departments to institute, and ten thousand and more officers to appoint, and send to every corner of the Confederacy; and all the complex machinery of government to set in motion; and this, too, in time of war. No man born of woman, could have accomplished all this, without committing many grave and serious blunders and errors, and making many bad appointments. . . .[7]

Whether he realized it or not, Representative Gholson spoke at a critical moment in the history of the Confederacy. Southern despondency and war-weariness, as well as wishful thinking about the terms of peace Lincoln might agree to, had reached such proportions that Jefferson Davis in January, 1865, reluctantly participated in the train of developments that culminated in the famed peace conference at Hampton Roads, Virginia, on February 3. President Lincoln and Secretary of State William H. Seward represented the United States at the meeting, and Vice-President Alexander Stephens, Senator Robert M. T. Hunter of Virginia, and Assistant Secretary of War John A. Campbell spoke for the Confederacy.

An influential Confederate senator from North Carolina, William A. Graham, reported on the development in a private letter and also afforded an interesting insight into the way that at least some Confederates interpreted Lincoln's policy thus far of freeing the slaves of "rebels" while not disturbing those of "loyal" men:

The intervention of F. P. Blair who has passed two or three times back & forth from Washington to this city recently, has resulted in the appointment today, by the President, of an informal commission, consisting of Messrs. A. H. Stephens, R. M. T. Hunter & J. A. Campbell, to proceed to Washington, and confer with a like board there on the subject matters of difference between the Northern & Southern States, with a view to terms of peace. The action of the Senate was not invoked, it is presumed, because the appointment of formal Ministers

[7] "Speech of Hon. Thos. S. Gholson of Virginia . . . Delivered in the House of Representatives . . . on the 1st of February, 1865" (Richmond, 1865). Pamphlet in the Flowers Collection, Perkins Library, Duke University.

might be considered inadmissible until the question of recognition should be settled in our favor. I trust that a termination of hostilities will be the result. From several conversations with Mr. Hunter, in concert with whom I have been endeavoring to reach this form of intercourse [with the Lincoln administration] since the commencement of the session of Congress, I am satisfied the first effect will be to establish an armistice of as long duration as may be allowed; and then to agree upon terms of settlement. Upon the latter I anticipate great conflict of views. The Northern mind is wedded to the idea of restoration, and notwithstanding the extravagances of the violent republicans, I am convinced would for that, guarantee slavery as it now exists, and probably make other concessions, including of course amnesty, restoration of confiscated property except slaves, and perhaps some compensation for a part of these. On the other hand, while the people of [the] South are wearied of the war, and are ready to make the greatest sacrifices to end it, there are embarrassments attending the abdication of a great Government such as now wields the power of the South, especially by the agents appointed to maintain it, that are difficult to overcome. The commission is a discreet one, and upon the whole, is as well constituted as I expected, and I trust that good will come of it. . . .

. . . Genl. Lee has addressed a letter to a member of the Va. Senate advocating the enlistment of slaves as soldiers with emancipation of themselves & families and ultimately of the race. With such wild schemes, and confessions of despair as this, it [is] high time to attempt peace, and I trust the commission above named may pave the way to it. . . .[8]

☞ The sort of ideas that Graham had privately expressed were known and anathematized by the Richmond *Enquirer* (January 28, 1865), which foresaw trouble brewing between Virginia and

---

[8] William A. Graham to David L. Swain (former governor of North Carolina), January 28, 1865, in William A. Graham Papers, North Carolina Department of Archives and History, Raleigh. Robert P. Dick, state senator from Guilford County (Greensboro) and a prominent leader in the peace movement, declared in the state senate, ''Prudent negotiation and speedy peace may yet postpone the doom of slavery.'' Dick went on to add: ''Can our [Confederate] rulers be so mad as to believe that free born Southern white men will stand side by side with the degraded negro in a war for liberty? Has despair made them lose all their reason? . . . The corn field is the only battle ground where the negro can assist us in winning our independence.'' *North Carolina Standard*, January 13, 1865.

certain of her sister states concerning the ultimate purpose of the war:

It is stated that there are certain members of Congress, representing large slaveholding constituencies, who have openly declared their preference for reconstruction, with Federal guaranty of slavery, to the emancipation of slaves as a means of securing the independence of the Confederate States.

We know of no propositions for emancipation by the States. That subject is surrounded by so many legal and social obstacles, its effect in securing the only object which would justify its adoption, is so doubtful that there is little probability of its being even considered. But we contemplate with astonishment the declarations to which we have referred.

Can it be possible that men representing slaveholding constituencies would prefer returning to the Union to the dedication of their property to the cause of independence[?]

What constituted the proximate cause of this war? The prohibition of slavery extension and the unwarrantable interference with the institution of slavery within the States.

Why have our people rallied to this cause? Only because they regarded it [as] one form of interference with the rights of property within the States.

Is the army of defence composed exclusively of slaveholders? They have responded nobly to the vindication of the public rights. They have contributed their means and their lives to the common defence. But, as a class, they have enjoyed certain practical exemptions from the general conscription. Men owning slaves have been able to employ substitutes. They have been exempted from military service because they owned fifteen hands or less.

The non-slaveholders have, on the contrary, enjoyed no similar privileges. They have not sought them.

Now what contributions to the cause have been made by the non-slaveholding sections of this and other States? Take the Valley of Virginia for instance. There the slave property has been carried away; the houses burned and the country abandoned to conflict between the contending armies. The men from this region have endured the fate of war. They have been mutilated and beggared by the war. They have lost the special interest which in chief part occasioned the war. Have they flinched from or abandoned the cause because their interest in the cause has been extinguished? On the contrary, they cling the closer to the principle of independence when their property interest in its preservation has been diminished.

Can it, then, be possible that those so deeply interested in the cause as the slaveholders from the interior of the cotton States should prefer, under any circumstances, the security of their property to the independence of these States? It would be in effect to say to all other interests: "You have fought for the integrity of slave title, your country has been desolated, your lives and limbs have been sacrificed to the success of this object, but we doubt your ability to guarantee, by your valor, the safety of our title. You even propose to sacrifice this title to the success of your cause. As the object of the war was the safety of slave title, we must seek that object by another course. We shall throw ourselves upon the protection of the enemy. They will grant us, at least, the temporary use of our own slaves."

This is the alledged [sic] proposition of certain slaveholding members translated. We cannot admit that any sacrifice of interest or institution is too great to be made, if such sacrifice will secure peace and independence. We repeat, that we do not believe emancipation will ensure independence and we would not, therefore, make the experiment.

But if any ill-advised slaveholder should resort to reconstruction for the protection of his property, let us see what he would gain. The mythical proposals of Blair and Singleton [Francis P. Blair, Sr., and General James W. Singleton, Northern envoys who paved the way for the Hampton Roads conference] affirm the supremacy of the Federal Constitution. Now, under that Constitution, a proposition has been introduced in the Federal Congress for so amending the Constitution as to authorize the abolition of slavery.

This proposition requires a few votes to become a law. It is said, we think by Mr. Seward, that Congress will adopt the measure during the ensuing session. The Federal Constitution moreover authorizes that the Legislatures of three fourths of the States may change their Constitutions. Now, upon reconstruction, there would be ten slave States and,

175

we think, some twenty-four or -five free States, with other territorial States either admitted or ready for admission. The number of slave States is fixed, that of the free States will be increased by the formation of new States from national domain and alien population. How long, then, would the protection of slavery last? For how many months or days? Long enough, say some, to reap the profits of their labor for the maintenance of their owner. Then we should have a premature peace to secure to a comparative few the temporary use of their property? These men would have given life, limb, property, and a great cause, for the special gain of a few.

Now we repudiate the sentiment attributed to certain members of Congress, as the sentiment of the slaveholding class. We know hundreds who have given property, and life, to the cause of independence. We know hundreds that would be willing—if any guarantee of freedom could be given—to subscribe every slave they possess to the success of the cause. Such a concession is wholly unauthorized by the slaveholders of Virginia.

We have no disposition to discuss questions before they arise. But we have no idea of permitting such declarations to go before the world, as binding any more than the individuals who may have uttered them, and, possibly, the constituents which they represent.

It would be a singular spectacle if it should appear that either one of those States, which invited Virginia into this conflict, finding their interests likely to suffer by the further prosecution of the war, should compound for their own safety, by a surrender of the principles of State Sovereignty involved in the war.

Such States might be seen sitting by the side of the reconciled Federal authorities, when Virginia, like the noble British Queen, should be led in, manacled, to receive the sentence incurred by having come to the rescue of those who have deserted her. We apprehend no such spectacle.

☞ The Richmond *Enquirer* might be horrified by what it suspected to be "reconstructionist" thinking among leaders like Senator Graham. William W. Holden's *North Carolina Standard* (January 17, 1865), however, simultaneously managed to appeal to those who were afraid for the institution of slavery, those whose fears of and prejudices against the Negroes ran strong, and—

perhaps the largest group among Tarheels—those who desperately longed for peace:

The *Confederate*, of this City [Raleigh], is out in full blast in favor of arming the slaves. It copies, with marks of approbation, an article from the Wilmington *Carolinian,* in which that paper says—"We would have each State provide a homestead for the black soldier on his return home—this as a reward. And then we would give him freedom as a means of enjoying the property given him. We would give him the right to hold any species of property which a white man could hold."

Such is the doctrine put forth by a public journal in the midst of a slaveholding people. Aside from the wretched war policy which it urges, it is abolition doctrine, and incendiary in its character. It is Lincoln doctrine. It is the very doctrine which the war was commenced to put down. Surely we ought to have peace now, since extremes have met!—since the partizans of Mr. Lincoln and the partizans of Mr. Davis have united not only in the advocacy of abolition, but in the same means of effecting it! Negroes are not only to be conscripted and placed in camp and on the field on a level with our white soldiers, but they are to have their freedom and a *homestead* at the end of the war, as their reward! The negro soldier is to have a homestead, but the white soldier is promised nothing! No homestead is to be provided for him. His wife and children, already beggared by the war, must toil on, and the children must grow up in ignorance and rags, because he is white; but the negro is to have his freedom and a homestead,—the *negro* is to be the pet, and the gallant white veteran, with the scars of fifty battles on his body, is to be turned off to work as a tenant, if he have no land, and must be jostled and insulted in his neighborhood as long as he lives, by his black comrade, who is to have a homestead provided for him by the State! If this is not *negrophobia* [negrophilia?] run mad, we know not what is. Why, our enemies have not yet proposed to divide our lands among our negroes. Aggressive and harsh as they are, they have appeared disposed thus far to spare us this humiliation. They offer freedom to our slaves, but not homesteads. But if they should go farther hereafter, and tell our slaves that if they will abandon their masters and fight under their flag, they will give them our lands as their reward, they might plead the above offer as an extenuation of their crime, and declare to the world that some of our own leading journals had set them the example by proposing such a policy.

The *Confederate,* in copying the *Carolinian's* article, says:

"Without concurring entirely in the sentiments therein contained, there is much to commend it to the public. Since the attest of our military leaders from two points of observation has declared in favor of the employment of negro soldiers, the spirit of the press is very properly conforming to this standard authority. Of the right, we never doubted; of the expediency we are now convinced. If the Southern negro be appealed to, with the proper moral inducements to enlist his sympathies, we doubt not either his capacity, or his willingness, or his fidelity; and with this element of strength, our independence is certain. The soldiers are almost unanimous in favor of it. They need reinforcements, and *their wishes* ought to be a controlling influence."

It is not true that the press of the country is "conforming to this standard authority." A poor, contemptible, subsidized press, many of whose Editors are detailed men [assigned the duty by the army], are "conforming" under orders, as we admit, to this black "standard," —but the *free* presses of the land, whose Editors speak for the people instead of power, regard the proposition with abhorrence. Nor is it true that the negro possesses either sufficient capacity, willingness, or fidelity to make a good soldier. . . . As to their willingness, they would show it at once by taking to the woods as soon as they heard of the order for their conscription; and so far as their fidelity is concerned, the few who might be forced into the ranks would illustrate that by deserting to the enemy. Nor is it true that the soldiers are in favor of arming the slaves. On the contrary, they regard it not only as an insult to themselves, but as fraught with the most alarming consequences to their families at home. . . .

The Destructive [Holden's synonym for Confederate] leaders are certainly very fertile in expedients to keep themselves out of the war. First, peaceable secession was to give us independence; then King Cotton was to do it; then foreign intervention was to do it; next, we should *certainly* whip the enemy when we got him away from his gunboats; and now, all these expectations having failed, we are to get our independence through the negro. Anything that will keep these same leaders out of the range of bullets. But they are going after a while. They cannot go just now, but they will "send a hand." If the negro should

178

fail to whip the enemy, which is hardly probable, and if they should be needed, they will consider the propriety of determining at some future day whether they will go; and if meanwhile any Conservative should refuse to go, or should make disparaging remarks about them, or should even intimate that the administration at Richmond is not the wisest administration in the world, they will denounce him as a traitor of the worst stamp—call him "Red String," and threaten to have him hanged. It is thus that patriotism is kept alive among us, the enemy driven back, and our independence secured.

But seriously, it is apparent that we are rapidly approaching that point in our progress which will involve us, unless some check is interposed, in all the horrors of the French revolution. The two sections are vieing [sic] with each other in the work of emancipation. The negroes are to be armed, and society is to be not merely upset, but destroyed. Every evil which followed in the wake of French emancipation [in Santo Domingo] will afflict us here, if this policy be adopted. We call upon the Legislature of this State, now in session, to rise to the magnitude of the occasion, and not only to stamp this infamous proposition with the seal of its reprobation, but to adopt promptly the most vigorous measures to ensure an honorable PEACE, which can alone close this Pandora's box of ills untold, and put us again in the enjoyment of prosperity, freedom, and happiness.[9]

❧   The war's threat to slavery had, at least since 1863, been one of Holden's most potent arguments for peace. At the time of the Hampton Roads conference, the *Standard* (February 3, 1865) was still pushing the idea that only peace could save the peculiar institution.

A WORLD TO SLAVEHOLDERS.—A radical abolition Convention has been held in Tennessee and slavery abolished. If the peace commissioners [to the Hampton Roads conference] should, on their return, report against peace, and if the war should go on, in less than twelve months the same result will take place in North Carolina. Tennessee is destined to be a *peon* State, but North Carolina is yet in a condition

[9] The Augusta (Ga.), *Chronicle and Sentinel* (as reprinted in the *Standard*, January 13, 1865, among other occasions) expressed many of the same ideas as had Holden.

to save her slave property, at least for a time. Let slaveholders be warned. So far as their interests are concerned it is now or never.

🐎 The variety of arguments used by the Southerners who opposed any Confederate tampering with slavery ranged from those of zealous Confederate diehards to those of extremists in the peace movement, like Holden. One pious South Carolinian who wrote to the Charleston *Courier* (January 24, 1865) expressed the idea, bizarre to later generations though then seriously held by many religious Southerners, that slavery was among the "God-ordained relations" with which mere mortals dared not interfere:

It is to maintain slavery, God's institution of labor, and the primary political element of our Confederate form of Government, state sovereignty, that we have taken the sword of justice against the infidel and oppressor. The two must stand or fall together. To talk of maintaining our independence while we abolish slavery is simply to talk folly. Four millions of our fellow-men in the domestic relation of slaves have, in the providence of God, under His unalterable decree . . . been committed to our charge. We dare not abandon them to the tender mercies of the infidel. Like the marriage, parental and fraternal relations, slavery enters into the composition of our families, and like those God-ordained relations, it has the sanction of His law and His gospel. The family relations are incorporated into civil government, and with us slavery is one of those relations.

African slave labor is the only form of labor whereby our soil can be cultivated, and the great staples of our clime produced. The testimony of ample experience proves that the white man is not physically adapted to that end, and that he sickens, degenerates and dies, if he undertakes it. By the removal of African slave labor from this land, our productive and fruitful fields must become barren waste[s] and impenetrable swamps. By yielding to abolition infidelity, and emancipating our slaves, we will destroy the household, disorganize the family, and annihilate our Government—act contrary to the will and instruction of God—bring down His just wrath upon our heads, and doom ourselves to utter humiliation, contempt and wretchedness as a people. The last hope of true Republican liberty on the American continent would be lost, the progress of the human family, by the light of religion, science and true philosophy, toward peace and happiness, blackened for centuries, and the triumph of the rulers of the darkness of this world advanced.

. . . And shall we look to other sources than the Almighty arm and the sword He has placed in our hands for protection? Is it for human aid and foreign help we sigh? Let us go forth to battle, *Deo vindice,* and see that we bear not the sword in vain.

⌛ In Texas a bishop in the Episcopal church, Alexander Gregg, used phrases remarkably similar to those of the South Carolinian and upheld the faithful in clinging to slavery and scorning Yankee heresy (Galveston *Tri-Weekly News,* March 31, 1865):

. . . Those among us, therefore, who are discussing the subject of emancipation as a *possible,* it may be *probable* necessity, in a certain event, or at best, as *choice of evils,* are not only introducing an element of division which may prove dangerous, and manifesting a weakness and want of confidence in our cause and our institutions, which is recreant to our fathers and unworthy of the South; but they are ministering therein to that morbid and arrogant spirit of fanaticism to which I have referred. Away with such weak-kneed and faint-hearted patriots! Shame upon those, wherever to be found, who have so far given in to the claim of Yankee power and Puritanic dominance, as to suppose for a moment, that they can, at will, change the course of nature, dictate the relations of races, and overthrow the social fabric of the world. . . .

Instead of this great moral dominion, the mad-men of the North— for they are nothing less—who are leagued together for our ruin, are doomed, I am persuaded, and that ere long, to a depth of bitter humiliation, which will be the well-earned moral penality of an *arrogance* and *presumption,* to speak of nothing else, such as the world has never seen!

Let us have *faith* in *God* and in the *justice* of our *cause,* and prosecute it without wavering, and all will be well.

⌛ With so many mortal men plus the Deity being arraigned against his ideas, Jefferson Davis understandably might have simply given up. He did nothing of the sort, of course. Rather, he, Benjamin, and their allies tried to rouse public pressure that might prod the Confederate Congress, as well as the legislature of Virginia, into some action other than unending debate, much of it in secret session, and time-hallowed parliamentary maneuvering.

Benjamin, who dared to have and express ideas that were literally unthinkable to many Southerners, wrote candidly to seek help from an old friend and former classmate, Frederick Porcher, in Charleston, South Carolina:

I have your favor of the 16th instant, and have read your views with the more interest from the fact that for a year past I have seen that the period was fast approaching when we should be compelled to use every resource at our command for the defense of our liberties. Without entering into any lengthened discussion of the considerations which should guide our policy on this point, it appears to me enough to say that the negroes will certainly be made to fight against us if not armed for our defense. The drain of that source of our strength is steady, fatal, and irreversible by any other expedient than that of arming the slaves as an auxiliary force. I further agree with you that if they are to fight for our freedom they are entitled to their own. Public opinion is fast ripening on the subject, and ere the close of the winter the conviction on this point will become so widespread that the Government will have no difficulty in inaugurating the policy foreshadowed in the President's message. The effect of that message, followed up by that of Governor Smith, has been great, and if you could get your newspapers, or any one of them, to commence a discussion on this point the people would rapidly become educated to the lesson which experience is sternly teaching.

While agreeing with you thus far, I cannot concur in your opinion that the Confederate Government should assume powers not vested by the Constitution, on the allegation that our safety depends on the exercise of such power. Without dilating on this point it is enough to say that I do not see the necessity for such assumption. Matters of this sort are always best settled by degrees, and it is enough for the moment that the Confederacy should become the owner of as many negroes as are required for the public service and should emancipate them as a reward for good services. The next step will then be that the States, each for itself, shall act upon the question of the proper status of the families of the men so manumitted. Cautious legislation providing for their ultimate emancipation after an intermediate stage of serfage or peonage would soon find advocates in different States. We might then be able, while vindicating our faith in the doctrine that the negro is an inferior race and unfitted for social or political equality with the white man, yet so modify and ameliorate the existing condition of that inferior race by providing for it certain rights of property, a certain degree of personal liberty, and legal protection for the marital and parental relations, as to relieve our institutions from much that is not only unjust and impolitic in itself, but calculated to draw down on us the odium and reprobation of civilized man. It is well known that General Lee, who commands so largely the confidence of the people, is strongly in favor of our using the negroes for defense, and emancipating them, if necesssary, for that purpose. Can you not yourself write a series of articles in your papers, always urging this point as the true issue, viz, is it better for the negro to fight for us or against us? The action of our people on this point will be of more value to us abroad than any diplomacy or treaty making, even if we had the power to treat upon this point. In the absence of the power the President would never consent to open this subject, nor would I consent to be his agent for such a purpose under any circumstances. If the Constitution is not to be our guide I would prefer to see it suppressed by a revolution which should declare a dictatorship during the war, after the manner of ancient Rome, leaving to the future the care of re-establishing formal and regular government. . . .[10]

Not surprisingly, Benjamin had little luck in converting the Charleston press to emancipation. Secretary of War Seddon fared no better when he broached the subject to the famed Georgian Howell Cobb and received this scorching reply:

Your letter of the 30th of December received by yesterday's mail. I beg to assure you that I have spared no efforts or pains to prosecute vigorously the recruiting of our Army through the conscript camp. It is true, as you say, there are many liable to conscription who have not been reached, and for reasons I have heretofore given I fear never

[10] Judah P. Benjamin to Frederick A. Porcher, December 21, 1864, *O.R.*, Series IV, Vol. III, 959–60.

will be reached. Rest assured, however, that I will not cease my efforts in that regard. In response to your inquiries, how our Army is to be recruited, I refer with strength and confidence to the policy of opening the door for volunteers. I have so long and so urgently pressed this matter that I feel reluctant even to allude to it, and yet I should not be true to my strong convictions of duty if I permitted any opportunity to pass without urging and pressing it upon the proper authorities. It is in my opinion not only the best but the only mode of saving the Army, and every day it is postponed weakens its strength and diminishes the number that could be had by it. The freest, broadest, and most unrestricted system of volunteering is the true policy, and cannot be too soon resorted to. I think that the proposition to make soldiers of our slaves is the most pernicious idea that has been suggested since the war began. It is to me a source of deep mortification and regret to see the name of that good and great man and soldier, General R. E. Lee, given as authority for such a policy. My first hour of despondency will be the one in which that policy shall be adopted. You cannot make soldiers of slaves, nor slaves of soldiers. The moment you resort to negro soldiers your white soldiers will be lost to you; and one secret of the favor with which the proposition is received in portions of the Army is the hope that when negroes go into the Army they will be permitted to retire. It is simply a proposition to fight the balance of the war with negro troops. You can't keep white and black troops together, and you can't trust negroes by themselves. It is difficult to get negroes enough for the purpose indicated in the President's message, much less enough for an Army. Use all the negroes you can get, for all the purposes for which you need them, but don't arm them. The day you make soldiers of them is the beginning of the end of the revolution. If slaves will make good soldiers our whole theory of slavery is wrong —but they won't make soldiers. As a class they are wanting in every qualification of a soldier. Better by far to yield to the demands of England and France and abolish slavery, and thereby purchase their aid, than to resort to this policy, which leads as certainly to ruin and subjugation as it is adopted; you want more soldiers, and hence the proposition to take negroes into the Army. Before resorting to it, at least try every reasonable mode of getting white soldiers. I do not entertain a doubt that you can by the volunteering policy get more men into the service than you can arm. I have more fears about arms than about

men. For heaven's sake try it before you fill with gloom and despondency the hearts of many of our truest and most devoted men by
resorting to the suicidal policy of arming our slaves. . . .[11]

☜ Taking the opposite view from Howell Cobb, John Forsyth, editor of the Mobile *Register,* staunchly supported the President's
efforts to change southern policy. Jefferson Davis personally
wrote to thank Forsyth:

You will readily understand why during the session of Congress my
private correspondence should be in arrears. I have now, though it
may seem late, to thank you for your letter of [the] 31st of December.
The article inclosed from the Register and Advertiser is a substantial
expression of my own views on the subject of employing for the defense of our country all able-bodied men we have, without distinction
of color. It is now becoming daily more evident to all reflecting persons that we are reduced to choosing whether the negroes shall fight
for or against us, and that all arguments as to the positive advantages
or disadvantages of employing them are beside the question, which is
simply one of relative advantage between having their fighting element
in our ranks or in those of our enemy.

On the other topic suggested by you, making use of this subject as
an aid for negotiations, you will appreciate the obligation of reticence
imposed on me in these matters, and I can only say that I perceive no
discordance in the views you express from what wise policy would dictate. So far, therefore, from obstructing any effort that the Government may be, or may have been, making in the hope of securing our
independence, the influence of your journal in the line which you propose to take would be a valuable assistance. . . .[12]

☜ The efforts of Davis, Benjamin, and others in the Richmond government to rally support were as nothing compared to the
impact of events themselves. In December, 1864, the Army of Tennessee suffered a crushing defeat. As Christmas approached, Savannah fell to Sherman. In mid-January, 1865, the Federals

[11] Howell Cobb to James A. Seddon, January 8, 1865, *ibid.,* 1,009–1,010. Immediately below Cobb's letter is printed a letter to Jefferson Davis from one Samuel
Clayton of Cuthbert, Georgia, ''an agriculturalist'' who had lost two sons in the
war and who urged that ''Congress should make haste and put as many negro
soldiers in the field as you and General R. E. Lee may think necessary.''
[12] Jefferson Davis to John Forsyth, February 21, 1865, *ibid.,* 1,110.

captured Fort Fisher, which protected the last important Confederate seaport, Wilmington, North Carolina, and Sherman's army headed into the Carolinas. These events alone were grim enough for the Confederates.

But the outcome of the Hampton Roads conference had the truly electrifying impact on the South. Lincoln made it emphatically clear, even to those who much wanted to believe otherwise, that there would be no armistice nor any convention of the states (as Stephens, Governor Brown of Georgia, and many others had incessantly urged); there would be peace when there was a restored Union without slavery. Jefferson Davis reported on the outcome to the Confederate Congress:

. . . I herewith submit for the information of Congress the report of the eminent citizens above named [Stephens, Hunter, and Campbell], showing that the enemy refused to enter into negotiations with the Confederate States, or any one of them separately, or to give to our people any other terms or guarantees than those which a conqueror may grant, or to permit us to have peace on any other basis than unconditional submission to their rule, coupled with the acceptance of their recent legislation, including an amendment to the Constitution for the emancipation of all the negro slaves, and with the right on the part of the Federal Congress to legislate on the subject of the relations between the white and black population of each State.

Such is, as I understand, the effect of the amendment to the Constitution which has been adopted by the Congress of the United States.[13]

[13] *Journal of the Congress* . . . , VII, 545. The truth about the terms that Lincoln somewhat tentatively held out was not quite as simple and categorical as Davis implied. For an interesting study that emphasizes Lincoln's interest in compensation for southern slaveowners and the political reasons for such a policy, see Ludwell H. Johnson, ''Lincoln's Solution to the Problem of Peace Terms, 1864–1865,'' *Journal of Southern History*, XXXIV (November, 1968), 576–86.

CHAPTER VI

The Confederate Revival of February, 1865

🜚 EMOTIONS OF ANGER, fear, disappointment, despondency, and determination were curiously mixed among Southerners in their reactions to the outcome of the Hampton Roads conference. The most pervasive note was struck by the declaration of the Richmond *Sentinel* (February 6, 1865):

. . . There are no peace men among us now! There is no room for one; not an inch of ground for one to stand upon. We are all war men henceforth. We must take our measures accordingly. We must summon every resource to the public defence. The people must be devoted and enthusiastic—the authorities must be wise, energetic, sleepless. No time for trifling! No time for shrinking from duty! No time for dealing tenderly with inefficient officers. Every man to his post, and the right men in the right places, and we will put forth an effort that will confound our enemies, and astonish the world. We are full able to defend our liberties and to vanquish our foes, and by the blessing of God, we *will certainly do it!* All that is needed is that firm concord, that united resolve, which, if they had [been] wanting before, Lincoln has now supplied. With "brave hearts in our bosoms and God overhead," we are certain to win independence, liberty and undying fame!

Let our legislative bodies, *for mercy's* sake, now stop debate, and *act.* To the Virginia Legislature we would say—for we are anxious that our dear old Commonwealth should lead off—lay all your wire-drawn resolutions, and your elaborate bills, *on the table,* and pass one simple resolution, devoting *the whole power of the State in men and material,* to the public defence, and placing all at the call of the Governor. Virginia is to be the great fighting ground. Her capital is to be the gage of battle. Whatever we have that can help Gen. Lee, should be placed at his disposal. Better far that we be sunk by an earthquake than over-run by the Yankees.

🔫 The same sentiment as the *Sentinel's* was echoed by countless other newspapers, as Holden and other leaders in the peace move-ment temporarily subsided, and a series of great public meetings —really Confederate revival services—began in Richmond and then in other towns throughout the unconquered portions of the South. At the first of these meetings in the capital on the evening of February 6, 1865, Jefferson Davis, who was widely considered too dignified or aloof for impassioned oratory, appeared unex-pectedly. He spoke so movingly that even one of his bitterest critics, who was in the audience, called it the ''most remarkable speech'' of Davis' life, ''the most splendid and dramatic oration he had ever made,'' the essence of which was ''imperious uncon-querable defiance to the enemy.''[1] The reporter for the Rich-mond *Enquirer* (February 9, 1865) wrote the following account of the impromptu speech:

The mass meeting at the African Church [the largest auditorium in the city] on Monday night was one of the most enthusiastic ever held in Richmond. Ten thousand persons were present, within and without the building, and of course two-thirds were compelled to be content with only occasional glimpses of the speakers, and fragmentary parts of the speeches, from window seats and out-of-door standing room.

Governor Smith opened the proceedings with a brief speech, prefa-tory of . . . resolutions, which were unanimously adopted. . . .

His Excellency, President Davis, then appeared upon the stand, and was greeted with thunders of applause. In response he said that he would have been pleased if the meeting had been called to commemo-rate a victory. But it was not only pleasant, he felt a proud and ec-static joy to see his countrymen looking whatever disasters there had been in the face, and plucking from adversity new courage and resolu-tion; and it was at this spectacle that his heart beat high with hope. It

[1] Edward A. Pollard, *Life of Jefferson Davis* . . . (Atlanta, 1869), 470–72. Dur-ing the war Pollard was associated with the Richmond *Examiner*, which was edited by John Moncure Daniel. Douglas Southall Freeman characterized Daniel as ''half genius, half misanthrope,'' and it seems fair to add that Pollard was not a little erratic himself.

was well that there should commence here in Virginia that reactionary movement of the people in preparation for a new proclamation to meet the demands of the hour. All must now be laid on the altar of country. If such a feeling should now take possession of the hearts of the people, if they should give a hearty and unanimous answer to the demands of the present exigency upon them, then he could say we stood now upon the verge of successes, which would teach the insolent enemy, who had treated our propositions with contumely, that in that conference in which he had so plumed himself with arrogance, he was, indeed, talking to his masters.

He had never, he continued, hoped anything from propositions of peace made to the enemy unless accompanied with victories of our arms; that the true hope of the Confederacy was in brave soldiers in sufficient number to contest her claims in the military field; but he would have been more or less than man not to have yielded to a natural desire to testify, on every occasion, his anxiety, his yearning anxiety, for peace. He had received a notice from Mr. Lincoln opening the way to an unofficial conference on the subject. He did not feel at liberty to decline the invitation which it implied. In the notes which passed between Mr. Lincoln and himself in the matter, there was one marked difference. He (President Davis) spoke always of two countries. Mr. Lincoln spoke of a common country. He could have no common country with the Yankees. His life was bound up with the Confederacy; and if any man supposed that, under any circumstances, he could be an agent of the reconstruction of the Union, he mistook every element of his nature. With the Confederacy he would live or die. Thank God he represented a people too proud to eat the leek or bow the neck to mortal man.

Although he anticipated that nothing in the way of peace could come out of recent conferences with the enemy, yet he was not prepared for such extravagance of insolence as they had shown. They had not so much as proposed that these States might come back even on those conditions, which was the first occasion of their separation from the Union; but they were to come back as a conquered people, submitting to all the recent legislation of the Washington Government, including the abolition clause in the Constitution recently enacted in Congress, and pushed with the greatest haste through that body, before the Commissioners should arrive at Fortress Monroe. And, but a few days before this, one of Mr. Lincoln's Cabinet had sat at the feet of Beecher in Baltimore, gloating over the picture drawn by that Yankee artist of words of a long procession of the public men of the Confederacy moving to the gallows to expiate the crime of "rebellion." Perhaps Lincoln's heart softened at the length of the procession when he suggested that, in case of our submission, he might be *merciful.*

He would never have occasion to show that mercy. Words of cheer and encouragement had recently come from the armies of the Confederacy. If only half the absentees were back in Gen. Lee's army, he was sure that Grant would be taught a lesson such as he had never received even in his eventful routs from the Rapidan to the James. Beauregard held another army in Sherman's path, and it might soon be shown that Sherman's march through Georgia was his last. If there had been mistakes in the past, let us accept them as lessons of wisdom for the future. Let us improve the errors of bygones; let us unite our hands and hearts, lock our shields together, and we may well believe that before the next summer solstice falls upon us, it will be the enemy who will be asking us for conferences and occasions in which to make known our demands.

The President was frequently interrupted with applause, and at the conclusion of his speech was cheered again and again. . . .

☞ At the second of these mass meetings in Richmond at noon on Thursday, February 9, 1865, Senator Robert M. T. Hunter of Virginia, one of the most powerful foes of Davis' policy, and Secretary of State Benjamin were among the featured speakers. Hunter used the occasion not only to reaffirm his devotion to the Confederate cause but to reassert his belief in slavery. The *Examiner* (February 10, 1865) had this account:

NOON MASS MEETING AT THE AFRICAN CHURCH—ANOTHER OUTPOURING OF THE PEOPLE—THE RESOLUTIONS, SPEECHES, &C.—In pursuance of a call for a mass meeting of the citizens of Richmond at noon, yesterday [February 9, 1865], at the African Church, that edifice was again filled to its utmost capacity. The hour appointed for the meeting was twelve, M., but hundreds of citizens, among them many ladies, took time by the forelock, and filled the spacious body of the church several hours earlier. The main centre doors were kept closed, and the aisle open for the ingress of the speakers, officers of the meeting and others who were to occupy the platform, and by the excellent arrangements of Chief of Police Seal, assisted by a posse of police, the uncomfortable crowding experienced on the occasion of the former meeting was greatly obviated.

The officers and speakers of the occasion assembled at the Governour's mansion at half past eleven o'clock, and at twelve, M., proceeded in procession to the church. The Armory band occupied the choir gallery, and as the speakers and officers entered the church and mounted the stand, struck up the Marseilles Hymn.

Rev. Moses D. Hoge, of the Presbyterian Church, inaugurated the proceeding by a prayer.

Hon. R. M. T. Hunter, the President of the meeting, then came forward, and was received with great enthusiasm. He commenced by saying that it perhaps became him, as one of the returned commissioners, to explain to his fellow citizens the occasion of this noon day call, this assembling for counsel, and the consideration of the great end and aim of the struggle upon which we have entered. He need not tell them that all that was held dear in the cause of freedom, or revered in the affections of men were involved in the contest. For four long years the war has been going on, a war such as has not been known since the days of modern civilization; an effort is made to secure an honourable peace, when your comissioners are informed, and Lincoln, himself, told them so, that there can be no peace but upon the condition of grounding our arms. If anything were wanting to disclose to these people the depth of the degradation in store for them if they are subdued; if anything was wanted to raise the heart and stir up the blood, the people of this Confederacy have that one thing now made plain to them—Lincoln will not treat with us for peace with arms in our hands, because, forsooth, we are rebels. In 1778 Great Britain sent three commissioners to the then revolted colonies, and peace negotiations were the result; but not so with Lincoln. We are to be held criminally responsible for a war we did not begin. We are to atone for all the blood that has been shed; confess that we have kept up a wicked war, and submit to all the laws as they are. If we go back to the bonds of the Union we go back without representation in Congress, as Mr. Lincoln intimated; three millions

191

of slaves loosed in the midst of Southern society; we ourselves slaves, and our slaves freedmen. Such were the terms of submission and re-union; it was subjugation in either form—nothing more, nothing less. And what was to become of the slave himself? Those best acquainted with the negro's nature know that perish he must in time off the face of the earth; for, in competition with the white man, the negro must go down. The only hope of the black man is in our success. Europe may fold her arms and look, in philanthropick zeal, for the coming of the day of salvation for the negro; but the day of his freedom is the day of his doom. Well may good men exclaim, "Philanthrophy, oh, philanthrophy, how many cruelties are committed in thy name."

The speaker drew a picture of the condition of the Confederacy in the event of our successful maintenance of the war, and he did not for a moment admit a doubt of it. With victory and independence wrested from the enemy, in the frowning face of all Europe, with our ports locked and cut off from all the sympathy of nations, a glory would attach to our name such as never was before known. We may say the world, if not in arms against us, is against us in sympathy. The odds are such as no people ever contended against, and so much greater in proportion will be the renown if we fight out this contest and establish our nationality. The speaker would not hold out delusive hopes, for he spoke to men of stout hearts and strong hands. The struggle would result in no easy victory; but the issue was such that we had better lose our lives than lose this contest. We must have faith in the cause, faith in the government, faith in ourselves, and faith in one another. It was a French general who, when his legion was wavering, shouted forth the "Marseilles Hymn," and changed his flying legion into a charging column. It was a Roman leader who saw the blazing cross in the sky when going forth to battle, and drew from the sign assurance of victory. We must discard the possibility of failure, and admit nothing but the certainty of success.

At the conclusion of Mr. Hunter's remarks, there were cries from the throngs outside of "adjourn to Capitol square," "send out a speaker to us," . . .

🏵 Judah P. Benjamin, the third speaker, took the opposite tack from Hunter on the matter of emancipation and seized the opportunity to make a dramatic appeal for the freeing and arming of the slaves through joint action of the Confederate government and Virginia. Since hope for President Davis' original proposal had now clearly died, the administration tried another course of action. Benjamin had long been under the bitterest sort of attack from the political and journalistic foes of the Davis government, and this speech, his first public advocacy of emancipation, became one of the factors that led a large group of congressmen to demand his ouster from the cabinet. Nevertheless, the Louisianian neither minced words nor wrapped himself in patriotic generalities. One of the fullest accounts of Benjamin's speech appeared in the Richmond *Dispatch* (February 10, 1865):

The number of persons composing this meeting, the cheers with which I hear you greet every expression of patriotic sentiment, shows the defiance with which your breasts are swelling, and the hot flush which all feel, at the bare thought of the ignominy which an arrogant Government has proposed to you, that you should bend the knee, bow the neck, and meekly submit to the conqueror's yoke; and all give assurance that the fire of freedom burns unquenchably in your souls. How different from one short week ago! It seems an age, so magic has been the change. Then, despondency and hope deferred oppressed and weighed upon us, men were querulous, and asking if it were true that no honorable peace were attainable except by continued warfare. Then, it was said it was our perverse indisposition to negotiate that led to the arrogance of the invader. This delusion went so far that it penetrated the legislative halls, and threatened a disruption of the harmony of our councils. Now, cheerful voices are heard all around, and hope beams on every countenance. Now, the resolute and war-worn soldier is nerved anew. . . . What then is the cause of this change? It is the knowledge which has come home to the understanding and the hearts of the people. We now know, in the core of our hearts, that this people must conquer its freedom or die. (Cheers.) No Southern man ever dreamed of such arrogant propositions as were brought from Fortress Monroe. Thank God, we know it now. The people know, as one man, the path which they must tread or perish.

. . . What is our present duty? We want means. Are they in the country? If so, they belong to the country, and not to the man who chances to hold them now. They belong either to the Yankees or to the

Confederate States. I would take every bale of cotton in the land. I have a few bales left in my distant Southern home, which is a free gift to my country. . . . I now ask, has any man the right to hold a bale of cotton from his country? (No.) I say the same thing in regard to tobacco. Take all the cotton and tobacco, and make it the basis of means, without which we cannot go on. (Applause.) I want more. I want all the bacon—everything which can feed the soldiers—and I want it as a free gift to the country. Talk of rights! what right do the arrogant invaders leave you!

I want another thing. War is a game that cannot be played without men. (Cheers.) Where are the men? I am going to open my whole heart to you. Look to the trenches below Richmond. Is it not a shame that men who have sacrificed all in our defence should not be reinforced by all the means in our power? Is it any time now for antiquated patriotism to argue a refusal to send them aid, be it white or black? (A voice—''Put in the niggers''—and cheers.)

I will now call your attention to some figures, which I wish you to seriously ponder. In 1860, the South had 1,664,000 arms-bearing men. How many men have the Yankees sent against us? In 1861, 654,000; in 1862, 740,000; in 1863, 700,000; in 1864, they called out 1,500,000. Here you have the figures that they brought out 3,000,000 men, against 1,664,000 Confederates, who lived at the beginning of the war to draw the sword in their country's service. Our resources of white population have greatly diminished; but you had 680,000 black men of the same ages; and could Divine prophecy have told us of the fierceness of the enemy's death-grapple at our throats—could we have known what we now know, that Lincoln has confessed that without the 200,000 negroes which he stole from us he would be compelled to give up the contest, should we have entertained any doubt upon the subject? (A voice—''We will make him give it up yet.'')

I feel that the time is rapidly coming on when the people will wonder that they ever doubted. Let us say to every negro who wishes to go into the ranks on condition of being made free—''Go and fight; you are free.'' If we press them, they will go against us. We know that every one who could fight for his freedom has had no chance. The only side that has had the advantage of this element is the Yankee—a people that can beat us to the end of the year in making bargains. Let us imitate them in this—I would imitate them in nothing else. My own negroes have been to me and said: "Master, set us free, and we will fight for you; we had rather fight for you than for the Yankees." But suppose it should not be so—there is no harm in trying. With all my early attachments and prejudices, I would give up all. It can only be done by the States separately. What States will lead off in this thing? (A voice—"Virginia.") . . . South Carolina, I know, will follow Virginia, as well as every other Southern State, if she but give the lead. When shall it be done? ("Now.") Now. Let your Legislature pass the necessary laws, and we will soon have twenty thousand men down in those trenches fighting for the country. You must make up your minds to try that, or see your army withdrawn from before your town. I came here to say disagreeable things. I tell you, you are in danger unless some radical measure be taken. . . .

☞ With Richmond having set the example, public meetings now became the order of the day in much of the South. The Richmond *Whig* (February 28, 1865) carried a story on one in Mobile, Alabama:

Mobile, Feb. 14.—One of the largest meetings ever assembled in Mobile was held at the Theatre last night, which was presided over by Hon. Judge Forsyth.

Resolutions were unanimously adopted declaring our unalterable purpose to sustain the civil and military authorities to achieve independence—that our battle-cry henceforth should be—"Victory or Death"—that there is now no middle-ground between treachery and patriotism—that we still have an abiding confidence in our ability to achieve our independence—that the Government should immediately place one hundred thousand negroes in the field—that reconstruction is no longer an open question.

That at this time an order reinstating Gen. Joseph E. Johnston in command of the Army of Tennessee will effect more to restore confidence, and increase the army, and secure the successful defence of this Department, than any other order that could issue from the War Department—urging better discipline in the army, and thanking [the army?] for its heroic conduct, and pledging all for liberty, which, with the Divine assistance, is assured.

The meeting was enthusiastic, and speeches were delivered by Judge Tucker of Missouri, Judge Phelan of Mississippi, and Judge Jones and Col. Langdon of Mobile.

☞ In Lynchburg, Virginia, the patriotic Confederates rallied, but candidly confessed their perplexity about freeing and arming the slaves:

PUBLIC MEETING IN LYNCHBURG.

In response to a call by the Mayor, a very large number of ladies and gentlemen convened at Dudley Hall, on Tuesday night, the 28th ult. [February], for the purpose of giving expression to their views on the state of the country, and Lincoln's insulting and degrading proposition of unconditional submission, lately tendered our commissioners at Fortress Monroe, as the only terms upon which he would allow us peace.

On motion, John M. Speed, Esq., was elected President, Col. B. P. Walker and Major John H. Flood were chosen Vice-Presidents, and R. H. Glass and Major Stephen T. Peters, Secretaries.

Messrs. John O. L. Goggin, A. M. Trible, C. W. Button, J. R. Mc-Daniel and Rev. J. D Mitchell were appointed a committee to prepare resolutions expressive of the views of the meeting, who retired for consultation.

During the absence of the Committee, Maj. James Garland being called on, responded in an able address, which was frequently interrupted with applause.

The committee reported the following preamble and resolutions, which were adopted unanimously:

Whereas, the government of the United States, while hypocritically professing an anxious desire for peace upon terms just and honorable to both parties, has, through its accredited agents, the President and Secretary of State, most emphatically and insultingly rejected the offer of negotiations to that end, made by the Government of the Confederate States, and has defiantly announced to the Confederate Commissioners that there can be no peace, and no negotiations for peace, except upon the humiliating and unconditional acknowledgment of their absolute authority, and of abject submission to their hated tyranny, by the government and people of the Confederate States; and, whereas, we have still, as we have ever had, an unshaken confidence in the justice of our cause, in the sufficiency of our resources, in the energy and integrity of our Government, in the undismayed and unfaltering courage of our soldiers, in the tried valor and consummate skill of our Generals, in the exalted patriotism of the masses of our people, and, above all, an abiding faith in Him "who ruleth in the kingdom of men," and whose favor is vouchsafed to the cause which is just—with humble gratitude and adoration, too, acknowledging the kind Providence, which, in the seemingly darkest hours of our struggle, has covered our arms with glory, and wrought out so many signal deliverances for us—accepting the reverses and disasters with which we have been visited, as designed in the ordinations of God's providence, to chasten us for our sins, to make us worthy of our cause, to teach us its true value by the price which we pay for the civil and religious liberties it involves, and to prepare us, when He shall have given us the victory, for His own crowning benediction, "Blessed is that nation whose God is the Lord"; [be it] therefore resolved,

1. That with "our hands prepared for war and our fingers to fight," we accept the necessity which our enemies have forced upon us, to continue this war, and that "here, in this presence and in the face of the world, reverently invoking" the continuance of God's favor, we dedicate ourselves and all that we have *anew* to the cause in which we struggle; that to maintain it we will shrink from no duty, fear no sacrifices, shun no dangers, complain of no hardships, know no weariness, no fainting, no despondency, and that, with God as our helper, we will conquer.

. . . 5. That while there have been differences of opinion amongst us as to the necessity and policy of enlisting a portion of our slaves in the army, and whether, if done, it should be upon a voluntary or compulsory system of enlistment, and whether with or without changing the social status of the slaves, yet holding our independence to be paramount to all other considerations, and understanding it to be the declared opinion of the President and of Gen. Lee, who are charged with the conduct of the war, that such a measure in some form is demanded by the present exigencies of the country, we compromise all differences of opinion, and urge upon our Congress and State Legislature the immediate adoption of some plan to put as many of our slaves in the army as the Commander-in-Chief may deem necessary, believing that such a measure means war and war to the end, and will therefore succeed, whatever real or supposed objections there may be to it. . . .[2]

☞   If the citizens of Lynchburg were baffled and perplexed—but yet determined to follow the lead of Davis and Lee—many Texans had not come to feel any such sense of crisis or urgency. In Goliad, Texas, on February 15, 1865, news of the Hampton Roads meeting had clearly not arrived (Galveston *Tri-Weekly News,* March 6, 1865) :

. . . *Resolved,* That the discussion of the question, whether it is expedient or politic to abolish Southern slavery, is premature, unwise and unnecessary, and impresses the Northern mind with the belief that we feel unable to sustain the institution. The man who advocates any change in our laws on this subject, is doing more harm to the interests of the Confederate States than he could accomplish in the ranks of the Federal army. We especially condemn this class of writers.

Resolved, That the prosperity and happiness of our country depend upon our system of slavery and whether this doctrine be true or not, it is the institution of our choice, not to be wrested from us by any power on earth. We are fighting for the sacred right of making our own laws, as a free and independent people, unaffected by the insolent dictation of other nations; and to yield this right is, so far, to be subjugated and allow the vandals of the North to be our victors. Rather than submit to such degradation, our people should fight for another term of four years, or, by the grace of God, longer if necessary. Let us imitate our revolutionary sires, who, under every discouragement and hardship, fought for seven years, rather than pay a paltry tax, imposed upon them without their consent.

. . . *Resolved,* That whilst we are not surprised to learn that abolition and traitorous articles are written for the press in Texas, (knowing as we do that both traitors and abolitionists are to be found in the State,) yet we are surprised and incensed to see such communications

---

[2] Richmond *Whig,* March 6, 1865. For Confederate rallies in various Georgia towns where the issue of freeing and arming the slaves was largely ignored, see the Macon *Telegraph and Confederate,* February 18, 20, 22, and March 13, 1865.

appear in our leading State journals, and that the excuse for publishing them is "to provide for the possible contingency of abolishing slavery in the South." . . .

☞ Texans remote from the heart of the Confederacy were not, of course, the only Southerners who remained unconvinced by the passion of Davis and the eloquence of Benjamin. The Richmond *Examiner* (February 16, 1865) sourly yielded ground on the arming of blacks but gave not an inch on emancipation:

The idea of employing negroes to help in the defence of their homes, has greatly ripened in the publick mind; and especially since the atrocious *ultimatum* of the enemy at Hampton roads [*sic*] has fully brought home to us all the imperative necessity of bringing out and using all the elements of force which we can possibly command. It is also very well known that General Lee, who has accepted the powers and responsibilities of General-in-chief, urgently calls for a large force of negroes to be placed at his disposal, to be used according to his best judgment. The country will not venture to deny to General Lee, in the present position of affairs, *anything* he may ask for.

In the President's Message at the opening of the present session, the subject was most injudiciously presented for the first time to publick attention. . . .

. . . Upon every ground of justice and humanity, this Southern people feels itself entitled, and indeed bound, to hold its existing relation with the black race, so long as possible. If compelled by the strong necessity of self-preservation to abandon or to modify that relation, it will be under strong protest, and taking heaven and earth to witness that the blood of those simple creatures does not stain our hands.

It is also very certain that negroes are not intended for soldiers, and will never fight when they can avoid it; and that if we could but collect and bring back the absentees without leave, now on the rolls of our armies, we should never have to consider the project of alloying with this base material the pure metal of our Confederate ranks.

Yet when all this has been said, still comes back the urgent question —how to meet the formidable and multitudinous hosts of a vindictive invader this very spring;—and also the not less urgent demand of the great soldier on whom we all depend to command our armies, for power to use negroes in defence of the country. Who will take the responsibility of refusing that appeal?

Congress has now several Bills before it, intended to authorize this description of force. But Congress is somewhat slow and timid this session; its legislation aims at too much exactitude in providing for every contingency and prescribing forms and restrictions; and the consequence is, that time passes, and the needful thing still remains to be done. As we have a Commander-in-chief—as this species of force is to be created at his express request, and as he will have the care of organizing and disposing it, something should be trusted to his discretion. And with this view we should greatly approve the simple amendment proposed on Tuesday, enacting "that the General-in-chief be and is hereby invested with the full power to call into the service of the Confederate States, to perform any duty to which he may assign them, so many of the able-bodied slaves within the Confederate States as, in his judgment, the exigencies of the publick service may require." This makes no allusion to the future *status* of the slaves so to be employed. Congress cannot change that *status,* nor empower the General to change it. Therefore it leaves all that for future consideration in State Legislatures—it also avoids all special provisos as to the proportion of those taken from a particular plantation, to those who are left; trusting that to the practical sagacity and justice of General Lee. It clothes him with great power, and loads him with heavy responsibility. If he is willing to wield that power, and shoulder that responsibility, in the name of God let him have them.

It has been too generally assumed in discussing this matter, that you cannot fairly expect negroes to fight for the country without promising them freedom. Why? Would they have more stake in the country as free men than as slaves? Would they have a better cause to fight for as freemen than as slaves? If so, then they would be elevated and made happier by being made freemen? If so, here is abolitionism again; abolitionism pure and simple. Those who thus affirm either are abolitionists in their hearts, or else they can give no good reason why they are not. We desire to see this most urgent practical question cleared and disembarrassed of theories and arguments. The thing to be done is, to take the slaves and to get their service. It would not be the first time that slaves have fought for their country; and certainly negro slaves have a far stronger interest in defending a country where they have a master and protector and an assured home, than one in which they would be left exposed, without defence, to the cruel benevolence of Yankee abolitionists. If we must use negroes in defence of our homes, let us do so; but for their sake as well as for our own let us beware of giving any consent or adhesion to the doctrine that people of that race gain by being turned wild—or "made free," if we are to use that improper Yankee cant.

☞ Like the *Examiner*, the Richmond *Whig* was slow in coming around. But the *Whig,* too, moved—a bit. As late as January 30, 1865, however, it proffered a preposterous idea that had earlier been advanced by a Confederate congressman:

The New York *Times*, that has heretofore ridiculed the idea of the slave being made to fight with and for his master, can not conceal its delight that we have permitted, as it alleges, the time to pass within which slaves could be brought into the army and organized, disciplined and instructed in time for the Spring campaign. The *Times* could not more emphatically declare the alarm with which it has regarded the proposition. Nor is this leading journal alone in this apprehension. Whatever our own people may think of the value of the negro as a soldier, there is no doubt the enemy look upon him as a foeman not to be despised. Nothing would gratify them more than to be assured that we will, under no circumstances, employ that resource for recruiting our armies. For this reason, we are glad to observe that the House of Representatives refused by a very decisive vote . . . to commit itself against the policy. The question is thus kept open, and the power reserved to arm the slaves and employ them against the invader—their enemy no less than ours—whenever we think it necessary or politic. Nor is the *Times* correct in its theory as to the length of time that would be required for bringing them into the service, and qualifying them for its demands. There is a plan that we have heard suggested by an influential member of Congress that would require but a little while to be put in practice, and would be attended by other important advantages. That is for the Confederate Government to buy and present to each soldier in the field a young and able-bodied negro man, armed and equipped—to be instructed by his new master in the art of handling his weapon, and to be carried into battle by his side. This plan would serve, first, to transform the negro into a soldier by the readiest and most efficient process, and thereby at once double the number of our troops. Second, to diffuse the interest in this species of property, and thereby remove all discontent resulting from the idea that this is the non-slaveowners' fight for the slaveowners' property. Third, to overcome all repugnance our soldiers might feel to having the negro introduced into the army as a comrade in arms. Fourth, to pay our brave troops in something substantial and valuable for their toils and sacrifices. We refer to this matter at present rather for the purpose of giving information to the anxious people of the other side, than to urge its adoption. When once it has been determined to put the negro in the ranks, we expect to find the scheme having many advocates. It suffices for the present to say, in answer to the *Times*, that it is not now, and never can be, too late to adopt the policy of arming our slaves, for the time has not come and will never come when the master race will not be able to cope with their enemy, until the negro could be prepared for such service as he would be capable of as a soldier.

But the tide of events had swept past such voices as those of the *Examiner* and the *Whig*. In his speech on February 9, Judah Benjamin had warned, "I tell you, you are in danger unless some radical measure be taken." Indeed such "radical" measures were finally introduced in the Confederate Congress, but none of them was passed. The measure that was ultimately enacted was introduced by Representative Ethelbert Barksdale of Mississippi on the day after Benjamin's speech. It contained no provision for emancipation, as its crucial last section made clear:

AN ACT TO INCREASE THE MILITARY FORCE OF THE CONFEDERATE STATES.

The Congress of the Confederate States of America do enact, That in order to provide additional forces to repel invasion, maintain the rightful possession of the Confederate States, secure their independence, and preserve their institutions, the President be, and he is hereby, authorized to ask for and accept from the owners of slaves, the services of such number of able-bodied negro men as he may deem expedient, for and during the war, to perform military service in whatever capacity he may direct.

Sec. 2. That the General-in-Chief be authorized to organize the said slaves into companies, battalions, regiments and brigades, under such rules and regulations as the Secretary of War may prescribe, and to be commanded by such officers as the President may appoint.

Sec. 3. That while employed in the service the said troops shall receive the same rations, clothing and compensation as are allowed to other troops in the same branch of the service.

Sec. 4. That if, under the previous sections of this act, the President shall not be able to raise a sufficient number of troops to prosecute the war successfully and maintain the sovereignty of the States and the independence of the Confederate States, then he is hereby authorized to call on each State, whenever he thinks it expedient, for her quota of 300,000 troops, in addition to those subject to military service under existing laws, or so many thereof as the President may deem necessary to be raised from such classes of the population, irrespective of color, in each State, as the proper authorities thereof may determine: *Provided,* that not more than twenty-five per cent of the male slaves between the ages of eighteen and forty-five, in any State, shall be called for under the provisions of this act.

Sec. 5. That nothing in this act shall be construed to authorize a change in the relation which the said slaves shall bear toward their owners, except by consent of the owners and of the States in which they may reside, and in pursuance of the laws thereof.

Approved, March 13, 1865.[3]

☞ Even for this cautious and limited proposal to be passed by the Confederate Congress, the public intervention of Robert E. Lee was required.

[3] *O.R.,* Series IV, Vol. III, 1,161. Since Professor Stephenson in his 1913 article skillfully untangled and traced the various measures introduced in February, 1865, and the legislation that the Congress finally passed, no attempt will be made here to give more than a brief summary of that phase. The dissenting minority report (from the special House committee whose majority reported the Barksdale bill) of Representative Samuel S. Rogers of Florida and the longer minority report, signed by Representatives William Porcher Miles of South Carolina, Thomas S. Gholson of Virginia, W. N. H. Smith of North Carolina, Julian Hartridge of Georgia, and Stephen H. Darden of Texas, are available in pamphlet form in the Virginia State Library.

❧ CHAPTER VII ❧

Lee's Views Become
Public Knowledge

🜚 THE NAME OF Robert E. Lee had early entered the debate that
rocked the Confederacy during the last six months of its existence.
Undoubtedly, a number of the political and military leaders knew
that Lee favored a bold break with the past. The public at large,
however, only knew what others alleged the ideas of the charis-
matic general to be. The editor of the Lynchburg *Virginian* (February 18, 1865) made this explicit by stating that the "people at
large have not seen or heard anything emanating directly from
Gen. Lee upon this subject [of freeing and arming the slaves]."

John B. Jones, the gossipy, news-hungry clerk in the Confederate War Department, made this entry in his diary on January 25,
1865:

I saw Mr. [James] Lyons [former Confederate congressman from
Virginia] to-day, who told me Mr. Hunter dined with him yesterday,
and that Gen. Lee took tea with him last evening, and seemed in good
spirits, hope, etc. Mr. Lyons thinks Gen. Lee was always a thorough
emancipationist. He owns no slaves. He (Mr. Lyons) thinks that using
the negroes in the war will be equivalent to universal emancipation,
that not a slave will remain after the President's idea (which he don't
seem to condemn) is expanded and reduced to practice. He favors
sending out a commissioner to Europe for aid, on the basis of emancipation, etc., as a dernier ressort. He thinks our cause has received most
injury from Congress, of which he is no longer a member.

If it be really so, and if it were generally known, that Gen. Lee is,
and always has been opposed to slavery, how soon would his great
popularity vanish like the mist of the morning! Can it be possible that
he has influenced the President's mind on this subject? Did he influ-

ence the mind of his father-in-law, G. W. Park Custis, to emancipate his hundreds of slaves? Gen. Lee would have been heir to all, as his wife was an only child. There's some mistake about it.[1]

🖙 There was, of course, no mistake about the tea-time conversation that the shocked diarist found unbelievable. Lee now publicly, and with incredible influence on southern opinion, lent his support to the policy of Davis and Benjamin. The secretary of state appealed first for help from Lee:

You may perhaps have seen that at the public meeting on Thursday [February 9, 1865] I spoke of the necessity of instant re-enforcement for your army. In order to disarm opposition as far as possible and to produce prompt action, I proposed that those slaves only who might volunteer to fight for their freedom should be at once sent to the trenches. From what I can learn, this would add promptly many thousand men to your force. Now, although this proposal seemed to meet with decided favor from the meeting, some of the opponents of the measure are producing a strong impression against it by asserting that it would disband the army by reason of the violent aversion of the troops to have negroes in the field with them. It occurs to me that if we could get from the army an expression of its desire to be re-enforced by such negroes as for the boon of freedom will volunteer to go to the front, the measure will pass without further delay, and we may yet be able to give you such a force as will enable you to assume the offensive when you think it best to do so. If this suggestion meets your approval, the different divisions ought at once to make themselves heard, and there will be no further effective opposition in any of our legislative bodies, State or Confederate.[2]

🖙 Quick to accede to Benjamin's request, Lee soon had the satisfaction of seeing the newspapers filled with resolutions sent in by

---

[1] John B. Jones, *A Rebel War Clerk's Diary* (2 vols.; Philadelphia, 1866), II, 398. That Lee's unorthodox ideas about slavery were not just a wartime development is indicated by a letter he wrote to his wife on December 27, 1856. After deploring the abolitionists and their ideas and tactics, Lee declared, in Jeffersonian but most un-Calhounian terms: ''In this enlightened age, there are few I believe, but what will acknowledge, that slavery as an institution, is a moral & political evil in any country.'' Freeman, *R. E. Lee*, I, 372.
[2] Judah P. Benjamin to Robert E. Lee, February 11, 1865, *O.R.*, Series I, Vol. XLVI, Pt. 2, p. 1,229.

numerous units in the army. But before the full impact of those communications could be felt, Congressman Barksdale received the hoped-for answer in Lee's letter of February 18, 1865. It was this letter that apparently turned the tide of opinion, in and out of Congress. Undoubtedly with Lee's permission, the letter quickly appeared in the Richmond newspapers and then gradually began to be published in countless other southern journals. Views that Lee had expressed earlier on several occasions now became public knowledge:

I have the honor to acknowledge the receipt of your letter of the 12th instant [February], with reference to the employment of negroes as soldiers. I think the measure not only expedient but necessary. The enemy will certainly use them against us if he can get possession of them; and, as his present numerical superiority will enable him to penetrate many parts of the country, I cannot see the wisdom of the policy of holding them to await his arrival, when we may, by timely action and judicious management, use them to arrest his progress. I do not think that our white population can supply the necessities of a long war without overtaxing its capacity, and imposing great suffering upon our people; and I believe we should provide resources for a protracted struggle,—not merely for a battle or a campaign.

In answer to your second question, I can only say that, in my opinion, the negroes, under proper circumstances, will make efficient soldiers. I think we could at least do as well with them as the enemy, and he attaches great importance to their assistance. Under good officers and good instructions, I do not see why they should not become soldiers. They possess all the physical qualifications, and their habits of obedience constitute a good foundation for discipline. They furnish a more promising material than many armies of which we read in history, which owed their efficiency to discipline alone. I think those who are employed should be freed. It would be neither just nor wise, in my opinion, to require them to serve as slaves. The best course to pursue, it seems to me, would be to call for such as are willing to come with the consent of their owners. An impressment or draft would not be likely to bring out the best class, and the use of coercion would make the measure distasteful to them and to their owners.

I have no doubt that if Congress would authorize their reception into service, and empower the President to call upon individuals or States for such as they are willing to contribute, with the condition of emancipation to all enrolled, a sufficient number would be forthcoming to enable us to try the experiment. If it proved successful, most of the objections to the measure would disappear, and if individuals still remained unwilling to send their negroes to the army, the force of public opinion in the States would soon bring about such legislation as would remove all obstacles. I think the matter should be left, as far as possible, to the people and to the States, which alone can legislate as the necessities of this particular service may require. As to the mode of organizing them, it should be left as free from restraint as possible. Experience will suggest the best course, and it would be inexpedient to trammel the subject with provisions that might, in the end, prevent the adoption of reforms suggested by actual trial.[3]

Lee had earlier responded to an inquiry from a member of the state senate of Virginia, Andrew Hunter. Although this letter was not made public at the time, Lee had written on January 11, 1865, a somewhat fuller statement of his views than he had in the letter to Barksdale:

I have received your letter of the 7th instant, and without confining myself to the order of your interrogatories, will endeavor to answer them by a statement of my views on the subject. I shall be most happy if I can contribute to the solution of a question in which I feel an interest commensurate with my desire for the welfare and happiness of our people.

Considering the relation of master and slave, controlled by humane laws and influenced by Christianity and an enlightened public sentiment, as the best that can exist between the white and black races while intermingled as at present in this country, I would deprecate any sudden disturbance of that relation unless it be necessary to avert a greater calamity to both. I should therefore prefer to rely upon our white population to preserve the ratio between our forces and those of the enemy, which experience has shown to be safe. But in view of the preparations of our enemies, it is our duty to provide for continued war and not for a battle or a campaign, and I fear that we can-

---

[3] Lee to Ethelbert Barksdale, February 18, 1865, in James D. McCabe, Jr., *Life and Campaigns of General Robert E. Lee* (Atlanta, 1866), 574–75.

not accomplish this without overtaxing the capacity of our white population.

Should the war continue under existing circumstances, the enemy may in course of time penetrate our country and get access to a large part of our negro population. It is his avowed policy to convert the able-bodied men among them into soldiers, and to emancipate all. The success of the Federal arms in the South was followed by a proclamation of President Lincoln for 280,000 men, the effect of which will be to stimulate the Northern States to procure as substitutes for their own people the negroes thus brought within their reach. Many have already been obtained in Virginia, and should the fortune of war expose more of her territory, the enemy would gain a large accession to his strength. His progress will thus add to his numbers, and at the same time destroy slavery in a manner most pernicious to the welfare of our people. Their negroes will be used to hold them in subjection, leaving the remaining force of the enemy free to extend his conquest. Whatever may be the effect of our employing negro troops, it cannot be as mischievous as this. If it end in subverting slavery it will be accomplished by ourselves, and we can devise the means of alleviating the evil consequences to both races. I think, therefore, we must decide whether slavery shall be extinguished by our enemies and the slaves be used against us, or use them ourselves at the risk of the effects which may be produced upon our social institutions. My own opinion is that we should employ them without delay. I believe that with proper regulations they can be made efficient soldiers. They possess the physical qualifications in an eminent degree. Long habits of obedience and subordination, coupled with the moral influence which in our country the white man possesses over the black, furnish an excellent foundation for that discipline which is the best guaranty of military efficiency. Our chief aim should be to secure their fidelity.

There have been formidable armies composed of men having no interest in the cause for which they fought beyond their pay or the hope of plunder. But it is certain that the surest foundation upon which the fidelity of an army can rest, especially in a service which imposes peculiar hardships and privations, is the personal interest of the soldier in the issue of the contest. Such an interest we can give our negroes by giving immediate freedom to all who enlist, and freedom at the end of the war to the families of those who discharge their duties faithfully (whether they survive or not), together with the privilege of residing at the South. To this might be added a bounty for faithful service.

We should not expect slaves to fight for prospective freedom when they can secure it at once by going to the enemy, in whose service they will incur no greater risk than in ours. The reasons that induce me to recommend the employment of negro troops at all render the effect of the measures I have suggested upon slavery immaterial, and in my opinion the best means of securing the efficiency and fidelity of this auxiliary force would be to accompany the measure with a well-digested plan of gradual and general emancipation. As that will be the result of the continuance of the war, and will certainly occur if the enemy succeed, it seems to me most advisable to adopt it at once, and thereby obtain all the benefits that will accrue to our cause.

The employment of negro troops under regulations similar in principle to those above indicated would, in my opinion, greatly increase our military strength and enable us to relieve our white population to some extent. I think we could dispense with the reserve forces except in cases of necessity.

It would disappoint the hopes which our enemies base upon our exhaustion, deprive them in a great measure of the aid they now derive from black troops, and thus throw the burden of the war upon their own people. In addition to the great political advantages that would result to our cause from the adoption of a system of emancipation, it would exercise a salutary influence upon our whole negro population, by rendering more secure the fidelity of those who become soldiers, and diminishing the inducements to the rest to abscond.

I can only say in conclusion that whatever measures are to be adopted should be adopted at once. Every day's delay increases the difficulty. Much time will be required to organize and discipline the men, and action may be deferred until it is too late.[4]

☞ The Richmond *Sentinel* (February 23, 1865) prefaced its publication of Lee's letter to Barksdale with what seems to have been the sentiment of the great majority:

. . . With the great mass of our people, nothing more than this letter is needed to settle every doubt or silence every objection. The few civilians who may insist on opposing their opinion, whether as to military

[4] Lee to Andrew Hunter, *O.R.*, Series IV, Vol. III, 1,012–1,013.

necessity or military expediency, to that of Gen. Lee, will incur not
only the imputation of presumption, but a responsibility to the country which no man could support. The opinion of Gen. Lee may be repudiated or it may be adopted—it is too clear and unequivocal to be com-
promised or evaded.

🌫 Even before the widespread publication of General Lee's views,
the Richmond *Enquirer* (February 18, 1865) thought that the
tide of opinion had turned, and the *Enquirer* began to emphasize
the necessity of discipline for Negro recruits:

The question of negro soldiers, we consider as settled. Public opinion
has definitely declared in favor of arming the negroes; the resolution
introduced in the Virginia Legislature, giving the consent of the State
to the measure, will pass, and may be followed, and should be, by instructions to [Confederate] Senators to vote for the measure and thus
put the matter at rest. As to giving the slaves their freedom, this
should be the reward for faithful service, at the end of the war, if desired by the slaves. To some it may be a boon, a reward—others may
not even desire freedom. Negroes are divided in opinion as to whether
they would prefer freedom to slavery, but by all means leave the choice
with them, let them decide the matter. We do not expect the reward to
make soldiers of them; *discipline* only will do that. It must be a discipline differing, very much, from that which now holds together, with
loosened bands, the armies of the Confederate States. It must be a discipline sharp, severe, exacting, which first teaches them their duty and
then compels them to perform it. There never has been discipline in
the armies of this Confederacy, but instead thereof a kind of universal
suffrage, which fights when it chooses and straggles when it feels like it.
All this must be changed with the negro troops; they have not the motives that impel the white man to this fight; they must be kept up to
the mark by *fear of punishment* more than by hope of reward.
. . . This arming of the negroes is a most important step in the
progress of this war; rightly and properly managed it will give most
material strength to our armies, and, without doing the least injury
to the institution of slavery, effect much towards the independence of
these States. But it will require much patience and much labor to
make the negroes efficient soldiers. The selection of the proper officer

to undertake their drilling is most important; upon him will depend the success or failure of the experiment. If he is a disciplinarian he will succeed, but if he is not, no matter how brave, how great a strategist, the experiment will be a failure. If, in the effort to drill the negroes and discipline them into soldiers, there should be developed a system by which our present noble armies may be improved and perfected, and their unsurpassed courage become disciplined courage, there will be no more disasters like those in the Valley [of Virginia] and at Nashville. It is upon such trying occasions that discipline develops its real effects and brings out its great results. Perhaps, in drilling the negroes, our officers may learn how to discipline the whites.

☞ Lee had emphasized emancipation, but the *Enquirer* seemed more interested in discipline for the Negro soldiers. Another high Confederate officer, Brigadier General Francis A. Shoup, shared the disciplinary emphasis in an article that appeared in the Richmond *Whig* (February 20, 1865):

The proposition to put negroes in the army has gained favor rapidly of late, and promises, in some form or other, to be adopted. So far from exciting the repugnance on the part of the army at first apprehended, it has been called for by the resolves of many regiments and brigades, and is known to be favored by nearly all the principal officers. We [the *Whig*'s editors] do not profess to be very sanguine of good results from the measure, but we do not feel that, as civilians, we would be justified, in the present emergency, in opposing the use of any means which our leading military men assure us can be made efficient. To them this cause is trusted, and especially to the General-in-Chief. It is known that he urges—with a warmth he has not, perhaps, exhibited in regard to any other matter of legislation—the passage of a law subjecting the negro element to military use. His opinion, at all times entitled to great weight, becomes imperative as to such a matter, when we reflect that the whole responsibility of our defence has been devolved upon him. . . .

. . . A paper on this subject, written by Brigadier General Shoup, presents the military view of the subject very clearly and forcibly; and as it is a matter in regard to which our people desire all the light that can be thrown upon it, we assure ourselves that we will meet their wishes in extracting largely from what he has written. After stating that the subject has engaged his earnest attention from the very beginning of the war, Gen'l S. says:

"Napoleon declares as a maxim that 'the first quality of a soldier is the power to endure hardships and fatigue.' It will not be denied, I take it, that the negro possesses this element in the highest degree. The common opinion is that courage is the highest quality, and, as if to meet that opinion, Napoleon goes on to say, in the same maxim, 'courage is altogether secondary.' It is to be understood, of course, that he here speaks of the private soldier. That courage is necessary in an army, and that of the highest order, is entirely manifest—but to understand this maxim it is necessary to consider the nature and organization of an army. There are, as everybody knows, three separate and distinct grades or estates—the private soldier, the non-commissioned officer and the officer. . . . Real soldiers come to have no will of their own, but obey simply because they are ordered by proper authority. You will hear it said that this is a West Point notion; but in truth it is the notion underlying the whole military world. On this continent we are new hands at war. We are just beginning to learn what soldiers are. When discipline is properly enforced the soldier is so entirely in the hands of his officers, that the tone, character and courage of a command is entirely determined by these properties in the officers and non-commissioned officers. Whenever there is misconduct on, or off, the field, it is to be charged to misconduct or neglect on the part of the officers. All soldiers know this. Thus while courage may be dispensed with in the private, it is most important in the two higher classes. . . . There is no necessity to make anything but a private soldier of the negro. The officers and non-commissioned officers should be taken from the most gallant and meritorious officers and soldiers of the army. . . .

"So much for the theory. What has experience shown? It is by no means certain that the negro is so deficient in courage as is generally believed. If we are to credit the statements of travellers in Africa, the native negro is the most sanguinary warrior in the world. In their battles hand to hand, they fight till either party is almost annihilated; and our very slaves are in great part the descendants of prisoners captured in war. We see the negro altogether in his servile condition. He naturally shrinks, without regard to appearances. He, however, makes a fearless sailor and fireman. The English have long used him as a soldier, and he has done good service. But the experiences of this war are abundantly sufficient to show his adaptability as a soldier. The enemy has taught us a lesson to which we ought not to shut our eyes. He has caused him to fight as well, if not better than, have his white troops of the same length of service. Our prisoners from Ship Island and elsewhere declare that they are far the best sentinels and most thoroughly drilled of the federal troops. I have myself seen them, in the hands of a single engineer officer, entirely without organization, work under fire, where certainly he could not have held white men. Now, if the enemy has succeeded in making any kind of troops of these people, with all their non-commissioned officers and a great part of their officers black, how much better could we make with all these white!

". . . But it is alleged by those who oppose the measure, and here seems to lie the greatest difficulty, that they will not fight in our cause. Here again let us go to that highest of all authorities—Napoleon. He says in one of his maxims of war, 'a good general, good officers, commissioned and non-commissioned, good instruction, and strict discipline, make good troops without regard to the cause in which they fight.' By 'cause' we are to understand the particular sentiments or preferences of the troops. This is the broadest and most positive enunciation of a principle which goes to the very foundation of the whole matter. It is strictly true, and proceeds from the very nature of army organization and discipline. It will be observed that he assumes the two higher orders, officers and non-commissioned officers, to be good. Such would be the case in the plan proposed. The truth is, troops always hold the sentiments and opinions of their officers, whatever they may be. Even the negroes that have served with our armies as cooks and teamsters, are as thoroughly enlisted in our cause as are their masters; and in many cases have been known to fight as gallantly as they. It is altogether a mistaken notion to suppose that it is pay or bounties that induce men to fight. These considerations may cause them to enlist, but once made soldiers, they find themselves in the hands of a giant that leaves them no power to escape—discipline. One who is not a soldier can hardly understand this, but it is not the less true. Nor is it patriotism, nor any other sentiment, that holds a soldier at his post. Give our troops—brave and patriotic as they are—liberty to go home to-day—removing all influence of officers—and how much of an army would you have to-morrow? The negroes, however, should be given pay, etc.

. . . "I speak now of heavy infantry. With the other arms a somewhat different rule holds—since more individuality is required—but the same is substantially true throughout. Thus the negro is excellently adapted for a soldier.

"The negro does not fight for the enemy because he is free. He has been tricked and forced into his service, and he cannot help it. Those who have been re-captured say they would rather fight on our side, because we know better how to treat them.

"It is not true, then, that to make good soldiers of these people, we must either give or promise them freedom. On the contrary, it is my firm conviction that to do either would be to impair their efficiency and tractability. But the greatest possible advantage can be had by skilfully using their desire for freedom. The President should have power to declare free such of them as may from time to time be recommended for such reward, by their officers, for gallant or meritorious conduct. This would act as an ever-present spur. It should not be to take effect at the end of the war, but be declared at once in general orders, and the soldier should be given honorary chevrons to distinguish him during the remainder of his service. To say that all should be free at the end of the war would have little effect. The uncertainty and vagueness would altogether fail to impress a simple-minded negro beyond a week. As well might one promise to free one's cook at some indefinite period with the expectation of thereby securing good dinners. But if it be held out as a boon within his immediate grasp, and which he sees conferred upon others every day, it must have a most excellent effect. Besides, to either give or promise freedom wholesale, would have a most pernicious influence upon the whole race. It is wholly unnecessary, and should not be done, as a mere matter of expediency.

"But, it is alleged, he would desert. No soldier who understands the potency of discipline could hold such an opinion. . . .

". . . It is said, again, they would revolt. Nothing could be more impossible. No scheme could be kept from the non-commissioned officers constantly at hand. Even if a regiment were to succeed sufficiently to come to an outbreak, others could not act in concert, and would be brought to crush the refractory ones at once. Besides, the cavalry and artillery (white) would be ever at hand to destroy any that might attempt it. Mutiny is scarcely known where discipline is maintained. . . .

". . . My proposition, then, is to let the slavery question remain just where it is—put into service as many negroes as we can provide with arms and equipments—organize them strictly as heavy infantry, to be held for the day of battle—convert the white troops into cavalry, artillery and *elite* infantry—take all officers and non-commissioned officers from the most gallant and meritorious of our present armies, and introduce the strictest possible system of discipline—all with the greatest rapidity. The time required to accomplish this would be less than at first thought. The greatest obstacle in making troops is to teach and give experience to the officers. In this case we would have them, in great part, already made. The soldier is taught everything so far as the drill goes when he knows the school of the company. All drill beyond that depends upon the officer almost entirely, so that the time required would be that necessary for experienced officers to drill one company. Thus an army would spring into existence in a remarkably short time."

🙢   Although the suggestion was not followed, the Virginia Military Institute made an offer to the Confederate secretary of war to undertake the task of organizing and drilling the blacks:

The present state of the country justifies any one in presenting for the consideration of the Government well-meant suggestions, even if they should appear crude to those who are better informed.

The tone of public sentiment and the tenor of present legislation indicate that the call of General Lee for negro troops will be responded to.

I suggest that the maximum number allowed to be raised should be half a million.

I do not suppose that so many are required or could be obtained. But to place the maximum at this figure would, I believe, inspire dread in the minds of our enemy, who exaggerates, through ignorance, our power in this particular; and further, to call for half a million would, by the effect upon the minds of owners and slaves, facilitate and insure the raising of 200,000.

The second suggestion I would make is, that in the event of the troops being raised you might command the services of our corps of cadets with their officers to perform the work of organization and drilling in the shortest time, and with the greatest efficiency.

In 1861, between the 20th of April and the 20th of June, the cadets drilled 15,000 men of the Army of Northern Virginia, and if a large camp of instruction were established at Camp Lee the same work could be done for all of the negro troops that would be sent there.

Allow me to say that these suggestions are the result of conversation among some of the officers of our school, and the last one is contained in a letter to me from General Smith, our superintendent, who is now absent at Lexington.[5]

Robert E. Lee's views were finally clear enough to all, but what did the Confederate army think of black comrades in arms? Congressional and journalistic opponents of the President's policy certainly placed great emphasis on the alleged aversion of the Confederate soldiers to the idea. And it was true that in the army, as in southern society at large, opinion initially was clearly divided, with scattered individual opponents of the notion perhaps making the first claim for notice. After the Hampton Roads conference, however, and even more so after Lee wrote his letter to Barksdale, the army spoke out publicly in a remarkable fashion.

There had been no wholesale change of opinion and enough dissent cropped out to support the authenticity of the evidence. The main point was that the larger part of Lee's Army of Northern Virginia, and possibly of the other Confederate armies, accepted the idea of freeing and arming the slaves. There had not been, of course, any more of a Damascus-road type of conversion than there had been two or so years earlier in the northern army. It was clearly a case, for most of the southern soldiers, of welcoming almost any development—if it meant help in the struggle to fend off the Yankees.

A Confederate congressman, Thomas L. Snead of Missouri, had seen the handwriting on the wall and commented, not without some sarcasm, perhaps:

---

[5] J. T. L. Preston (acting superintendent) to John C. Breckinridge, February 17, 1865, *ibid.*, 1093.

. . . The opposition to the employment of negro troops is growing weaker daily, and I think it almost certain that at least 100,000 of them will be put in the Army next spring. General Lee, whose opinions on all subjects are omnipotent, advocates the measure warmly, and the army here seems to be anxious for the experiment to be made. The simple truth is that there is no alternative for it, in the opinion of General Lee and many of our wisest men. . . .[6]

🖜 Not all of Lee's corps commanders shared his views:

It is deemed desirable, and a request is made through General Lee, that the several corps of this army give an expression of opinion on the subject of putting negroes, who for the boon of freedom would volunteer as soldiers, into the field. The effect of such a measure on this army is doubted, and consequently the matter is submitted to your discretion for obtaining the sense of your division on the subject. It may not be amiss to say that the opinion of the lieutenant-general commanding [James Longstreet] is that the adoption of such a measure will involve the necessity of abolishing slavery entirely in the future, and that, too, without materially aiding us in the present.[7]

🖜 Major General John B. Gordon, unlike Longstreet, evinced a
    more positive attitude toward the swiftly developing idea:

I have the honor to report that the officers and men of this corps are decidedly in favor of the voluntary enlistment of the negroes as soldiers. But few have been found to oppose it. The aversion to the measure has in no instance been found strong. The opposition to it is now confined to a very few, and I am satisfied will soon cease to exist in any regiment of the corps. I respectfully suggest that these reports be immediately forwarded to the authorities at Richmond.[8]

🖜 A wry example of the early expression of an individual and un-
    identified soldier's opinion appeared in the Richmond *Sentinel*
    (January 4, 1865). A soldier at the front in the "6th Texas"

[6] Thomas L. Snead to Sterling Price, January 10, 1865, *O.R.*, Series I, Vol. XLVIII, Pt. 1, p. 1,321.
[7] O. Latrobe to J. B. Kershaw, February 16, 1865, in *O.R.*, Series I, Vol. XLVI, Pt. 2, p. 1,236. Same letter to G. E. Pickett and H. L. Benning.
[8] John B. Gordon to W. H. Taylor, February 18, 1865, *O.R.*, Series I, Vol. LXI, Pt. 2, p. 1,063.

wrote thanking the newspaper for "supporting us, *our* war and *our* administration," and then added:

. . . Where is the spirit of '61? Where are the blood and thunder orators, who promised us to be the first here . . . ? We need them now, and promise them war, dirty clothes, scant rations, and glory to their hearts' content. . . . To the "Convention of all the States" men, I will say that we are here, representatives from every State, and would like to have a *few more delegates;* and we want white ones. If the negroes must be "put in," make Home Guards of them, and clear the woods of conscripts and deserters.

☞ The Richmond *Examiner* (January 6, 1865) printed resolutions from "Jordan Battery, Captain J. D. Smith commanding." The eighty or so soldiers involved pledged that they renewed their "vows of allegiance to the Confederate States of America" and affirmed their "steadfast determination to prosecute the war with the most untiring zeal." But they also resolved: "That we view with utmost abhorrence the idea of arriving at a settlement of our difficulties by sacrificing slavery or by yielding dishonorably in any way, thereby inviting the aid of any foreign power."

By February 11, 1865, the *Examiner* explained that it was so overwhelmed with "patriotick" statements from the army that they had to be abridged for publication. Given the paper's editorial policy, this may have resulted in the omission of certain resolutions; but even the *Examiner* (February 17, 1865) found itself printing this affirmation, among others, from the 17th South Carolina Regiment: "That we believe it to be the duty of Congress to tax heavily to redeem our currency; that we believe the liberty of the white man is better than the bondage of the slave, and, if necessary, one hundred thousand negroes should be freed and armed to assist us."

And on the following day, this appeared in the *Examiner* from "Thomas's brigade": "That when, in the opinion of President Davis and General R. E. Lee, it shall become necessary to arm a portion or all of the slaves capable of bearing arms, and make soldiers of them, we will accept it as a necessity and cheerfully acquiesce, preferring, as we do, any and all sacrifices to subjugation."

The *Sentinel* (February 13, 1865) also reported that it was inundated with communications about the question of freeing and arming the slaves and, happily, supporting that paper's policy—"with a singular unanimity, *all* are in favor of it." One army officer urged Congress to show greater decisiveness and more confidence in the plan and he repudiated the notion that white soldiers would be degraded by black comrades: "Many of us have ploughed all day by the side of the negro, and were not injured by it."

Typical of the longer letters from the army that appeared in the newspapers after mid-February was this one in the *Sentinel* (February 21, 1865) :

Camp Davis's Brigade
Near Petersburg, Va., Feb. 14, 1865

At a meeting of the officers and men of Davis's brigade held this day, the meeting being called to order, on motion of Colonel B. O. Reynolds, 11th Mississippi, Private W. C. McDougal, 26th Mississippi, was called to the chair, and on motion of Captain J. C. Donaldson, 42d Mississippi, Lieutenant M. D. McNeely, 42d Mississippi, was appointed Secretary; Private Wm. F. Price, 11th Mississippi, presented the following preamble and resolutions, which, after considerable discussion, were adopted :

Whereas the enemy, in his efforts to subjugate these Confederate States, is resorting to every expedient to effect the consummation of the same; he has stolen our negroes and placed them in his armies; he has recruited his wasted legions from the pauper and prison houses of Europe, and is now threatening us with a negro draft of three hundred thousand men, and we, the soldiers of this brigade, fully appreciating the great issue at stake, upon the result of which depend the destiny of our people, and everything that freemen hold dear and sacred, believe the time has come when the war material of our country, regardless of color, should be fully developed : Therefore be it resolved,

1. That we are in favor of the introduction of the negro, as a soldier, into the military service of the Confederacy, upon such conditions as Congress and the wisdom of our rulers may see fit to determine.

2. That we most earnestly invite the attention of Congress to the necessity of immediate action to secure this end, assuring them that it

will create no dissatisfaction in our ranks, but will be hailed as an evidence that everything will be subordinated to the interest of the cause, and as the harbinger of speedy success in the bloody struggle in which we are engaged.

3. That if Congress in its wisdom should deem it inexpedient to pass a law bringing negro troops into the service, we respectfully request the Legislature of our State to raise, arm and equip, one or more negro brigades, and place them in active service.

4. That a copy of these resolutions be forwarded to the members of Congress from our State, and to Governor Clarke, with the request that they be presented by him to the Legislature at its next session.

☞ The Richmond *Enquirer* (February 21, 1865) had received a report from the 15th Alabama Regiment that the editor no doubt gleefully publicized:

The opinion of the soldiers of the army upon the question of putting negroes in the ranks, not having been given in any official and positive form, has left opportunity for great misunderstanding upon this point. There are many persons who really believe that the army is opposed to it. This is not the fact. We have many assurances to the contrary, but the strongest we have yet seen is the following from the 15th Alabama regiment. The letters will explain themselves:

Hd'qrs 15 Alabama Regiment
February 11, 1865.

"Lieut. Col. W. H. Taylor:

Colonel—With this find a paper, which, in a great degree, explains itself. It is the work of the enlisted men alone, and was handed to me after they had signed it. I then submitted it to the officers, all of whom, who were present with the regiment, signed it. There are present for duty two hundred effective men, out of that number, you will see that one hundred and forty-three signed this paper; and of that one hundred and forty-three, and to whose names are annexed cross marks, there are eighty-eight (88) men who are willing to take the negroes in the ranks with them. The officers present all consent to taking them in the ranks. The man who sent me the paper tells me that several more would have signed it if they had thought it would have any effect towards bringing about the desired object of putting the negroes in the army. Thinking that Gen. R. E. Lee might like to get all the information he could as to the feeling in the army on the subject, I concluded to have a copy of this paper made for his use and send it to you with the request that you hand it to him. Some of the Congressmen seem to be very tender-footed on this point, but I think here is evidence that at least one regiment means political independence at any price. It is due that I should state that the eighty-eight men who are willing to take the negroes into the ranks are among the best men in the regiment, young men of good families in point of position and property. I am satisfied that there are two other regiments in this (Law's) brigade that are anxious to have negroes put in the army, but of course I cannot speak as definitely as of my own regiment. These two regiments are the 4th and the 44th Alabama. I send the original paper, signed by the men in pencil, with the request that you hand these papers to General Lee.

> I am, Colonel, respectfully,
> A. A. Lowther,
> Colonel 15th Alabama regiment.''

"We, the undersigned, soldiers of the 15th regiment Alabama volunteers, infantry, seeing the determination of the Federal government to finally subjugate us, confiscate our lands and property, free our slaves, believe the time has come for the arming and putting into the Confederate States service two hundred thousand (200,000) negroes, and most respectfully urge that Congress pass a law to that effect or authorize the President to receive them in any way that is constitutional.''

(Signed by one hundred and forty-three names.)

Here is a regiment in earnest, and which means ''independence,'' and which will not permit any questions of taste or *smell* either to stand between them and freedom.

A gentleman, over the signature of ''on the shelf,'' writes:

"When I left my home in South Carolina, a few days ago, the principal reasons urged against placing negroes in the ranks was that our brave boys would not tolerate the admixture or association, but all men were willing, with few exceptions, to lend their slaves to the cause whenever General Lee thought them needed. I have just come from a visit to Bratton's brigade and others below here, and, having sounded almost every man, I was pleased to hear them, so far from urging an objection, enthusiastically in favor of being placed side by side with the faithful slaves from home.''

We never contemplated putting negroes in the regiments with the old soldiers against the wishes of the whites. We would not see any single soldier forced to fight by the side of a negro. But when the regiment is willing to have its ranks filled up and its regimental organization preserved, with all its glorious name and fame, by negro recruits, there can be no objection urged. Every soldier who objects to fighting with the negroes might be transferred to some other regiment. . . .

. . . We call upon the commanders of regiments to take the sense of their men, and permit every soldier to give his wishes in this matter. The example set by the 15th Alabama may well be followed by every regiment. Let Congress act promptly. Precious time is passing away. Every day now lost is a delay prejudicial to the country and its cause.

☞ One group of Virginia soldiers, including a significant proportion from slaveholding families, tellingly revealed their grudging assent to the revolutionary proposal in a letter to the Richmond *Whig* (February 23, 1865):

Camp 56th Virginia Regiment,
Near Dutch Gap, Feby. 14th, 1865.

To the Editor of the Whig:

Enclosed please find a copy of resolutions passed by the 56th Va. Regiment, to-day, which I send you for publication. In obedience to one of the resolutions, I am requested to call your attention particularly to the resolution expressing the approbation of the regiment of the enlistment of negroes as soldiers; the resolution was passed with great spirit and entire unanimity, and is, so far as known, the first voice uttered in definite form and solemn meeting that has gone from the army on that subject. It is also worthy of note that the 56th Va. Regiment is composed of companies from the most populous slave districts in Virginia, and its members, perhaps, own in the aggregate, as many slaves as any other regiment from Virginia.

Henry G. Allen, Secretary.

. . . *Resolved,* That slavery is the normal condition of the negro— that the right of property in slaves is just and perfect, and is entitled to the same protection, by constitutional guarantees and legislative enactments, as any other right of property—that involuntary servitude is as indispensable to the moral and physical advancement, prosperity and happiness of the African race as is liberty to the whites; but if the public exigencies require that any number of our male slaves be enlisted in the military service in order to the successful resistance to our enemies, and to the maintenance of the integrity of our Government, we are willing to make concessions to their false and unenlightened notions of the blessings of liberty, and to offer to those, and those only who fight in our cause, perpetual freedom, as a boon for fidelity of service and loyalty to the South. . . .

☞ The Third Virginia Cavalry revealed its dissension concerning the central question of the day and finally shied away from the idea of emancipation (Richmond *Sentinel,* February 25, 1865) :

. . . 1st. That the conduct of our illustrious chief magistrate in designating *"Independence"* as the only basis on which we could or ought to enter into negotiations for peace with the United States, meets with our cordial approbation, believing, as we do, that it is the sentiment of our whole people.

2d. That we take up the gauntlet which the enemy has again thrown down, and hereby announce our determination to meet him on the field of battle, and submit to the arbitrament of the sword, the issue of independence or subjugation.

3d. That on the subject of recruiting our armies, it is our deliberate opinion that wisdom in legislation and firmness in the execution of laws would speedily raise a sufficient force of white troops to guarantee our independence. That we contemplate with anxiety and apprehension the proposition to enlist negro troops in our armies, seriously doubting both its expediency and practicability, dreading its effects upon our social system, and earnestly desiring to see the independence of our country established by the strong arms of her white people, who have bravely resisted her enemies thus far.

4th. That we hail the appointment of Gen. Robert E. Lee to General-in-Chief, as an augury of a vigorous prosecution and glorious termination of the war, and that we would rejoice to see all the military resources of the country placed at his disposal during this great struggle.

. . . Whereupon, it being proposed to vote upon each resolution

separately, the preamble and first and second [and fourth] resolutions
were unanimously adopted. The third resolution elicited an animated
and protracted discussion, resulting in the adoption of the following
substitute . . . :

Resolved, That we are in favor of putting the entire country on a
military footing. We are in favor of putting every man in the country,
between the ages of 17 and 45 in the army, and as many negroes, without changing their social status, as the Commander-in-Chief may deem
necessary to redeem our sacred soil from the pollution of an insolent
foe, holding our independence as paramount to all other considerations. . . .

☞ Bolder than the Virginia cavalrymen above, "Captain W. S. Grif-
fin's company, A, 18th Va. battalion artillery," meeting "in the
trenches on Chaffin's farm," reported to the *Sentinel* (February
25, 1865) that they had resolved:

. . . That we have unlimited confidence in the wisdom and patriotism
of our representatives in Congress and the Virginia Legislature, and
we earnestly solicit them, (if in their judgment the crisis demands it)
to tender to our beloved President the slaves of Virginia, to aid in driving from our soil the nefarious invader who now pollutes it. . . .

CHAPTER VIII

Congressional
and Legislative Action
at Last

WITH JEFFERSON DAVIS and Robert E. Lee as their reference points, the majority of the Confederate soldiers in Virginia had apparently agonized their way into an acceptance of what was to them a most drastic change. As magic as Lee's name had already become, however, not even his opinion was the final word for many powerful Southerners. The members of two crucial bodies, the Confederate Congress and the Virginia legislature, proved remarkably hard to move. True, certain newspapers that earlier had stoutly opposed the idea now capitulated. For example, the Richmond *Examiner,* held out until February 25 when it speculated that Lee just might not be a "good Southerner." But the *Examiner,* protesting to the last, nevertheless yielded:

The question of employing negroes in the army is by no means set at rest by the Senate majority of one. The debates having been secret, the publick can have no knowledge of the reasons and arguments urged on either side. Undoubtedly the arming of negroes, whether as slaves or not, is a very serious step; justifies earnest deliberation, and accounts for honest differences of opinion. It is a great thing which General Lee asks us to do, and directly opposite to all the sentiments and principles which have heretofore governed the Southern people. Nothing, in fact, but the loud and repeated demand of the leader to whom we already owe so much, on whose shoulders we rest so great a responsibility for the future, could induce, or rather coerce, this people and this army to consent to so essential an innovation. But still the question recurs—can we hope to fight successfully through a long war without using the black population? Evidently General Lee thinks not; because at the same moment that he makes new efforts to recall the absentees and deserters to their posts, he also urgently demands that Congress and the several States pass at once such legislation as will enable him to fill his ranks with negro troops. On this point of military necessity, there are few in the Confederacy who would not defer to the judgment of the General.

There is another very material consideration. If we arm negroes can they be made serviceable soldiers? This journal has heretofore opposed the whole project upon the last named ground; and has not changed its opinion. Yet General Lee has, on this question also, very decidedly expressed a different judgment in his letter to a member of Congress. And this is another question purely military; upon which, therefore, the whole country will be disposed to acquiesce silently in the opinion of the commander who undertakes to use that species of force efficiently for our defence. There are many other considerations, which are not military, but moral, political and social, relating to the future of the black race as well as of the white,—all of which oppose themselves strongly to the revolutionary measure now recommended. On these General Lee cannot be admitted as an authority without appeal: indeed, his earnestness in providing that "those who are employed should be freed," and "that it would be neither just nor wise to require them to serve as slaves," suggests a doubt whether he is what used to be called a "good Southerner"; that is, whether he is thoroughly satisfied of the justice and beneficence of negro slavery as a sound, permanent basis of our national polity. Yet all these considerations must also give way, if it be true that, to save our country from Yankee conquest and domination it is "not only expedient but necessary" to employ negroes as soldiers. *He* is the good Southerner who will guaranty us against that shameful and dreadful doom. To save ourselves from that, we should of course be willing not only to give up property and sacrifice comfort, but to put in abeyance political and social theories, which in principle we cannot alter.

The whole matter depends practically on the question—Is this necessary, or not necessary, to the defeat of the Yankee invaders and the establishment of Confederate independence? The Senators who voted against the measure are entitled to credit for purity of purpose. It would be very invidious, and is unnecessary, to assume that any of them refuse the aid of negroes in this war from any silly and sneaking sort of a lingering secret hope that if the country is subdued they will not perhaps be deprived of their slaves by the Yankee conquerers. If any Senator, or any constituent of any Senator, is at this day so hopelessly idiotick as to imagine that in case of subjugation the enemy will not take from him both his negroes and his plantation to boot, that Senator, or constituent, is not to be argued with. Leaving that out of the question, then, it may be assumed that the majority of the Senate objected to the employment of negro soldiers, either because they think the ''Necessity'' spoken of by General Lee does not exist— or because they are of opinion that negroes would make bad soldiers; and that if the whites confess themselves unable to continue the contest, negroes would not save them; or because they are inflexibly opposed in principle to altering the relative *status* of white and black from these moral, political and social considerations alluded to before. As to the two first objections, the only answer that can be made is that General Lee is of a different opinion; he thinks he can make efficient soldiers of negroes, and he thinks the time has come when it is necessary to take and use them. It is one thing to be quite converted to his opinion, and another to acquiesce in his decision. As to those other and larger considerations, which do not depend upon military necessity, nor on the present exigency, but go down to the foundations of society and the natural relation of races, those Senators who hold that it would be a cruel injury, both to white and black, to sever their present relation of master and slave; that to make ''freedom'' a reward for service, is at war with the first principles of this relation, and is the beginning of abolition, and that abolition means the abandonment of the black race to inevitable destruction upon this continent, those Senators are undoubtedly right. This is the true Southern principle, and the only righteous principle. But what then? What good will our principle do if the Yankees come in over us? Will there be any comfort in going down to perdition carrying our principles with us intact? The principle of slavery is a sound one; but is it so dear to us that rather than give it up we would be slaves ourselves? Slavery, like the Sabbath, was made for man; not man for slavery. On this point also, as well as all the others, the only practical question now ought to be: Is it necessary, in order to defend our country successfully, to use negroes as soldiers—not abandoning any principle, but reserving for quieter times the definitive arrangements which may thus become needful? If it is necessary, as General Lee has said—that is, if the alternative is submission to the enemy—then no good Southern man will hesitate. It may be under protest that we yield to this imperious necessity; but still we yield.

🖙 The *Examiner* might have officially yielded, but the editor and his close associates probably had not changed their own opinions one whit. No more editorials slashed out against the proposal, but the *Examiner* (March 4, 1865) carried a comment from the *Globe* of Toronto, Canada, that cast a dubious eye on the Confederacy's great experiment that was approaching:

The rebel Congress at Richmond, it seems, is at last about to toe the mark, and to pass a bill for the arming of two hundred thousand slaves. . . . If this had been done in the first or second year of the war, there might have been some little reason in the experiment, though even then it would have been extremely hazardous. But now, when every man in the South, black or white, must pretty thoroughly understand how fast the South is losing ground, the experiment is doubly dangerous. How long will it take to collect these two hundred thousand slaves? . . . They must, at the best, be of little avail for the next summer's campaign, and by the end of that who knows that the rebel leaders will have any use for them, or, at all events, any important army of whites left to co-operate with them?

🖙 The Raleigh, North Carolina, *Confederate* (March 9, 1865) printed other comment from outside the South. Apparently the New York *Tribune* did not know just what to believe about developments in Richmond:

It is idle to suppose the majority of one in the Rebel Senate will hold out against the almost unanimous opinion of the Rebel leaders, and Rebel journals, and Rebel people—a few Hunkerish planters excepted who, like our Conservatives at the North, never learn anything and never forget anything. The only doubt in the case is not whether the Rebels mean to raise a negro force, but whether they have not already raised that force. It is shrewdly suggested that this appearance of debate and delay has no other purpose than to cover the proceeds of organization now actually going on. The appointment of Lee as General-in-Chief when he was known as an advocate of arming the negroes, showed that he was to have his own way, and we have a report from a source that ought to be well informed, that the Rebels have been for weeks if not months busily engaged in drilling an army of negroes, and that at this moment they are about ready to enter the field. It is asserted that they are to bear the brunt of Sherman's advance and that without evacuating Richmond or even Petersburg, the Confederacy, by the help of this new negro army, will prove itself able to risk a battle for the possession of North Carolina. We do not vouch for the report. There are many probabilities against it. The Richmond papers are too much in earnest to be counterfeiting. The reluctance to overturn the "corner-stone" of the Confederacy has been too real. It is but lately that the opposition seemed in the way of being silenced. But the report itself is another evidence that the fact is about to be accomplished.

☞ Greeley's *Tribune* was not the only important newspaper that had difficulty in separating fact from rumor about Confederate affairs. The London *Times* (as reprinted in the Raleigh *Confederate*, March 9, 1865) also mixed wild hearsay with some hard *realpolitik:*

We are assured from New York that President Davis has the game in his hands, and can secure the independence of the South either with the assent of the North or in *despite of it,* according to his pleasure.

The clue to this startling mystery is to be found in the statement, firmly credited in America, that the Emperor of Mexico has conveyed in trust to the Emperor of the French the northern portions of the Mexican territory, to be held and administered by a French viceroy, in liquidation of the claims of France upon the Mexican Government. This cession it is assumed in the North, could not possibly occur without the recognition of the Southern Confederacy by France, and that recognition, it is further assumed in the North, would at once be followed by this country and the other great powers of Europe. The presumption[s] current on this subject are strengthened by the anticipation [of a change of] policy on the part of the Confederate Government. It is expected that General Lee will decree the liberation of the negroes of the South, and call them as freemen into the ranks of his armies. Such a measure, it is argued, would not only furnish the Confederacy with two hundred thousand soldiers, but would remove the obstacle which prevents the governments of Europe from recognizing the independence of the Southern States. The new Confederacy would no longer represent a slaveholding power, the injurious stigma would be effaced, and the European States might welcome the Southern republic without offence or scandal. From all this it follows that President Davis, if the Federals will not grant him acceptable terms of peace, may continue the war on conditions more favorable than before, with France probably for any ally, and the other Powers of Europe for friends, and that the North, rather than encounter this new opposition at the present period of the struggle, should come at once to terms, even on the basis, if necessary, of political separation. . . .

The Southerners have for some time persuaded themselves, and are now fully convinced, that if the South would but break with the institution of slavery we should be ready to step out of our neutrality and recognize the government of President Davis. We venture to assert that there can be no foundation whatever for this persuasion, though we are not altogether surprised at its prevalence. The more ardent partisans of the North in this country have so strenuously and persistently represented the whole war as a mere struggle for slavery on one side and emancipation on the other, that the Federals may perhaps have regarded our neutrality as due only to our national abhorrence of the Southern institution. They may not unnaturally suppose, therefore, that the removal of this barrier would allow our sympathies to set in towards the South, and terminate the impartiality which we have hitherto maintained. We do not hesitate to say that such a presumption *is based on complete ignorance of the real opinions* of Englishmen. Our neutrality has not been founded on any balance of Northern and Southern claims to favor. Discrimination of that kind has doubtless determined the private sympathies of individuals, but it has not regulated the policy of our government. We have been neutral in this war from mere abstract principles of public policy. We have stood aloof because it would have been the extreme of political folly to interfere, because the war was none of our war, and because we desired to remain at peace. Our recognition of Southern independence would, when it was made, be dictated by considerations applicable not to this case merely, but to all such cases, and would be whol[l]y unconnected with the professions, whether political or moral, of the new confederacy. International law and usage give us ample guidance for our conduct. It is well known and established under what circumstances new government[s] may be recognised without offence, and when the Confederates have achieved the necessary position they will obtain recognition apart from any reference to their proposed institutions. . . .

☞ As the press and governments of the Atlantic world watched Richmond, and even as such powerful foes of the Davis administration as the *Examiner* swung into line, much of the old opposition within the South yielded. But not the Charleston *Mercury*. Even as Sherman's army approached, the Rhetts clung to their dogmas, and the *Mercury* (January 13, 1865), growing increasingly hostile toward Virginia, sank to a strange level of argument for a presumably paternalistic voice of the so-called aristocracy:

The wild talk prevalent in the official and the semi-official organs at Richmond grates harshly upon the ear of South Carolina. It is still more grievous to her to hear the same unmanly proposition from those in authority in the old State of Virginia. Side by side Carolina and Virginia have stood together against all comers for near two centuries—the exemplars and authors of Southern civilization. Side by side it is our earnest hope they will stand to all time against the world. But we grieve to say there are counsels now brewing there that South Carolina cannot abet—that she will not suffer to be consummated, so far as *she* is concerned in them.

There are men in Virginia, and there are men in South Carolina, who have supposed that there is jealousy existing between these States, in the race of fame and ambition. These men are small pettifoggers and petty creatures. There is no State in the Union that has the solid, calm respect for the merits of Virginia, that exists here in South Carolina. But we are not mouthers, or worshipers. We have no demonstrations to make. It is not our habit. We act. John C. Calhoun, the idol, the demi-god of South Carolina, could have made his most magnificent effort of genius before a Charleston audience, and the only response, at the climax of one of his grand syl[l]ogisms, would have been a slight, a very slight rapping on the floor. Men who worshiped him, found it not congenial to their natures to *demonstrate*. Calm and quiet approval is our habit—our custom—to all. We are sufficiently confident in our own position—sufficiently confident in our own intelligence—in our conduct—in our history, to be jealous of no State— not even of Virginia. We are prepared to stand upon the basis of our record, with a satisfaction too complete to admit of envy towards any people. As equals, as dear friends, who have most confidence in each other from long experience and good deeds done, and good feeling, we meet Virginia in counsels of war or of peace. When Virginia wants a sword to assist in her defence, Carolina's will ever be the first unsheathed.

But, we are no *followers*.

In 1860 South Carolina seceded alone from the old union of States. Her people, in Convention assembled, invited the *slaveholding* States (none others) of the old Union to join her in erecting a separate Government of *Slave States,* for the protection of their common interests. All of the slave states, with the exception of Maryland and Kentucky, responded to her invitation. The Southern Confederacy of slave States was formed.

It was on account of encroachments upon the institution of *slavery* by the sectional majority of the old Union, that South Carolina seceded from that Union. It is not at this late day, after the loss of thirty thousand of her best and bravest men in battle, that she will suffer it to be bartered away; or ground between the upper and nether mill stones, by the madness of Congress, or the counsels of shallow men elsewhere.

By the compact we made with Virginia and the other States of this Confederacy, South Carolina will stand to the bitter end of destruction. By that compact she intends to stand or to fall. Neither Congress, nor certain make-shift men in Virginia, can force upon her their mad schemes of weakness and surrender. She stands upon her institutions—and there she will fall in their defence. *We want no Confederate Government without our institutions.* And we will have none. Sink or swim, live or die, we stand by them, and are fighting for them this day. That is the ground of our fight—it is well that all should understand it at once. Thousands and tens of thousands of the bravest men, and the best blood of this State, fighting in the ranks, have left their bones whitening on the bleak hills of Virginia in this cause. We are fighting for our system of civilization—not for buncomb, or for Jeff Davis. We intend to fight for *that,* or nothing. We expect Virginia to stand beside us in that fight, as of old, as we have stood beside her in this war up to this time. But such talk coming from such a source is destructive to the cause. Let it cease at once, in God's name, and in behalf of our common cause! It is paralizing [*sic*] to every man here to hear it. It throws a pall over the hearts of the soldiers from this State to hear it. The soldiers of South Carolina will not fight beside a nigger—to talk of emancipation is to disband our army. We are free men, and we chose to fight for ourselves—we want no slaves to fight for us. Skulkers, money lenders, money makers, and blood-suckers, alone will tolerate the idea. It is the man who won[']t fight himself, who wants his nigger to fight for him, and to take his place in the ranks. Put that man in the ranks. And do it at once. Control your armies—put men of capacity in command, re-establish confidence—enforce thorough discipline—and there will be found men enough, and brave men enough, to defeat a dozen Sherman's. Falter and hack at the root of the Confederacy—our institutions—our civilization—and you kill the cause as dead as a boiled crab.

The straight and narrow path of our deliverance is in the reform of our government, and the discipline of our armies. Will Virginia stand by us as of old in this rugged pathway? We will not fail her in the shadow of a hair. But South Carolina will fight upon no other platform, than that she laid down in 1860.

☞ Having flatly affirmed that it wanted no part of a Confederacy without slavery, the *Mercury* (January 31, 1865) pursued the matter of the crucial differences that it perceived between the Upper and Lower South:

The soil, climate, and productions of the Border States, and the non-cotton producing States generally, of this Confederation, differ materially from those of the more Southerly and cotton States. A fact upon which may hinge a vast deal in the present, touching the most essential interests of these latter States, and no little as to their future relations and duties. In Virginia, the greater part of North Carolina, Kentucky, Tennessee and Missouri, the institution of African slavery is one merely of choice on the part of these States. That is to say, their productions could go on, and their prosperity continue, under the free labor of the white man. Doubtless, any sudden overthrow of slavery in those States would precipitate ruin upon many, and would temporarily paralyze the general industry. But the soil and the climate are such that in time, with the influx of white labor, their general prosperity could be restored. In time, Virginia would become another Pennsylvania, and Kentucky another Ohio. So with the others. Should the institution of slavery be done away with in those States, the form of labor would be changed, and the race of the laborers with it. *Farming* would succeed to *planting,* the German and the Irishman to the negro—and the negro, like the Indian, would in a few generations pass away—be trampled out of existence, or driven Southward to seek life elsewhere. But pecuniary prosperity might, nevertheless, continue, and external progress supervene. We do not mean to be understood as arguing that this change of labor and of institutions would be for the *better.* By no means. For we think, should this change be effected, it would be in every way advisable for those States to get the lease of some respectable Emperor to look after their political welfare. They will want a Maximilian by all means—and the sooner the better. We do not believe in mobocracies being any better institutions in Southern than in Northern States. Indeed, we think that that system of Government (if *Government* it can be called) is better adapted to the cold-blood, calculating nature of Northern men, than to our own. Both must live in spasmodic energy, lawlessness, riots, revolutions, upturnings of society, blood, and final *Empire.* ''There is no new thing under the sun, and what hath been, that it is which shall be''—sayeth the wise man. And certainly, as regards the laws of human nature and human conduct, the great sage never announced a wiser apothe[g]m. And history tells us, through all time past, that this is the broad road to destruction, down which all Democratic (or mobocratic) Governments, unballanced [*sic*] by the conservative institution of slavery, quickly descend.

The produce of the Cotton States of this Confederation are, on the contrary, those of a tropical climate and a tropical soil. To labor in the field under a tropical sun, to withstand the malaria of a tropical region, to bring forth the fruits from a tropical soil, the negro is indispensable. Without the systematized labor of the negro, our great productions, cotton, rice, and sugar, the basis upon which rests all other forms of industry in the Cotton States, must quickly be swept away. With them must crumble every branch of our industry, every trace of our prosperity, every vestige of our present form of civilization, society and government. The whole must go by the board, and sink like a house built of cards. It is absurd to suppose that the African will work under a system of voluntary labor. The experience of four thousand years all over the world has proved the contrary. Time can prove no more, or anything more certainly. To perform his part in the roll of human life and human duties, the labor of the negro must be compulsory—he must be a slave. Withdraw the condition of his slavery here, and the richest portions of the Cotton States lapse into a state of nature. A most charming hunting ground it will make to be sure—one that will not be surpassed by the thickest jungles of India. . . . *A most magnificent jungle* over all our bottom and sea coast lands extending from the Cape Fear to the Mississippi rivers—and all well stocked with wild cats, wild niggers, wild turkeys, deer, and almost every variety of game—nothing wanting but the importation of a few tigers and lions, and the thing would be perfect —a second Africa brought to light! What a fascinating idea! In the meantime, with the work of miscegination [*sic*] going bravely on, we may fairly and reasonably hope almost to rival the condition of refinement, civilization and morals attained by the Mexicans, and finally to establish a mongrel, half nigger, half white-man, universal-freedom, beggarly Republic, not surpassed even by Hayti. The prospect is refreshing to the heart of every patriot. And it is encouraging to see how many devoted patriots are longing for this paradise. . . .

☞ As for Robert E. Lee, the *Mercury* (February 3, 1865) distorted historical fact and reached for time-honored invective to call him what most Southerners had come to regard as an ugly name— "an hereditary Federalist and a disbeliever" in slavery:

There have always been two classes of political thinkers in America, since the days of Alexander Hamilton and Thomas Jefferson. The one class are known as Federalists, the other as States Rights men. The Federal party which existed in all the States except South Carolina, was gradually year by year dying out in the Southern States under the pressure of the Northern people, the development of facts, and the growing knowledge of the true theory of our General Government, and our State interests. At the head of the one party, until within a year or two of the war, stood Daniel Webster. At the head of the

other, John C. Calhoun. Ingrained deeply into the very fibers of the
Federal party has ever been the principle of *emancipation*—the disbelief in the institution of slavery, whether as a social, a political, or
an economical institution. A fanatical faith in the Union, in the con-
centration and consolidation of power in the hands of the General
Government, have been its cordial principles.

In South Carolina alone, of the old States, this system of ideas never
found a *party*. *Individuals* here, of course have entertained those
opinions; but never a sufficient number to make a *party*. In Virginia,
although a staunch States Rights State, this party has always been a
strong, obstinate and influential one. From the days of Washington,
(who was himself a Federalist,) to those of General Robert E. Lee, it
has always numbered in its ranks some of the strongest and most influential names and individuals in Virginia—in the past and in the
present. A profound disbelief in the institution of slavery lies at the
very base of most of these men's political opinions.

. . . Gen. Lee, the advocate, if not the author, of this scheme of
nigger soldiers and emancipation, is said by those who are acquainted
with the families and the family opinions of men in Virginia, to be
an hereditary Federalist, and a disbeliever in the institution of slavery.
It is with these sentiments then that he comes to us to advise us. What
else then could his advice be than what it is? But are we in the Cotton States, after all the long teachings and labors of Calhoun and our
other sages, at this time of day, to turn a summersault [*sic*] in all of
our political and social views, and to lay down our arms at the feet
of Southern Federalism and Abolitionism. To recast all of our opinions, ignore our past actions, and proclaim ourselves to have been all
wrong in the past, and our leaders to have been blind guides. . . .

☞ The Richmond *Whig* (February 17, 1865), now converted from
its own earlier opposition to the Confederate experiment with
Negro soldiers, deplored the *Mercury*'s divisiveness and attempted to reassure the Charlestonians that there was no "unsoundness" in Virginia about slavery:

We regret to see, in the Charleston *Mercury,* an article on the subject
of arming negroes, which has a tendency to provoke resentments and
animosities among our people, just at a time when harmony and good

feeling are most imperatively needed. We can very well account for decided differences of opinion on this important question; for, without such differences what now appears to be the prevailing sentiment in favor of the proposition could never have been reached. A sudden conversion from unanimous opposition to unanimous support, on the part of a reflecting people, would be an extraordinary phenomenon in the history of public questions. But the very fact that this question exhibits those phases of transition which seem to indicate an approaching affirmative decision, should, we think, have suggested to so candid a journal as the *Mercury,* the propriety of abstaining from unqualified impeachments of the integrity and patriotism of those who support the measure.

There can be no doubt that the expedient of using the services of the negroes in some direct way against the common enemy has grown in popular favor the more thoroughly it has been debated. The highest military authorities recommend it; and people just as sagacious as any others in the country urge it upon Congress. The *Mercury* is simply mistaken in assuming that this idea originated in Virginia, or that it is the reflection of unsoundness in this State, on the subject of slavery. It was the natural development of the necessities of the crisis, one among the many projects and devices to which the uneasiness of the past few weeks has given birth. If the most of the others have fallen still-born, while this one has survived and grown in strength, that fact shows that it possesses superior vitality, and is more congruous with the demands of the times. The *Mercury* does, indeed, limit its denunciations to those who propose to confer emancipation on the negro as a compensation for his military services. But it seems to infer that emancipation is the real object of those who favor the measure, thus attributing a kind of Abolitionism to a very large number of our people; while, in fact, emancipation is suggested only as an incident by those who imagine that in this way alone could the main expedient be rendered effective. In regard to this point also there may be a latitude of opinion, which does not by any means imply treason or abolitionism, either on the one side or the other. People who think that the gift of emancipation would better enable us to utilize the resources presented by our supply of negroes, are not therefore abolitionists. The expedient of arming the slaves being once adopted, the question might present itself—how best can we render this expedient effective? The question would not be, as it has been asserted, whether freedom or slavery is best for the negro; but whether the negro himself would so consider it. That large numbers of them do think it is a desirable boon, is proved by the fact that they run off to the Yankees in quest of it. That almost all of these would return to us with the same inducement, we think unquestionable. But we sincerely hope that we shall not be driven to any such alternative. We may accomplish all that we desire by using the negroes simply as slaves. But we do say that we would not hesitate to use them in any way whatever to get rid of Yankee domination. We say this in order to meet fully the *Mercury*'s assertion that South Carolina entered into this struggle for no other purpose than to maintain the institution of slavery; that Southern independence has no other object or meaning, and that independence and slavery must stand together or fall together. We do not pretend to dispute the *Mercury*'s assertion. But we protest against applying it to the other States.

It is true that to preserve African slavery, menaced as it was by an unprincipled and imperious ochlocracy, was the proximate object of secession. So it is true that the stamp act and the tea tax were the proximate causes of the American Revolution. But we have yet to learn that the patriots of that day would have submitted to England, after declaring independence, if England had guarantied [*sic*] to them free tea and unstamped paper forever. Nor do we believe that this people would or ought to return to the Yankee Union, even if Lincoln could and would guarantee the perpetuity of African slavery. The *Mercury* will have it that slavery and independence must stand together or fall together; that neither of them can stand alone. As to slavery it is true. Without independence it must fall. How should we suffer, then, should we, in case of necessity, sacrifice it for the sake of independence? We hope to preserve it. We believe we can preserve it. So do we hope to preserve a portion at least of our houses and our lands. Would the *Mercury* declare that we should succumb to the Yankees rather than sacrifice any more of our property? Or must we be told that it is our duty to give every thing for independence— lands, houses, life itself—but not our slaves? These, to be sure, we shall lose at once should we be conquered; but is it better to be conquered, even to submit to the yoke we so much dread, and against which we have so desperately struggled, than to make use of this last, and, it may be, this most effective resource?

☞ With certain South Carolinians increasingly hostile and suspicious toward Virginia, certain North Carolinians questioned the patriotism of South Carolina. The Charleston *Courier* (February 15, 1865) attempted to answer the attack:

The Fayetteville (N. C.) *Telegraph,* referring to the proposal for admitting all that abolitionism charges, and for whitewashing the *African* and all the errors and defects and shortcomings of our conscription policy and practice, by enrolling the inferior dependent and servile race says:

It is said that South Carolina will bitterly oppose this scheme. This may be so; for there seems to be a strong disposition in that State to do all that can be done to thwart the aims of our Government. Some of the South Carolinians are hard to please, and we may expect the same opposition to this measure that is generally evinced to the policy of the Government in that State. We think they ought to give their hearty support to almost anything our Government may propose. They were the first to favor a severance from the United States Government, and they should now be found the last to raise objections to any measures that may be thought necessary to our success by the Confederate Congress.

The *Telegraph* is grossly wrong. We defy and challenge the production of any proof or instance of factious, local or sectional opposition in South Carolina as representing the State. We invite and challenge comparison with any State, and especially with our neighboring States, North Carolina and Georgia—both of whom have done generally well and nobly, and have not been questioned or aspersed in these columns.

The employment and use and services of the servants or of the servile race in this war is, was and should be a question for the States, and South Carolina, through her State action or her citizenship, has not been behind any State in her willingness to aid by all means in the common defence and the Confederate cause.

Many of our planters have offered everything at their command for the public welfare, and all, with a few exceptions, would do so under proper guarantees and regulations.

We do not, however, believe that the capacities of the Anglo American race for self government are to be decided by the Africans, and we seek and desire no privileges or immunities that cannot be maintained, vindicated and asserted by ourselves.

Let Abolitionists, and skulkers, and all who wish to enjoy privileges earned and achieved by African efforts, go to Liberia or New England.

☞ A bare majority of the Confederate senators proved to be almost as obdurate as the Charleston *Mercury* and the *Courier*, for the senate majority, after killing the relevant bills that had been introduced in the upper house, insisted on a restrictive and time-consuming amendment (the limit of 25 percent on the designated male slaves in any one state) to the Barksdale measure. Then the senate's passage of the bill by a 9–8 vote was made possible only because the Virginia legislature instructed its two senators to vote for it.[1]

Senator Graham of North Carolina on February 22, 1865, gave a private account of the situation as he and his allies in the opposition saw it:

. . . A Bill to conscribe negroes in the army was postponed indefinitely in the Senate yesterday, in secret session. I argued it at length as unconstitutional, according to the Dred Scott decision as well [as] inexpedient & dangerous. A Bill for this purpose, which had passed the Hs. [of] Reps. was laid on the table. There may be attempts to revive this fatal measure. All the influence of the administration & of Genl. Lee were brought to bear but without success. An effort is being made to instruct the Va. Senators to vote for it. Mr. Benjamin has been writing letters to induce the brigades of the army to declare for it. I rather regret, that I did [not] join in a vote of want of con-

---

[1] The nine were Albert G. Brown of Mississippi, Henry C. Burnett of Kentucky, Allen T. Caperton of Virginia, Gustavus A. Henry of Tennessee, Robert M. T. Hunter of Virginia, William S. Oldham of Texas, Thomas J. Semmes of Louisiana, William E. Simms of Kentucky, and John W. C. Watson of Mississippi. Opposing were Robert W. Barnwell of South Carolina, William A. Graham of North Carolina, Herschel V. Johnson of Georgia, Waldo P. Johnson of Missouri, Augustus E. Maxwell of Florida, James L. Orr of South Carolina, George G. Vest of Missouri, and Louis T. Wigfall of Texas. *Journal of the Congress* . . . , IV, 671. Since Virginia's two senators were originally opposed to the measure, it is readily apparent that the center of senatorial opposition lay in those seaboard states that were the last major bastions of Confederate resistance.

fidence in him which only [barely?] failed. Had I gone for it, I learn it would have been carried by a considerable majority. . . .[2]

🖙 Long after the war, in 1877 in fact, Jefferson Davis described Senator Hunter of Virginia as a "chief obstacle" to the timely passage of the measure for securing Negro soldiers. Hunter still continued to defend his course of action:

. . . He [Jefferson Davis] says that my opposition to the conscribing of negroes was a chief obstacle to the passage of a bill for it. That my opposition to this bill was some obstacle to its passage I had supposed, but that it was a chief obstacle, I had not imagined. I say this not to avoid the responsibility of opposition to that ill-starred measure. I wish I could have defeated it altogether, for I regard its approach to a passage as a stain upon Confederate history. It afforded, I believe, plausible ground against them for the accusation of falsehood in professing to secede from the United States Government, in part, and mainly on the plea that it was, by reason of their fear that the party in power would emancipate the negroes in defiance of the constitution and in violation of their pledge, which, as we believed, was implied in their adoption of that instrument, by which they bound themselves to protect the institution. And now it would be said we had done the very thing which we professed to fear from them, and without any more constitutional right than they would have had, if they had done the same thing. I never believed that our cause had the least chance of success under the Government which proposed the absurd and misch[i]evous law which so nearly passed the Senate. It was viewed, I think, by nearly all considerate people as a confession of despair by the Government, and I think they no longer had the least confidence in it. The effect of its passage, I believed, would be to drive the negro from us into the embraces of the Federals, from a place where he was doing us much good as a laborer, to another in which he would render the enemy some service as a soldier. Had that bill remained long on

[2] William A. Graham to David L. Swain, February 22, 1865, in the William A. Graham Papers, North Carolina Department of Archives and History, Raleigh. On March 12, Graham wrote further: "The Bill to arm slaves has become a law. It proposes to take them only with the consent of the masters, and in the event of failure in this, to call on the State authorities to furnish. I trust no master in N. C. will volunteer or consent to begin this process of abolition, as I feel very confident the Genl. Assembly will not." *Ibid.*

the statute book we should have had, I think, the same dispute as to
negro suffrage which we have lately witnessed, with this difference:
the actual dispute was between the conqueror and the conquered, in
that which probably would have been produced the character would
have been internecine, and as between neighbors and friends, far more
violent and bitter than between enemies; but it was an impracticable
measure, and incapable of execution from the beginning. . . .[3]

🖙 Hunter, Graham, and other opponents of the measure remained
unconvinced. But the arguments that ultimately triumphed in
the Confederate Congress are perhaps best exemplified in the
speech that Representative Barksdale delivered in the House
upon the occasion of his revelation of General Lee's letter. The
Sentinel later (March 6, 1865) carried the speech, which, aside
from Lee's letter, also included some interesting references to
historical precedents for the measure:

. . . The question is not free from embarrassing considerations, and
must be viewed in its varied social and moral phases, and with reference to its bearing upon the productive interests of the country; but
the end which is paramount to all other considerations, and to which
all else is secondary, is the achievement of our independence and our
assured escape from Yankee domination. Taking this view of the subject, all concur in the opinion that if the employment of the negro
be necessary to the attainment of this object, the step should be taken
without delay. Does the necessity exist? The bill which I have introduced, and which has been reported favorably to the House by the
special committee, leaves the decision of this question to our military
authorities, and who be [so] competent to decide it as they? If they
determine it to be necessary, the bill prescribes the method by which
the object is to be accomplished. It is proposed to effect it, not by
wholesale conscription—not by compulsion—not by the exercise of unauthorized power to interfere with the relation of the slave to his
owner as property, but by leaving this question, where it properly belongs, to the owner himself, acting in pursuance of the laws of his

[3] *Southern Historical Society Papers,* IV (December, 1877), 313–14. The *Whig*
(March 9, 1865) had editorially rebuked Hunter for making a speech against the
measure even as he obeyed the instructions of the Virginia legislature to vote for
it.

State, and by an appeal to the calm reason and patriotic spirit of the people. There are none so competent as the master to select from among his slaves those who would become serviceable soldiers. There is no agency so powerful as the means he can employ to obtain their consent to enlist in the service. Long observation of the peculiarities of the slave, and study of his character, well enable the owner to touch the chords by which his will is influenced and his action controlled.

The personal pledges of a kind master are worth more to the slave than all the proclamations your government can issue. And if the master, in response to the call of the authorities, patriotically determine to give the services of his slave to the cause, let us leave to him the exercise of the influence best calculated to effect the object. If, as a reward for faithful service in the war against the common enemy of both races, he should confer freedom upon the slave, no reasonable objection can be urged against it. To me, this plan of rewarding the slave for meritorious public service, is not new. It is engrafted upon the organic law of my own State, Mississippi, whose every interest is interwoven with the Institution of African slavery. Her Constitution confers upon the Legislature of the State power to provide for the emancipation of slaves "who shall have rendered distinguished service to the State." No "service" can be performed more worthy this testimonial of gratitude than that which may be rendered in repelling the savage foe who comes with fire and sword to bring ruin and misery on our land.

. . . Let us look at the objections urged against the measure. I admit that it is not wholly free from them even in the carefully guarded form in which it is proposed by the committee. But every step in life must be taken by a comparison of the good and evil that will attend it. The objections to the scheme are grouped together and ingeniously presented in a speech delivered in this body by a member from Virginia, (Mr. Gholson.) He insists that to employ the slave as a soldier "would be virtually staking our success on the capacity and fidelity of negro troops." There would be force in this objection if it was proposed to rely solely upon them. The fact is overlooked that it is proposed to make them merely auxiliary to our present tried veterans. . . .

By the same member, it is urged that "the introduction of slaves into the army would be obnoxious to a large portion of our soldiers."

If this be true, it would weigh strongly against my conviction that we should resort to it. I pray that I may do nothing to wound the sensibilities of the gallant men to whom their country owes a debt of lasting gratitude. But the gentleman from Virginia assumes too much. If his object is to gratify the army, let him send to it more muskets, no matter in whose hands they are placed, to aid in driving back the invader. . . . The soldiers, for whose sensibilities the member expresses so much concern, intend neither to be misunderstood nor misrepresented. They are holding meetings all along the line, and, with unexampled unanimity, are declaring in favor of the measure. Turning, naturally, first to the soldiers from my own State, I find that every command which represents it in the Army of Virginia, has deliberately proclaimed its wishes and addressed its petition [? word blurred] to Congress to pass a law in accord [?] with the pending bill.

Be it remembered that these are not the utterances of "timid and despairing men." They are the calm and deliberate expressions of brave men, who entered the contest with "a courage never to yield nor to submit," and who have never for a moment doubted the ultimate triumph of their cause. Nor are these opinions peculiar to the Mississippi troops in this army of heroes. Throughout the entire army the soldiers have held meetings, and to declarations of a determination to continue the struggle until our independence shall have been securely established, they have added an earnest call upon Congress to put a portion of the able-bodied negro population in the military service as soldiers. I have before me resolves of troops from Texas, Georgia, South Carolina and other States, and prominent amongst the rest, are the proceedings of soldiers from Virginia, the State of which the member (Mr. Gholson) is a representative. Their declarations are the best reply to the objection which he urges against this measure, that it would excite the repugnance of the army. I am at a loss to know how the member has reached his conclusion.

MR. GHOLSON—Those meetings were held after the delivery of my speech.

MR. BARKSDALE—(resuming)—Very well. The member was evidently egregiously mistaken in his opinion as to the wishes of the army. Their declarations show them to be precisely the reverse of what he imagined. They show that, on this subject, the soldiers are in advance of Congress. Perhaps they were designed to give inspiration to its sluggish spirit; and it is a reasonable supposition that the resolutions of the Virginians were intended as a protest against the speech from their representative. These expressions of the army are not confined to any particular branch of the service, nor do they come from the rank and file alone. The opinion in favor of employing the negro element is shared alike by officers and men. It is held in common by the private in the ranks and by the General-in-Chief commanding all our armies. He is a bold man who will rashly oppose his opinion to such an array of high military authority.

It is simply absurd to assume that the employment of the negro in the manner proposed, will put him on an equality with the white soldier. The two races in all communities where slavery exists, cultivate the same fields and labor in the same workshops, and it is a novel idea that the white man has disdained the tillage of the field or the toil of the workshop, because of the employment of the negro in such vocation. The God of nature has stamped the white as the superior race, and the negro, obeying the irreversible law of his being, takes his position of inferiority in all conditions of life. The unconquerable line of demarcation which nature has formed can never be overcome.

We are admonished that the "question of supplies for the army must not be overlooked." I concur in the opinion, but it has conducted me to the conclusion I have reached in favor of the measure of the committee. The "question of supplies must not be overlooked"; and, hence, you must increase your military strength so as to protect the lines of communication by which your armies are fed; and you must retake the producing regions now within the lines of the enemy. . . .

We are further told that "the plan proposed by those high in authority is to liberate the slaves introduced into the army at the termination of the war"—and it is asked, "what is this but abolition?" What is this but "doing precisely what our adversaries propose to do?" It is not the plan of the pending measure to interfere with the status of the negro. No "abolition" is proposed. The question is left where it belongs, with the owner himself, under such laws as his State may enact. If the owner choose to emancipate his slave on condition of faithful service, but few would seek to deny him the right. But do members not see the distinction between emancipating the slave who goes into our army and faithfully fights for the good of both races in a just cause, and the emancipation of the whole black population in accordance with the unscriptural dogma preached by the infidel reformers of the North? The question whether the emancipation of the negro soldier will be a blessing or a curse to him, is not to be considered. The real question is, how to make him available as a soldier, in order to secure the independence of these States, and to preserve their social, political and industrial systems, including the institution of African slavery. This is the end we are struggling to attain, and it is the part of true wisdom to venture boldly and to disregard every minor obstacle. The necessities of the contest may diminish the number of negroes now held as slaves, as a part of a cargo of a vessel in a storm at sea is thrown overboard to save the remainder, but if we triumph in the end, the institution itself will be preserved. . . .

The adaptability of the negro to the duties of a soldier has been a subject of controversy. It is urged that he is unfitted by nature for such a service. In order to form a correct opinion upon this point it is not necessary to enter into a rigid analysis of the negro character. . . . We need not go beyond the examples which have been furnished in the history of our own country, and during the present war [illegible phrase]. . . . We will not be without the encouragement which is afforded by the precept and the example of the fathers who, in the Revolution of 1776, achieved the independence which we are struggling to transmit unimpaired to future generations.

In a letter to James Jones, November 28th, 1780, Mr. Madison wrote:

"I am glad to find the Legislature persists in their resolution to recruit the line of the army for the war, though without deciding on the expediency of the mode under their consideration, WOULD IT NOT BE AS WELL TO LIBERATE AND MAKE SOLDIERS AT ONCE OF THE BLACKS THEMSELVES," &c.

But let us heed the words of him who was "first in war, first in peace, and first in the hearts of his countrymen," General Washington, the great leader of our revolutionary armies. Early in the war (December, 1775) at a meeting of his general officers, it was resolved that it was inexpedient to enlist negro soldiers. On being apprized of this proceeding, General Washington addressed a letter to the President of Congress, on the subject, saying:

"It has been represented to me that the FREE NEGROES WHO HAVE SERVED IN THIS ARMY are very much dissatisfied at being discarded. As it is apprehended that they may seek employment in the ministerial [British] army, I have presumed to depart from the resolution respecting them AND HAVE GIVEN LICENSE FOR THEIR BEING ENLISTED."

Here we have the highest authority for saying that negroes were "enlisted" for the war which our sires of revolutionary memory waged for independence, nor did these wise leaders pause to indulge nicely drawn speculations, as to the adaptability of the negro for such service.

Again: In 1779, Henry Laurens wrote to General Washington to this effect:

"Our affairs in the Southern department are more favorable than we had considered them a few days ago, nevertheless, the country is greatly distressed and will be more so, unless reinforcements are sent to its relief. Had we arms for three thousand such *black men* as I could select in South Carolina, I should have no doubt of success in driving the British out of Georgia, and subduing East Florida before the 2d of July."

To this letter General Washington replied as follows, under date of March 20th, 1779:

"The policy of *arming slaves* is, in my opinion, a moot point *unless the enemy set the example*. For should we begin to form battalions of them, I have not the smallest doubt if the war is to be prosecuted of their following us in it, and justifying the measure upon our own ground, the contest must then be, who can arm them fastest," &c.

It will be borne in mind that Gen. Washington had already, in the beginning of the war, enlisted free negroes, and when the proposition to arm the slaves was submitted to him, he said that it was a "moot point," not because there was doubt that they could be used as soldiers, but because the example would be followed by the enemy, who could arm them fastest. In the present war, "the example" has been set by our enemies, and according to the reasoning of Gen. Washington, our duty is plain. It is a "moot point" no longer, the enemy having "set the example."

Again: In a letter to Col. John Laurens, July 10th, 1782, alluding to the defeat of a plan brought by him before the Legislature of South Carolina, to raise a regiment of slaves—Gen. Washington wrote:

"I must confess that I am not at all surprised at the failure of your plan. That spirit of freedom which, at the commencement of this contest, would have gladly sacrificed everything to the attainment of its object, has long since subsided and every selfish passion has taken its place. It is not the public, but every private interest which influences the generality of mankind, nor can the Americans any longer boast [of being] an exception. *Under these circumstances* it would rather have been surprising if you had succeeded; nor will you, *I fear*, have better success in Georgia."

Gen. Washington, it will be seen, bitterly deprecated the failure of the plan to raise a command of slave troops in South Carolina. . . .

But all these precepts and examples from our revolutionary history are not required to render the argument unanswerable. It is found in the stern "logic of events" occurring in the present war. The enemy are [*sic*] employing all the slaves he can steal or entice away from their owners, for service as soldiers. Pending the Presidential election in the Northern States, Mr. Lincoln frankly admitted that so important had this element in the Federal army become, that to cease to use it would be equivalent to an abandonment of the contest. The posts they occupy are to a considerable extent garrisoned by negroes, and many of their lines confronting ours are held by the same description of troops.

But if doubts still exist whether negroes will make efficient soldiers and whether they are the requirements of our cause . . . , they should yield before the deliberate judgment of the General-in-Chief of our armies whose views upon a subject so important, and so purely military, I have thought it my duty to seek. They are clearly presented in the letter which I will now submit: [General Lee's letter to Barksdale follows.]

The adaptability of the negro for the duties of a soldier, and necessity of thus employing him, need not be further argued. I repeat, that sound policy and humanity accord in dictating the course proper to be pursued. It will be compassion to the slave to use him in the manner most conducive to the triumph of our righteous cause. The success of the enemy inevitably involves the extermination of the black population in those States, or its degradation to the condition of barbarism from which the negro would have never emerged but for the scheme of slavery as it exists here. . . .

🕀 The Virginia legislature helped to save the Barksdale bill allowing the Confederate government to arm black soldiers, but not even Robert E. Lee's counsel could persuade the legislature to embrace emancipation. Only slightly less dilatory than the Confederate Congress, the Virginia legislature on March 4 and 6, 1865, enacted the measures that were vital complements to the Barksdale bill. This group of joint resolutions was the first of the Virginia measures:

Resolved, That the General Assembly of Virginia do hereby authorize the Confederate authorities to call upon Virginia, through the Governor of the Commonwealth, for all her able bodied male free negroes between the ages of eighteen and forty-five, and as many of her able-bodied male slaves between the ages aforesaid, as may be deemed necessary for the public defense, not exceeding twenty-five per centum of said slaves, to be called for on the requisition of the General-in-Chief of the Confederate Armies, as he may deem most expedient for the public service.

Resolved, That whenever such call is made it shall be properly apportioned among the different counties and corporations of the Commonwealth, according to the number of male slaves between the ages of eighteen and forty-five in said counties and corporations, so that not more than one slave in every four between the ages indicated shall be taken from any one owner.

Resolved, That our senators are hereby instructed and our representatives requested to vote for the passage of a law to place at the disposal of the Confederate authorities as many of the male slaves and free negroes in the Confederate States of America between the ages of eighteen and forty-five, not exceeding twenty-five per centum of such slaves, as are necessary for the public defense, to be called for on the requisition of the President, or General-in-Chief of our armies, in such numbers as he shall deem best for the public service, each State furnishing its proper quota according to its slave population. But nothing in the foregoing resolutions shall be construed into a restriction upon the President or General-in-Chief of the Confederate army, or a prohibition to the employment of the slaves and free negroes for the public defense in such manner, as soldiers or otherwise, as the General-in-Chief may deem most expedient.[4]

⚓ The second of the Virginia measures merely repealed long-standing laws against the bearing of arms by blacks:

Be it enacted by the General Assembly, That it shall be lawful for all free negroes and slaves, who may be organized as soldiers, now, or at any time hereafter by the State or the Confederate Government, for the public defense during the present war with the United States, to bear arms while in active military service, and carry ammunition as other soldiers in the Army.

2. All acts, and parts of acts, in conflict with the foregoing, are hereby repealed.

3. This shall be in force from its passage.[5]

⚓ At long last, by mid-March, 1865, both the Confederate Congress and the Virginia legislature had acted. Other southern states, however, gave little indication that they would have any real part in the controversial experiment. For one thing, most of the governors of the other states, with majorities in their legislatures behind them, vigorously opposed any Confederate action that tampered or even threatened to tamper with slavery.

It is not surprising that Governor Joseph E. Brown of Georgia, who opposed almost every other Confederate measure, took a hard line against freeing and arming the blacks:

The administration, by its unfortunate policy of having wasted our strength and reduced our armies, and being unable to get freemen into the field as conscripts, and unwilling to accept them in organizations with officers of their own choice, will, it is believed, soon resort to the policy of filling them up by the conscription of slaves.

I am satisfied that we may profitably use slave labor, so far as it can be spared from agriculture, to do menial service in connection with the army, and thereby enable more free white men to take up arms; but I am quite sure any attempt to arm the slaves will be a great error. If we expect to continue the war successfully, we are obliged to have the labor of most of them in the production of provisions.

[4] *O.R.*, Series I, Vol. LXI, Pt. 2, p. 1,068.
[5] *Ibid.*, Series I, Vol. XLVI, Pt. 3, p. 1,315.

But if this difficulty were surmounted, we can not rely upon them as soldiers. They are now quietly serving us at home, because they do not wish to go in the army, and they fear, if they leave us, the enemy will put them there. If we compel them to take up arms, their whole feeling and conduct will change, and they will leave us by thousands. A single proclamation by President Lincoln—that all who desert us after they are forced into service, and go over to him, shall have their freedom, be taken out of the army, and permitted to go into the country in his possession, and receive wages for their labor—would disband them by brigades. Whatever may be our opinion of their normal condition, or their true interest, we cannot expect them, if they remain with us, to perform deeds of heroic valor, when they are fighting to continue the enslavement of their wives and children. It is not reasonable of us to demand it of them, and we have little cause to expect the blessings of Heaven upon our efforts if we compel them to perform such a task.

If we are right and Providence designed them for slavery, He did not intend that they should be a military people. Whenever we establish the fact that they are a military race, we destroy our whole theory that they are unfit to be free.

But it is said we should give them their freedom in case of their fidelity to our cause in the field; in other words, that we should give up slavery, as well as our personal liberty and State sovereignty, for independence, and should set all our slaves free if they will aid us to achieve it. If we are ready to give up slavery, I am satisfied we can make it the consideration for a better trade than to give it for the uncertain aid which they might afford us in the military field. When we arm the slaves we abandon slavery. We can never again govern them as slaves, and make the institution profitable to ourselves or to them, after tens of thousands of them have been taught the use of arms, and spent years in the indolent indulgencies of camp life.

If the General Assembly should adopt my recommendation by the call of a Convention, I would suggest that this, too, would be a subject deserving its serious consideration and decided action.

It can never be admitted by the State that the Confederate Government has any power, directly or indirectly, to abolish slavery. The provision in the Constitution which, by implication, authorizes the Confederate Government to take private property for public use only, authorizes the *use* of the property during the existing emergency which justifies the *taking*. To illustrate: in time of war it may be necessary for the Government to take from a citizen a business to hold commissary stores. This it may do (if a suitable one can not be had by contract) on payment to the owner of just compensation for the use of the house. But this *taking* cannot change the title of the land, and vest it in the Government. Whenever the emergency has passed, the Government can no longer legally hold the house, but it is bound to return it to the owner. So the Government may impress slaves to do the labor of servants, as to fortify a city, if it cannot obtain them by contract, and it is bound to pay the owner for just hire for the time it uses them, but the impressment can vest no title to the slave in the Government for a longer period than the emergency requires the labor. It has not the shadow of right to impress and pay for a slave to set him free. The moment it ceases to *need* his labor, the *use* reverts to the owner who has the *title*. If we admit the right of the Government to impress and pay for slaves to free them, we concede its power to abolish slavery, and change our domestic institutions at its pleasure, and to tax us to raise money for that purpose. I am not aware of the advocacy of such a monstrous doctrine in the old Congress by any one of the more rational class of Abolitionists. It certainly never found an advocate in any Southern statesman.

No slave can be liberated by the Confederate Government without the consent of the States. No such consent can ever be given by this State without a previous alteration of her Constitution. And no such alteration can be made without a convention of her people.[6]

🖙 Governor Zebulon Vance of North Carolina, although a staunch defender of his state's sovereignty and interests, was not the obstructionist to the Confederate war effort that Governor Brown was. Yet Vance had early dissociated himself from the idea of arming, much less freeing, the slaves:

. . . I will ask your [the legislature's] consideration of a copy of the resolutions adopted by a meeting of the Governors of the States of Virginia, North Carolina, South Carolina, Georgia, Alabama, and Mississippi, held in Augusta, Ga., on the 17th ult. [October], and request

[6] Joseph E. Brown to the Georgia legislature, February 15, 1865, in Allen D. Candler (ed.), *The Confederate Records of the State of Georgia* (5 vols.; Atlanta, 1909), II, 832–35.

you to regard them as a part of this message. This meeting was invited by me, in the earnest hope that something might be agreed upon to aid in reinforcing our armies and rendering uniform the action of the State[s] in many important particulars. . . .

Contrary to the impression sought to be made by some, the resolution relating to the impressment or conscription of slaves was by no means intended to include the arming of them, much less their final emancipation, which I take it would follow as a natural consequence. I supposed that as property their temporary services were within reach of the government like all other property, to be employed as pioneers, erecting fortifications, cooks, teamsters, hospital servants, laborers in the several departments, and wherever, in short, the negro could take the place of an able-bodied white man who could carry a musket. Under no circumstances would I consent to see them *armed,* which I would regard as not only dangerous in the extreme, but as less degrading only than their employment in this capacity by our enemies. The proposition to emancipate them by the Confederate Government, (which in conscience should be done if they fought in our armies) I regard as entirely out of the question. I imagine that such an idea as abolishing slavery by the General Government, advocated five years ago, would have made people stare, and caused some little excitement. This course would, it seems to me, surrender the entire question which has ever separated the North from the South; would stultify ourselves in the eyes of the world, and render our whole revolution nugatory—a mere objectless waste of human life. I need not allude at all to the constitutional question involved, which I presume must be understood by this time. Our independence, I imagine, is chiefly desirable for the preservation of our political institutions, the principal of which is slavery; and it is only to be won by the blood of white freemen. The slave, however, should certainly be made to do his part as a non-combatant. . . .[7]

Governor Henry W. Allen of Louisiana dared to rise above the parochialism and racial conservatism of the other governors and

---

[7] Raleigh *Confederate,* November 23, 1864. The repudiation of the policy of freeing and arming the blacks by Governor M. L. Bonham of South Carolina may be found in the Richmond *Sentinel,* December 12, 1864. Governor Charles Clark of Mississippi endorsed the idea of black soldiers but not their emancipation (Richmond *Sentinel,* March 25, 1865, and *Whig,* April 1, 1865).

join with Smith of Virginia in supporting the policy of Davis, Lee, and Benjamin. The Galveston, Texas, *Tri-Weekly News* (February 8, 1865) printed extracts from Allen's message to the legislature:

While looking for an early close of the war, it behooves us none the less to prepare for its duration for years. It is indeed wisest for us to act as though war were to be the permanent condition of our tenure of independence. Preparation for the worst, is the best means of warding it off. . . .

I have long been convinced that we have in our negro slaves the means of increasing the number of available fighting men. They are already, by the wise dispensation which placed them under our tutelage, disciplined to labor. They are peculiarly adapted to the endurance of our climate. Many of them are skilled in the ruder portions of mechanical work. . . .

It cannot be urged that our slaves are all needed to raise food for our people, and supplies for troops. Before the war, our Southern population was greater than it is now, including the army. We then produced a surplus of food, and three millions of bales of cotton, together with large quantities of rice, sugar, and tobacco. We now need no more food than then, and raise no cotton, and little rice or sugar. All having been the product of slave labor, it is evident that there are now more negro laborers than we actually need for agricultural purposes, and that the surplus can well be spared for army use, after making due allowance for those taken away by the enemy.

In view, also, of the possible calamities of a protracted war, it will be wise to have many thousands of negroes thus attached to our armies, mobilized, used to military discipline, habituated by army labor to action in concert, and thus made ready and ripe for that important step which the exhaustion of our armies may necessitate—the arming of negroes. It is the deliberate purpose of the ruling majority of our enemies to prosecute the war on such a scale as to exhaust our fighting men. In this Satanic game they seem willing to play three or four lives of their soldiers against every one of our own, as is shown by the last campaign. . . . If a master may, with the help of his faithful slaves, drive thieves from his corn crib, incendiaries from his cotton gin, and marauders from his house, why may not many masters, helped by their many slaves, act in concert to drive away armies of thieves, incendiaries and assassins?

There may now be differences of opinion as to the exigencies which shall call for this measure; but if we are driven to the wall, there will be none. Each section of the country should be the judge of the necessity. While in this [Trans-Mississippi] Department our army is still comparatively full, east of the Mississippi the want of troops has turned the thoughts of very many able statesmen, soldiers and journalists to the subject of putting negroes into the field. I hope the public mind in this State will be prepared for any action of the Confederate State Congress, and that our people will be ready for the emergency contemplated. Securing to the army a large number of organized negro laborers, appears to be the best possible preparation for this contingency. Should you concur in this opinion, I leave it to your wisdom to suggest such legislation as you may deem appropriate.

In the multiplicity of topics necessary to be called to your notice, I should have treated the subject of employing negroes in the army with more brevity, but for the capture and publication by the enemy of a letter to the Secretary of War, in the concluding paragraph of which I expressed the conviction that the time had come for putting negroes in the field. An expression of my views on this topic was naturally expected; and having no desire to withhold my opinion, in order to give it, I was obliged to state, in part, the reasons and facts on which it was based. . . .

President Davis in the long run had to look to the southern state legislatures and governors for support of the Confederate government's laws and policies. But the military crisis that Davis faced in the late winter and early spring of 1865 was of such intensity that he could hardly indulge in the luxury of long-run thought. It was the immediate, short-run reality of Grant's vast army and Lee's decimated one that loomed largest.

In the context of this crisis, no one could be surprised that bitter feelings had developed around the question of Negro soldiers, as well as concerning other issues not dealt with in this study. Nations, even new and short-lived ones like the Confederacy, do not suffer defeat, and final disintegration, without acrimony and passionate controversy. Under the circumstances, the recriminations exchanged between President Davis and some of the Confederate senators were remarkably controlled, although the bitterness and anger were apparent.

The President sent his special message to the Senate and House of Representatives on March 13, 1865:

When informed on Thursday last [March 9, 1865] that it was the intention of Congress to adjourn *sine die* on the ensuing Saturday, I deemed it my duty to request a postponement of the adjournment in order that I might submit for your consideration certain matters of public interest which are now laid before you. When that request was made the most important measures that had occupied your attention during the session had not been so far advanced as to be submitted for Executive action, and the state of the country had been so materially affected by the events of the last four months as to evince the necessity of further and more energetic legislation than was contemplated in November last.

Our country is now environed with perils which it is our duty calmly to contemplate. Thus alone can the measures necessary to avert threatened calamities be wisely devised and efficiently enforced.

Recent military operations of the enemy have been successful in the capture of some of our sea-ports, in interrupting some of our lines of communication, and in devastating large districts of our country. These events have had the natural effect of encouraging our foes and dispiriting many of our people. The Capital of the Confederate States is now threatened, and is in greater danger than it has heretofore been during the war. The fact is stated without reserve or concealment, as due to the people whose servants we are, and in whose courage and constancy entire trust is reposed; as due to you in whose wisdom and resolute spirit the people have confided for the adoption of the measures required to guard them from threatened perils.

While stating to you that our country is in danger, I desire also to state my deliberate conviction that it is within our power to avert the calamities which menace us, and to secure the triumph of the sacred cause for which so much sacrifice has been made, so much suffering endured, so many precious lives been lost. This result is to be obtained by fortitude, by courage, by constancy in enduring the sacrifices still needed; in a word, by the prompt and resolute devotion of the whole resources of men and money in the Confederacy to the achievement of our liberties and independence. The measures now required, to be successful, should be prompt. Long deliberation and protracted debate over important measures are not only natural, but laudable in representative assemblies under ordinary circumstances; but in moments of danger, when action becomes urgent, the delay thus caused is itself a new source of peril. Thus it has unfortunately happened that some of the measures passed by you in pursuance of the recommendations contained in my message of November last have been so retarded as to lose much of their value, or have, for the same reason, been abandoned after being matured, because no longer applicable to our altered condition, and others have not been brought under examination. In making these remarks it is far from my intention to attribute the loss of time to any other cause than those inherent in deliberative assemblies, but only urgently to recommend prompt action upon the measures now submitted. . . .

The measures passed by Congress during the session for recruiting the Army and supplying the additional force needed for the public defense have been, in my judgment, insufficient, and I am impelled by a profound conviction of duty and stimulated by a sense of the perils which surround our country, to urge upon you additional legislation on this subject.

The bill for employing negroes as soldiers has not yet reached me, though the printed journals of your proceedings inform me of its passage. Much benefit is anticipated from this measure, though far less than would have resulted from its adoption at an earlier date so as to afford time for their organization and instruction during the winter months. . . .

Having thus fully placed before you the information requisite to enable you to judge of the state of the country, the dangers to which we are exposed, and the measures of legislation needed for averting them, it remains for me but to invoke your attention to the consideration of those means by which, above all others, we may hope to escape the calamities that would result from our failure. Prominent above all others is the necessity for earnest and cordial co-operation between all departments of government, State and Confederate, and all eminent citizens throughout the Confederacy. To you especially, as Senators and Representatives, do the people look for encouragement and counsel.

To your action, not only in legislative halls, but in your homes, will their eyes be turned for the example of what is befitting men who, by willing sacrifices on the altar of freedom, show that they are worthy to enjoy its blessings. I feel full confidence that you will concur with me in the conviction that your public duties will not be ended when you shall have closed the legislative labors of the session, but that your voice will be heard cheering and encouraging the people to that persistent fortitude which they have hitherto displayed, and animating them by the manifestation of that serene confidence which in moments of public danger is the distinctive characteristic of the patriot who derives courage from his devotion to his country's destiny and is thus enabled to inspire the like courage in others.

Thus united in a common and holy cause, rising above all selfish considerations, rendering all our means and faculties tributary to the country's welfare, let us bow submissively to the Divine will and reverently invoke the blessing of our Heavenly Father that, as He protected and guided our sires when struggling in a similar cause, so He will enable us to guard safely our altars and our firesides, and maintain inviolate the political rights which we inherited.[8]

> A select committee of the Senate headed by James L. Orr of South Carolina answered the President's charges in an ingenious document that has to be read with caution:

The attention of the Congress is called by the President to the fact that for carrying on the war successfully there is urgent need of men and supplies for the Army.

The measures passed by Congress during the present session for recruiting the Army are considered by the President inefficient; and it is said that the result of the law authorizing the employment of slaves as soldiers will be less than anticipated in consequence of the dilatory action of Congress in adopting the measure. That a law so radical in its character, so repugnant to the prejudices of our people, and so intimately affecting the organism of society should encounter opposition and receive a tardy sanction ought not to excite surprise; but if the policy and necessity of the measure had been seriously urged on Congress by an Executive message legislative action might have been quickened. The President in no official communication to Congress has rec-

[8] *O.R.*, Series IV, Vol. III, 1,130–1,131, 1,133, 1,135–1,136.

ommended the passage of a law putting slaves into the Army as soldiers, and the message under consideration is the first official information that such a law meets his approval. Executive message transmitted to Congress on the 7th of November last suggests the propriety of enlarging the sphere of employment of the negro as a laborer, and for this purpose recommends that the absolute title to slaves be acquired by impressment, and as an incentive to the faithful discharge of duty that the slaves thus acquired be liberated with the permission of the States from which they were drawn. In this connection the following language is used: "If this policy should recommend itself to the judgment of Congress, it is suggested that, in addition to the duties heretofore performed by the slave, he might be advantageously employed as pioneer and engineer laborer, and in that event that the number should be augmented by 40,000. Beyond this limit and these employments it does not seem to me desirable, under existing circumstances, to go." In the same message the President further remarks, "The subject is to be viewed by us, therefore, solely in the light of policy and our social economy. When so regarded, I must dissent from those who advise a general levy and arming [of] the slaves for the duty of soldiers." It is manifest that the President in November last did not consider that the contingency had then arisen which would justify a resort to the extraordinary policy of arming our slaves. Indeed, no other inference can be deduced from the language used by him, for he says: "These considerations, however, are rather applicable to the improbable contingency of our need of resorting to this element of resistance than to our present condition." The Secretary of War, in his report under date of November 3, seemed to concur in the opinion of the President, when he said: "While it is encouraging to know this resource for further and future efforts is at our command, my own judgment does not yet either perceive the necessity or approve the policy of employing slaves in the higher duties of soldiers."

At what period of the session the President or Secretary of War considered the improbable contingency had arisen which required a resort to slaves as an element of resistance does not appear by any official document within the knowledge of your committee. Congress might well have delayed action on this subject until the present moment, as the President, whose constitutional duty it is "to give to the Congress information of the state of Confederacy," has never asked, in any authentic manner, for a passage of a law authorizing the employment of slaves as soldiers. The Senate, however, did not await the tardy movements of the President. On the 29th of December, 1864, the following resolution was adopted by the Senate in secret session:

"*Resolved,* That the President be requested to inform the Senate, in secret session, as to the state of the finances in connection with the payment of the troops; the means of supplying the munitions of war, transportation, and subsistence; the condition of the Army, and the possibility of recruiting the same; the condition of our foreign relations, and whether any aid or encouragement from abroad is expected, or has been sought, or is proposed, so that the Senate may have a clear and exact view of the state of the country, and of its future prospects, and what measures of legislation are required."

In response to this resolution the President might well have communicated to the Senate his views as to the necessity and policy of arming the slaves of the Confederacy as a means of public defense. No answer whatever has been made to the resolution. In addition to this, a joint committee was raised by Congress, under a concurrent resolution adopted in secret session on the 30th of December, 1864. That committee, by the resolution creating it, was instructed, by conference with the President, and by such other means as they shall deem proper, to ascertain what are our reliable means of public defense, present and prospective.

A written report was made by the committee on January 25, 1865, and although it had a conference with the President no allusion is made in the report to any suggestion by him that the necessities of the country required the employment of slaves as soldiers. Under these circumstances Congress, influenced no doubt by the opinion of General Lee, determined for itself the propriety, policy, and necessity of adopting the measure in question. . . .

If loss of time be a vice inherent in deliberative assemblies, promptitude is a great virtue in Executive action. . . .

Nothing is more desirable than concord and cordial co-operation between all departments of Government. Hence, your committee regret the Executive deemed it necessary to transmit to Congress a message so well calculated to excite discord and dissension. But for the fact that the success of the great struggle in which the country is engaged depends as much on the confidence of the people in the Legislative as in the Executive department of the Government the message would have been received without comment. Your committee would have preferred silence. It has been inducive to an opposite course, because they believe Congress would be derelict in its duty to permit its legitimate and constitutional influence to be destroyed by Executive admonitions, such as those contained in the message under consideration, without some public exposition of its conduct.[9]

☞ As the final crisis in the Confederacy's life approached, its Congress adjourned and the members scattered. The Richmond *Whig* and other anti-Davis journals praised the arguments of Senator Orr and the select committee, but the *Sentinel* (March 27, 1865) subjected the Senate document to close and telling scrutiny:

On the adjournment of Congress on Saturday, the 18th inst., the Senate disclosed the action taken by them in secret session on the evening of the preceding Thursday, relative to the important message sent by the President to both Houses on Monday, the 13th.

The report of the Senate Committee, published as adopted by that body, was of such a character, that we felt constrained to decline giving circulation to it in our columns, as requested, until we could ascertain, by reference to the record, the true merits of the controversy raised by that document, and thus present, with it, the materials for impartial judgment of its contents. That task we are now prepared to fulfil; and our readers will accordingly find in this issue the report printed at length.

We premise by saying that the course of the Senate during the past session has impressed the country as most remarkable. It was not such as the people and the States of the Confederacy expected, and had the right to expect, from those whom they had clothed with so high a trust and honored with their confidence . . . [portion illegible]. The paper which they have issued, and which they term a reply to Executive communications, is not confined, however, to a defence of themselves, but is a labored attempt to make the President responsible for that failure to pass the measures necessary for the public safety [? word blurred] of which the public has so justly complained.

The report was adopted, we are informed, without a call for the yeas and nays. This statement, carefully put forth to give additional con-

[9] *Ibid.*, 1,148–1,149, 1,152.

sequence to the Senate's action [? word blurred], has a wholly different effect when properly understood. It is intended to intimate unanimity; it discloses weakness. It is well known that towards the close of the session, the Senate had barely a quorum at its night sessions. This would afford to a few factious men the opportunity of giving to their own irregular action the appearance of formal legislation by shutting themselves up in secret conclave and abstaining from calling [the] yeas and nays, thus putting under a double concealment, the fact that the body was without a quorum. Apart from other good reasons for questioning the presence of a quorum in the night session of the 14th instant—the time when this report was adopted "without a division" —the very fact that the *secrecy of the session* was followed by *publication of its results* is unexplicable, unless there was something in the proceedings which it was deemed politic to hide [? word blurred]. The business was not of a nature to require secrecy. The message under consideration was public; for although delivered to the Senate by mistake in secret session, we have explained in a former issue that the mistake was corrected on the same day, by its delivery to the House in open session, and by its publication in the city papers before the action of the Senate, or of its Committee. What could there have been to conceal, unless it were the fact that a few senators, less than a quorum, were assuming to act in the name of the body?

The report of the Senate Committee is not simply uncandid in its statements and unfair in its reasoning. It is so full of assertions at war with notorious fact, that it is difficult to conceive how it could have been duly considered by those who bear its responsibility. It is with no pleasure that we address ourselves to the duty of exposing it—a duty imposed on us by our position as public journalists.

The first misstatement of the report is the attempt to impute the delay in organizing and disciplining the negroes, so as to prepare them for service as soldiers, to the absence of Executive recommendation. With this view, detached sentences are picked out of the [President's] message of November last, and the true issue is carefully avoided by the dexterous use of language well calculated to mislead on cursory perusal. Early in November, before the disasters in Tennessee or the fall of Savannah, or Charleston or Wilmington; before the devastation of Georgia and the Carolinas; the President stated in his message:

"*Until* our white population shall prove insufficient for the armies we require and can afford to keep in the field, to employ as a soldier the negro who has merely been trained to labor, and as a laborer the white man accustomed from his youth to the use of fire arms, would scarcely be deemed wise or advantageous by any; and this is the question *now* before us. But should the alternative ever be presented of subjugation or of the employment of the slave as a soldier, there seems no reason to doubt what should then be our decision." The message after further observation on this point, thus concludes on this subject: "If the recommendation above made, for the training of forty thousand negroes for the service indicated, shall meet your approval, it is certain that even this limited number, by their preparatory training in intermediate duties, would form a more valuable reserve force, in case of urgency, than threefold their number suddenly called from field labor; while a fresh levy could, to a certain extent, supply their places in the special service for which they are now employed."

For the recommendations of this message, the President was for three months constantly denounced by opponents in both Houses, as proposing to grant freedom to negroes to be employed in preparatory military service with the view to arming them for our defence when necessary. Nobody mistook, or could mistake the message. It said substantially, that legislation was needed to put more *white men* in the field, and recommended several measures for that end; that "*until* our white population should prove insufficient," it would be bad policy to arm the negro, and put the white man to labor as an agriculturist; but that it would be wise to prepare 40,000 negroes for service in case of need, by giving them their freedom and training them in other army duties, so as to habituate them to organization and discipline. The Senate did not give the white men asked for; neither passing a militia law, nor revoking class exemptions; and after having positively refused the latter, and having failed to act on the former for four full precious months from early in November to early in March, were on the eve of adjournment at the time the President's last message was sent in. Nor was *any* law passed about employing negroes as cooks, teamsters, engineer or pioneer laborers till the 28th of February, nearly four months after the meeting of Congress. Yet in the face of these *recorded facts,* the report of the Senate's committee broadly avers that "the Senate did not await the tardy movements of the President,'' and that ''Congress might well have delayed action on this subject until the present moment as the President whose constitutional duty it is to give to Congress information of the state of the Confederacy has never asked in any authentic manner for the passage of a law authorizing the employment of slaves as soldiers.''

But what are we to think of the assertion of the report, that ''the recommendation of the President to employ forty thousand slaves as cooks, teamsters, and as engineer and pioneer laborers, was assented to, and a law has been enacted at the present session for the purpose without limit as to number?''

The President stated his opinion that there ''should be a radical modification of the theory of the law'' about impressing slaves—that the Government should acquire the entire property, instead of impressing labor for short terms; and that the slave thus acquired by the Government should be freed as a reward for faithful service. *All this was positively refused by the Senate.* They passed a law the exact reverse of this system, and provided that the slave should remain the property of the private owner; that his wages should go to the owner, the slave receiving no pay, nor his freedom, nor any promise of reward for faithful service—nothing beyond his rations and clothes.

The report discloses some remarkable facts concerning the mode in which the relations of the Senate to the Executive have been conducted. It makes constant reference to secret action of the Senate, now revealed for use in assaulting the President in a manner which renders defence on his part utterly impossible. Thus the report refers to two secret resolutions; one, separate, passed in the Senate on the 29th December, and practically superseded by the other—a concurrent resolution of both Houses on the next day, appointing a joint Committee of Conference with the President upon substantially the same subject as embraced in the separate resolution. After inquiry from the best source, we learn that this conference was verbal; yet the report shows that it was made the subject of a written report in *secret session* on the 25th [of] January, was never seen by the President, who still remains ignorant of what he is represented to have said; yet, this *secret report* is made the basis two months later for *another secret report* charging the Executive with want of diligence in duty; and this *second secret report* is published after the adjournment, thus depriving him of any opportunity for official reply! A course less calculated to gain the public approval, it is difficult to conceive!

. . . If in our review of this paper we have spoken with some freedom, it has not been unwittingly. For the gentlemen of the Senate who have honestly and diligently labored for the good of their country during a session the most important that could occur in the lifetime of a nation, we have warm respect, and regard, and gratitude; and to this class belong some who have given their names to this report, under what influence it is, perhaps, bootless to inquire. But the country should know that there are men in the Senate who sometimes succeed in influencing its proceedings, and whose course during the past session was violent and factious beyond all precedent in our history, and who seemed oblivious of everything but how to whelm the President. Nor have these been so dangerous as others less prominent, who, under specious seemings, have pursued the same ends. We trust the Senate will meet in fuller body when it meets again, and that it may be our grateful pleasure in the future, as it has been in the past, to record a course of proceeding in harmony with the popular heart, animating to the public zeal, and responsive to the public necessities.

☞ Davis cared deeply about the issues at stake between him and the Confederate senators. That fact is indicated by a letter he wrote to an old friend, Mrs. Howell Cobb:

Accept my thanks for your kind consideration in sending me several newspapers with articles of interest in them.

Faction has done much to cloud our prospects and impair my power to serve the country. That such was not their purpose I am well assured and if we may be permitted to hope that when they see that the indulgence of evil passion against myself injures not the individual only but the cause also of which I am a zealous though feeble representative, the discovery will lead to a change of conduct and an earnest effort to repair the mischief done it may be in the end be [sic] well for us.

Near the close of the Session of Congress after the recommendations of my annual Message had been debated for four months without result, I sent as was my duty a message pointing out the necessitous condition of the country and urging legislation before adjournment. My style was not intended to provoke controversy and does not seem to me to have been wanting in decorum and deference. The Senate however took offence and in secret session appointed a committee to reply to the Message; after their adjournment it was published, and if not intended to destroy the confidence of the people in me, is certainly calculated to have that effect. No opportunity was afforded to me to reply and correct the many mis-statements of the report.

I send you a paper [the Richmond *Sentinel?*] containing an editorial which answers the main points of the report, by citations of the official record. Whether truth can overtake falsehood has always been doubtful, and in this case the race is most unequal, as many are interested in spreading statements for which they have hastily made themselves responsible, and the demand of the public taste for spicy articles will render it more to the interest of publishers to copy the assault than the defence.[10]

☞ Shortly before he wrote to Mrs. Cobb, Davis revealed in another letter, to J. D. Shaw of Greenwood, Mississippi, that he had virtually abandoned hope of Anglo-French recognition, even though he had not yet learned of the final failure of the Kenner mission:

A pressure of business has prevented me from replying sooner to your letter of September last. Your proposition, in regard to negotiating with European Powers respecting the slavery question, has been attentively considered. There would be difficulty, however, in carrying it into effect. In the first place, the Confederate Government can make no agreement nor arrangement with any Nation, which would interfere with State institutions, and if foreign Governments would consent to interpose in our behalf upon the conditions stated, it would be necessary to submit the terms to the different States of the Confederacy for their separate action.

It cannot be doubted that the obstacle to the recognition of the Confederacy has been an unwillingness to be embroiled in a quarrel with the United States. If slavery or any other cause had been the impediment, our advances to European Governments would have led to the disclosure of their reasons for not acknowledging our independence. As soon as these Governments are willing to negotiate with us upon

[10] Jefferson Davis to Mrs. Howell Cobb, March 30, 1865, in Dunbar Rowland (ed.), *Jefferson Davis, Constitutionalist: His Letters, Papers, and Speeches* (10 vols.; Jackson, Miss., 1923), VI, 524–25.

terms to which we can honorably accede, the declaration of their conditions will probably be made known to our Commissioners, so that the terms proposed may be submitted to the people, States and Government of the Confederacy.[11]

☛ Jefferson Davis may well have come to hope for nothing so far as Britain and France were concerned. He and General Lee, as well as numerous lesser Confederate leaders, gave every indication however, that they had real hopes pinned on the Confederate Negroes.

[11] Davis to J. D. Shaw of Greenwood, Mississippi, March 22, 1865, *ibid.*, 518–19. For James M. Mason's account of his futile interview with Lord Palmerston about Kenner's mission, see Mason to Judah P. Benjamin, March 31, 1865, *O.R.N.*, Series II, Vol. III, 1,270–1,276.

CHAPTER IX

Confederate Blacks and
Bootlegged Freedom

⚔ ALTHOUGH BOTH THE CONFEDERATE CONGRESS and the Virginia legislature had steered clear of any legal promise of emancipation,
Jefferson Davis and the War Department bootlegged freedom
into the plan when they promulgated the new policy. They did
this simply by adding their own regulations, printed beneath the
new Confederate law, for the fourth and ninth sections made
clear that no slave would be asked to fight for the Confederacy as
a slave:

> Adjt. and Insp. General's Office
> Richmond, Va., March 23, 1865.

General Orders, No. 14.

I. The following act of Congress and regulations are published for the
information and direction of all concerned: [Act printed above on pp.
202–203 follows]

II. The recruiting service under this act will be conducted under
the supervision of the Adjutant and Inspector General, according to
the regulations for the recruiting service of the Regular Army, in so
far as they are applicable, and except when special directions may be
given by the War Department.

III. There will be assigned or appointed for each State an officer
who will be charged with the collection, enrollment, and disposition of
all the recruits that may be obtained under the first section of this act.
One or more general depots will be established in each State and announced in orders, and a suitable number of officers will be detailed
for duty in the staff departments at the depots. There will be assigned
at each general depot a quartermaster, commissary, and surgeon, and

the headquarters of the superintendent will be at the principal depot in the State. The proper officers to aid the superintendent in enlisting, mustering, and organizing the recruits will be assigned by orders from this office or by the General-in-Chief.

IV. The enlistment of colored persons under this act will be made upon printed forms. . . . No slave will be accepted as a recruit unless with his own consent and with the approbation of his master by a written instrument conferring, as far as he may, the rights of a freedman, and which will be filed with the superintendent. The enlistments will be made for the war, and the effect of the enlistment will be to place the slave in the military service conformably to this act. The recruits will be organized at the camps in squads and companies, and will be subject to the orders of the General-in-Chief under the second section of this act.

V. The superintendent in each State will cause a report to be made on the first Monday of every month. . . .

VI. The appointment of officers to the companies to be formed of the recruits aforesaid will be made by the President.

VII. To facilitate the raising of volunteer companies, officers recruiting therefor are authorized to muster their men into service as soon as enrolled. As soon as enrolled and mustered, the men will be sent, with descriptive lists, to the depots of rendezvous, at which they will be instructed until assigned for service in the field. . . .

VIII. It is not the intention of the President to grant any authority for raising regiments or brigades. . . .

IX. All officers who may be employed in the recruiting service, under the provisions of this act, or who may be appointed to the command of troops raised under it, or who may hold any staff appointment in connection with them, are enjoined to a provident, considerate, and humane attention to whatever concerns the health, comfort, instruction, and discipline of those troops, and to the uniform observance of kindness, forbearance, and indulgence in their treatment of them, and especially that they will protect them from injustice and oppression.

By order:

S. Cooper,
Adjutant and Inspector General.[1]

[1] *O.R.*, Series IV, Vol. III, 1,161–1,162.

🖙 Clearly it was this promise of freedom, more or less smuggled in though it had been, that accounted for the fact that there were Negroes ready to fight for the Confederacy even at that stage of the war. Even while the matter was being discussed and the blacks' hopes for freedom being raised, a surgeon in charge of a military hospital reported a sampling that no doubt encouraged the Confederate leadership:

For my own gratification, as well as those who are taking great interest in the important question, with regard to the using of the slaves of the Confederacy as an assisting element to us in defending our homes, firesides, and country from those who would destroy us, I would respectfully say that this morning I caused the hired male slaves at this hospital to be convened, and after asking them the deliberate question, if they would be willing to take up arms to protect their masters' families, homes, and their own from an attacking foe, sixty out of seventy-two responded they would volunteer to go to the trenches and fight the enemy to the bitter end.[2]

🖙 The Confederate War Department on March 15, 1865, authorized Majors J. W. Pegram and Thomas P. Turner "to raise a Company or Companies of Negro Soldiers" under the act of March 13. Pegram and Thomas energetically tackled their task and published this notice in the Richmond newspapers (*Dispatch*, March 21, 1865):

COLORED TROOPS
AN APPEAL TO THE PEOPLE OF VIRGINIA.

It will be seen by the Order of the Secretary of War, published above, that the undersigned have been authorized to proceed at once with the organization of Companies composed of persons of Color, free and slave, who are willing to volunteer under the recent acts of Congress

---

[2] F. W. Hancock to R. S. Ewell, *ibid.*, 1,193. The *Examiner* (February 15, 1865) reported it had learned that "quite a military fever had broken out among negroes employed at the various hospitals here, and that they are already organizing volunteer companies to take the field against the Yankees. Several hundred of them have professed an anxiety to volunteer." Apparently some of these were the Negroes referred to in the *Dispatch* stories (March 22 and 23, 1865) about two black companies from the hospitals, but not in the regular Confederate army, who "were on the lines during the recent raids." Brewer, *The Confederate Negro*, 102–103, also mentions this.

and the Legislature of Virginia. It is well known to the country that Gen. Lee has evinced the deepest interest on this subject, and that he regards prompt action in this matter as vitally important to the country. In a letter addressed by him to Lt. Gen. Ewell, dated March 10th, he says, "I hope it will be found practicable to raise a considerable force in Richmond. . . . I attach great importance to the result of the first experiment, and nothing should be left undone to make it successful. The sooner this can be accomplished the better."

The undersigned have established a rendezvous on 21st, between Main and Cary streets, at the building known as "Smith's Factory"; and every arrangement has been made to secure the comfort of the new recruits, and to prepare them for service. It is recommended that each recruit be furnished, when practicable, with a grey jacket and pants, cap and blanket, and a good serviceable pair of shoes, but no delay should take place in forwarding the recruits in order to obtain these articles.

The governments, Confederate and State, having settled the policy of employing this element of strength, and this class of our population having given repeated evidence of their willingness to take up arms in the defence of their homes, it is believed that it is only necessary to put the matter before them in a proper light to cause them to rally with enthusiasm for the preservation of the homes in which they have been born and raised, and in which they have found contentment and happiness; and to save themselves and their race from the barbarous cruelty invariably practised upon them by a perfidious enemy claiming to be their friends.

Will not the people of Virginia, in this hour of peril and danger, promptly respond to the call of our loved General-in-Chief, and the demands of the Confederate and State governments?

Will those who have freely given their sons and brothers, their money and their property, to the achievement of the liberties of their country, now hold back from the cause their servants, who can well be spared, and who will gladly aid in bringing this fearful war to a speedy and glorious termination!

Let every man in the State consider himself a recruiting officer, and enter at once upon the duty of aiding in the organization of this force, by sending forward recruits to this rendezvous.

Every consideration of patriotism, the independence of our country, the safety of our homes, the happiness of our families, and the sanctity of our firesides, all prompt to immediate and energetic action for the defence of the country. Let the people but be true to themselves, and to the claims of duty, and our independence will be speedily secured, and peace be restored within our borders.

🖘 There were Tarheels too, unlike Senator Graham and his friends, who pinned desperate hopes on the new law. The Raleigh *Confederate* (March 22, 1865) emphasized the voluntary nature of the experiment:

. . . In a few days steps will be taken to commence the enrollment in North Carolina, and it is well to let the negroes know the terms upon which they will enter the service.

There will be no force employed to compel them to serve.

Their enlistment will be voluntary, with their own, and the consent of their master.

Free negroes will be received who choose to volunteer.

The boon will be freedom and a home among those with whom they have been raised—*a home of their own.*

An opportunity is now offered to the negro of serving his country, of establishing for himself a property and a home, of earning freedom, and winning the good opinion of mankind.

Gen. Lee has, long ago, announced that he looks to the negro as an element of strength that will enable him to resist all the efforts of the invader. He gives to this class his confidence, and tells them ''I will trust you—I will rely upon you—I will lead you in battle, and I expect that your courage, your fidelity, your love of country, and your love of home, will make you good soldiers, who will fight to win the boon of freedom.''

We hope the masters, in this State, will begin to explain this matter to their slaves, and put the choice to them freely, to say whether they will volunteer. Let no time be lost, they are needed now, great events are about to be accomplished.

🖘 Although the new law was destined to have only a brief time in which to be tried, scattered indications suggested that there were indeed slaveholders willing to break with the past and smash the cornerstone (Raleigh *Confederate,* March 31, 1865) :

The Lynchburg *Virginian* says, that the people of the Roanoke are responding nobly to the action of Congress and the call of Gen. Lee, for negro troops. Some thirty of the largest slave-holders, living at and near Salem, Va., headed by Nathaniel Burwell, Esq., who has fifty negroes of the military age, have joined in a paper tendering their negroes to the Government, and pledging freedom to them as a condition of their services, and employment at fair wages to all who may return after the war. This paper is being numerously signed, and the *Virginian* thinks there is a prospect of receiving large accessions to our army from that quarter.

The following is the pledge referred to:

"We whose names are herewith subscribed, mutually pledge ourselves to emancipate such of our negro men, between the ages of 18 and 45, as will volunteer as soldiers in the Confederate service; promising them that they will be permitted to return to their homes, and that proper provisions will be made for them and their families, when the war is over."

This is going the right way to work, and we hope that the slave-holders of this State will at once begin to move in this very important matter.

☞ Even in Georgia, which now received only delayed and often garbled reports, the Macon *Telegraph and Confederate* (April 15, 1865) hoped that Confederate Negroes would be forthcoming:

Negroes are now [being] enlisted, in several of the largest cities, for service in the Confederate army. Is it not time Macon, and this section of country, should be moving in this matter?

Private James B. Nelson, formerly of the 16th Georgia Battalion, but who has been a prisoner for sixteen months, is desirous of forming a company of negroes under the recent act of Congress. Those desirous of furnishing recruits can obtain any further information they desire at the store of W. T. Nelson, on Cherry street.

☞ General Cleburne did not live to see the Confederacy adopt the diluted version of his proposal that had so stirred up a few top Confederate leaders early in 1864. Late in the same year he was killed in the Confederate disaster at Franklin, Tennessee. Perhaps some of his ideas lived on among certain of his men, for one of them in Georgia, a Captain Thomas J. Azy (? last name blurred), echoed the brave Cleburne's phrases (Macon *Telegraph and Confederate,* April 17, 1865) :

Having served for four years as an artillerist with the gallant Gen. Cleburne, and owing to the severe campaign of the last twelve months, my command has been so greatly reduced in numbers, that I was assigned to the defenses of Macon, until my men could rest and recruit; and as I am desirous to do all I can for my country, I propose while performing the duties now imposed upon me, to receive, organize, drill, and discipline a battalion of negroes for artillery service.

The patriotic Virginians are nobly responding to the call of that illustrious Chieftain Gen'l Lee, and, we hope every planter in the South will show himself equally as magnanimous in, and as devoted to the cause of independence as those Virginians. Let them follow the Old Dominion's example, and independence, and peace will inevitably follow, and ere long happiness and plenty will bless our lovely South. Farmers, come forward at once and tender your able-bodied and most intelligent negroes to the Government, and by so doing, you will keep them from falling into the hands of the enemy, who will use them for you own destruction. Better give up half your negroes to defend your homes than let them all fall into the clutches of the North, to be used as spies, and guides, and to aid in your utter ruin. It is desired that the owners shall pledge themselves to emancipate such negroes as will volunteer in the Confederate service, promising them after we shall gain our independence, and they should desire to return to their old homes, that proper provisions will be made for them and their families, and fair wages given.

If 300 or 400 negroes shall be raised for this battalion, I propose to take my present command as officers and non-commissioned officers to control, drill and discipline said negroes. My command is composed of veterans who have made the enemy feel their vigorous blows on almost every battle field from Shiloh to Nashville. . . .

☞ Understandably enough, the recruitment of Confederate Negroes actually proceeded farthest in Richmond. A reporter for the *Examiner* (March 27, 1865) suggested the progress that was being made:

THE COMPANY OF NEGROES recruiting at the rendezvous for negro troops, corner of Cary and Twenty-first streets, is increasing in numbers daily under the energy displayed by Major Turner. The company now numbers thirty-five members, all uniformed and equipped. They are drilled daily for several hours by Lieutenant Virginius Bossieux, whose talent peculiarly adapts him to imparting instructions in the manual. About a dozen of the recruits are free negroes, who have enlisted of their own free will and choice. Recruits are coming in by ones and twos every day, and the negroes, being permitted to go out among their friends, are very good recruiting officers. We witnessed a drill of the company on Saturday afternoon, and the knowledge of the military art they already exhibit was something remarkable. They moved with evident pride and satisfaction to themselves. Their quarters in the rendezvous are neat, clean, warm and comfortable. Their rations are cooked at the Libby prison.

Major Turner hopes to recruit and equip a command of eighty or an hundred in a few weeks, and treat the citizens to a publick exhibition of their proficiency in the drill before turning them over to General Lee. Meanwhile, the owners of slaves have a duty to perform in sending forward recruits and infusing a spirit of emulation among the negroes. Let all hands go to work with energy.

☞   The *Examiner*'s reporter was corroborated by a story in the *Dispatch* (March 25, 1865) :

THE CAUSE PROGRESSING—Daily accessions are made to Major Turner's negro troops, now being drilled and organized at Smith's factory, on the corner of Twenty-first and Cary streets, by Lieutenant Virginius Bossieux. At 5 o'clock yesterday afternoon we witnessed a drill at their barracks, and have no hesitation in saying that, for the time they have been at it, as much aptness and proficiency was displayed as is usually shown by any white troops we have ever seen. . . .

☞   In case there were slaveowners whose pocket-nerves were more sensitive than their ties with the Confederacy, an advertisement addressed to them appeared in the Richmond papers (*Dispatch*, March 25, 1865) :

A gentleman, a refugee, has placed at the disposal of reliable parties in this city a large sum of money, to be expended in the purchase of slaves who will voluntarily enlist in the army. The manumission papers of the slaves so purchased will be placed in proper hands, to be delivered when they have performed meritorious services or been honorably discharged. It is hoped that patriotic masters will (if they cannot afford to manumit and offer their slaves as a free gift to the army) send them forward, and dispose of them at reduced prices, for the purpose of having them enter the military service of the country. Gentlemen in the country can direct their letters to "Major Turner, commanding rendezvous for recruiting colored troops, Richmond, Virginia." Any number of negroes for sale on reasonable terms can be disposed of readily if sent to this city.

☞ As some Southerners attempted to change not only their attitudes but also certain long-standing laws and customs concerning Negroes, there were ambiguities and occasional mix-ups. The *Whig* (March 31, 1865) sarcastically reported one such case:

Two negro soldiers, Ned, slave of J. H. Harwood, and Bob, slave of Thos. Edmonds, found their way into the criminal's box, this morning, having been arrested by the officers for having no pass, and for being supposed runaways. The Mayor returned them to the charge of Capt. Bossieux.

In regard to these negro soldiers there should be some definite understanding. Being soldiers to all intents and purposes, they should be furnished with passes, so as to walk the streets, if necessary, unmolested, and not be liable to arrest as runaways. Otherwise, the Mayor will be over head and ears in business of this nature, and the court-room will be crowded daily with detachments of the various black companies now in process of formation.—Sambo is going through the crucible at present, and it is hard to invest him with military attributes.—After awhile, however, we suppose that some system will be inaugurated whereby those black sons of Mars, who carry the musket and "follow the drum to Macedon," will be relieved of the supposition of being runaways—at least upon the city streets, if not upon the tented field.

☞ As the recruitment of the blacks progressed in the capital, President Davis and General Lee, although disappointed by the cautious legislation that had been enacted, continued to pin their hopes on the experiment, even though both leaders ruefully admitted that time was running out. Lee, even before the President had received the measure from Congress, suggested in a letter to Davis the urgency that he felt.

I do not know whether the law authorising the use of negro troops has received your sanction, but if it has, I respectfully recommend that measures be taken to carry it into effect as soon as practicable.

It will probably be impossible to get a large force of this kind in condition to be of service during the present campaign, but I think no time should be lost in trying to collect all we can. I attach great importance to the result of the first experiment with these troops, and think that if it prove successful, it will greatly lessen the difficulty of putting the law into operation.

I understand that the Governor of Virginia is prepared to do all that may be required of him under the authority he possesses. I hope it will be found practicable to raise some negro companies in Richmond, and have written to Genl Ewell to do all in his power to get them, as soon as he shall be informed in what manner to proceed. In the beginning it would be well to do everything to make the enlistment entirely voluntary on the part of the negroes, and those owners who are willing to furnish some of their slaves for the purpose, can do a great deal to inspire them with the right feeling to prepare them to become soldiers, and to be satisfied with their new condition. I have received letters from persons offering to select the most suitable among their slaves, as soon as Congress should give the authority, and think that a considerable number would be forthcoming for the purpose if called for.

I hope that if you have approved the law, you will cause the necessary steps to carry it into effect to be taken as soon as possible.[3]

☞ Although Lee, as much as the President, had emphasized the voluntary feature of the experiment, by March 24, 1865, he urged that Davis call upon Virginia for "the whole number of negroes" that could be obtained under the recent law:

I have the honor to ask that you will call upon the governor of the State of Virginia for the whole number of negroes, slave and free, between the ages of eighteen and forty-five, for services as soldiers au-

---

[3] Robert E. Lee to Jefferson Davis, March 10, 1865, in Dowdey and Manarin (eds.), *The Wartime Papers of R. E. Lee*, 914.

thorized by the joint resolution adopted by the Senate and House of Delegates of the State [of Virginia] on the 4th of March. The services of these men are now necessary to enable us to oppose the enemy.[4]

🖝 In his letter to Governor Smith of Virginia, President Davis made clear his continued preference for the voluntary approach:

Herewith I transmit the requisition made by General Lee in accordance with the suggestion I lately received from you. He informs me that it would have been made sooner if he had known that action on his part was waited for. He had previously written to you, but I infer, from the fact that you did not mention his letter, that it had failed to reach you. You have probably noticed that the order issued from the Adjutant-General's Office for the organization of colored troops looks only to the acceptance of volunteers, and, in a letter received this evening from General Lee he expresses the opinion that there should be compulsory enlistment in the first instance. My idea has been that we should draw into our military service that portion of the negroes which would be most apt to run away and join the army of the enemy, and that this would be best effected by seeking volunteers for our own army. If this plan should fail to obtain the requisite number there will still remain the process of compulsory enlistment.[5]

🖝 Governor Smith, in replying to the President, emphatically stated his own strong desire for emancipation of the Confederate Negroes, as well as his intention to push the Virginia legislature in the matter:

I received yours of the 25th covering Genl Lee's in reference to the raising of negro troops, and intended to call and see you the evening of its receipt, but was prevented by my company from so doing.

I had rec'd a letter from Gen. Lee, a few days previous, in reference to the same subject, calling for information as to the probable number that might be expected from the State. I replied to it as soon as the information could be obtained from the State Auditor, and he has doubtless received my letter. I suppose three or four thousand free negroes and four or five thousand slaves may be raised in Virginia.

Permit me to suggest that the new regulations just published are

[4] *O.R.*, Series I, Vol. XLVI, Pt. 3, p. 1,339.
[5] Jefferson Davis to William Smith, March 25, 1865, *ibid.*, 1,348–1,349.

not as well calculated to advance the object of embodying [*i.e.*, enlisting] the negroes as might be. In every village in Virginia we now have, I may say, a post organization. Why not assign to the officers at these places, such necessary duties as the service requires. Without a new officer, except those connected with the duty of getting the negroes into companies, every necessary duty might be performed by those already at posts. As fast as companies might be organized, they should be moved to the front and there be thoroughly organized and drilled. Why then the necessity of large depots, one or more? It seems to me that this policy of assembling the negroes in large numbers under any new organization will be unnecessarily expensive and is certain to produce complaint and dissatisfaction. I would advise a liberal use of gentlemen in the country, who are willing to engage in raising companies or battalions, with a promise, where required, that they shall have command of such force as they may raise, upon proof of fitness and competency. I am clear that the freedom of the slave should be secured to him when enrolled, at which time he should also be promised permission to remain at home, after the war, or when he shall obtain an honorable discharge.

As soon as the Legislature reassembles, which will be on Wednesday [March 29], I propose to submit a proposition distinctly providing for manumission of the slaves put into the army by purchase or otherwise, and, although the State is fully committed thereto already, to obtain a distinct pledge that the Slave, upon his honorable discharge, shall be permitted to live at home. This will involve the repeal of some existing laws; all of which I have no doubt will receive the favorable consideration of the Assembly.

I think the indications in the State are favorable, but I deem it all important that the simplest (which would be the cheapest) mode of collecting the negroes should be adopted. I think it particularly desirable to avoid all new post or depot officers and all collection of negroes in large numbers.

N. B. Do you wish me to issue my requisition for the slaves authorized by our statute at this time? I concur with Gen'l Lee that it would be better to forbear action at present.[6]

---

[6] Smith to Davis, March 27, 1865, in Jefferson Davis Papers, Perkins Library, Duke University, Durham.

☞ Jefferson Davis promptly informed Smith that steps had been taken to meet the objections that the governor had raised about procedures being followed with the Negroes:

Upon the receipt of your letter of the 27th instant, I had a conference with the Secretary of War and Adjutant-General, in relation to your suggestions as to the published order for the organization of negro troops, and I hope that the modifications which have been made will remove the objections which you pointed out. It was never my intention to collect the negroes in depots for the purposes of instruction, but only as the best mode of forwarding them, either as individuals or as companies, to the commands with which they were to serve. The officers at the different posts will aid in providing for the negroes in their respective neighborhoods, and in forwarding them to depots where transportation will be available to aid them in reaching the fields of service for which they are destined. The aid of gentlemen who are willing and able to raise this character of troops will be freely accepted. The appointment of commanders, for reasons obvious to you, must depend on other considerations than the mere power to recruit.

I am happy to receive your assurance of success, as well as your promise to seek legislation to secure unmistakable freedom to the slave who shall enter the Army, with a right to return to his old home, when he shall have been honorably discharged from military service.

I remain of the opinion that we should confine our first efforts to getting volunteers, and would prefer that you would adopt such measures as would advance that mode of recruiting, rather than that concerning which you make inquiry, to wit, by issuing a requisition for the slaves as authorized by the statutes of Virginia.[7]

☞ The President, increasingly worried about the possibility of Richmond's falling to the enemy, informed Lee that he was circularizing the governors for their aid in securing "liberal provisions" for the Negroes who would volunteer to don the gray uniforms:

I have been laboring, without much progress, to advance the raising of negro troops. You must judge how far you can consistently detach officers to recruit. I called for the recommendations made by you, and so few names were presented that I infer you do not find it desirable

[7] Davis to Smith, March 30, 1865, *O.R.*, Series I, Vol. XLVI, Pt. 3, 1,366–1,367.

to rely on officers sent to recruit for their own commands; therefore [I] have directed that orders be given to the commanders of Reserves in the several States to employ their officers to recruit negroes. If there be an officer or soldier to whose command the masters would prefer to intrust, and the slaves would prefer to go, he can be appointed when the company or battalion reaches its destination. I have prepared a circular letter to the governors of the States invoking their aid, as well by appeals to the owners as by recommendations to the legislatures, to make the most liberal provisions for those who volunteer to fight for the safety and independence of the State.

I have asked often, but without satisfactory reply, how many of the exchanged prisoners have joined the Army. Your force should have been increased from that source 8,000 or 10,000 men. The desire to confer with you would have caused me to go to Petersburg before this date but for the pressure which recent events have put upon me, and the operations in your vicinity prevented me from inviting you to come here.

To-day the Secretary of War presents propositions from the proprietors of the Tredegar Works which impress me very unfavorably. We will endeavor to keep them at work, though it must be on a reduced scale. There is also a difficulty in getting iron, even for shot and shell, but hope this may, for the present, be overcome by taking some from the navy, which, under the altered circumstances, may be spared. Last night we had rumors of a general engagement on your right. Your silence in regard to it leads to the conclusion that it was unwarranted. . . .

The question is often asked of me "Will we hold Richmond?" to which my only answer is, "If we can; it is purely a question of military power." The distrust is increasing, and embarrasses in many ways.[8]

~ For his part, Robert E. Lee obviously had less and less time even to think of the matter as Grant's forces began to push forward. Yet Lee informed Secretary of War Breckinridge of the practical, immediate steps that he was taking:

I have been awaiting the receipt of the orders from the Department for raising and organizing the colored troops before taking any action

[8] Davis to Robert E. Lee, April 1, 1865, *ibid.*, 1,370.

in the matter. I understand that orders have been published in the newspapers but have not seen them. In the meantime I have been informed that a number of recruits may be obtained in Petersburg, if suitable persons be employed to get them to enlist. Captain Cameron, assistant adjutant-general, Weisiger's brigade, and Private Stephen H. Britton, Second Company Washington Artillery, both citizens of Petersburg, have been recommended as the best persons to be employed for this purpose. Captain Cameron is willing to do all he can to raise the troops, though he does not desire a commission. I have not heard from Britton. As time is important I have ordered Captain Cameron to be assigned to that duty, and will also order Britton if he is not averse to it. I also propose to send Lieutenant Alexander, of the Virginia battalion, now acting as provost guard, to his residence in Mecklenburg County on the same duty. He has good reason to believe he can raise some men. I respectfully ask that these measures be approved by the Department, if not contrary to any of its regulations. I think it will be nearly useless, in the present temper of our people, to send recruiting officers to districts where they are not known, and where they have no personal influence or connections favorable to the new measure. The enemies of the system will do all they can to thwart their efforts, and will deprive their appeals to the people in a great measure of effect by representing that the officers are only seeking to raise commands for themselves. As far as practicable, men should be selected for this business who are known in the communities to which they are sent and have influential connections.[9]

☞ The last letter that Lee wrote to the President from Petersburg, on April 2, 1865—as the harrassed general-in-chief was constantly sending and receiving dispatches and couriers—discussed the recruiting of Negro troops and Lee's pleasure in the news that the President was appealing to all the governors:

Your letter of the 1st is just received. I have been willing to detach officers to recruit negro troops, and have sent in the names of many who are desirous of recruiting companies, battalions, or regiments to the War Department. After receiving the General Orders on that subject, establishing recruiting depots in the several States, I supposed that this mode of raising the troops was preferred. I will continue to

[9] Lee to John C. Breckinridge, March 27, 1865, *ibid.*, 1,356–1,357.

submit the names of those who offer for the service, and whom I deem competent, to the War Department; but among the numerous applications which are presented, it is difficult for me to decide who are suitable for the duty. I am glad Your Excellency has made an appeal to the Governors of the States, and hope it will have a good effect. I have had a great desire to confer with you upon our condition, and would have been to Richmond before this; but anticipating movements of the enemy, which have occurred, I felt unwilling to be absent. I have considered our position very critical, but have hoped that the enemy might expose himself in some way that we might take advantage of, and cripple him.

. . . I do not see how I can possibly help withdrawing from the city [Petersburg] to the north side of the Appomattox tonight. . . . I regret to be obliged to write such a hurried letter to Your Excellency, but I am in the presence of the enemy endeavoring to resist his advance.[10]

☞ On the same day, Lee sent the telegrams informing Davis that Richmond would have to be evacuated:

I think it is absolutely necessary that we should abandon our position tonight. I have given all the necessary orders on the subject to the troops, and the operation, though difficult, I hope will be performed successfully. I have directed General Stevens to send an officer to Your Excellency to explain the routes to you by which the troops will be moved to Amelia Court House, and furnish you with a guide and any assistance that you may require for yourself.[11]

☞ General Lee and the Army of Northern Virginia were on the road to Appomattox. Time had run out for the Confederacy.

[10] Lee to Jefferson Davis, April 2, 1865, in Dowdey and Manarin (eds.), *The Wartime Papers of R. E. Lee*, 927–928.
[11] Lee to Davis, April 2, 1865, telegram, *ibid.*, 925–926.

CHAPTER X

On the
Confederacy's Tombstone:
"Died of a Theory"

⚡ THE SOUTH HAD, despite all its misgivings and inhibitions, turned
to its Negroes at the last. But it had waited too late. Why did
the Confederacy, even as it watched Lincoln reap rich advantages
from his policy of emancipating and recruiting the blacks, fail
to achieve an effective and timely change in its own policy?
Surely the answers are many and complex, but two will be
hazarded here.

First, by late 1864 when southern leaders, or at least some of
them, faced up to the matter, the war had reached a cruel, grind-
ing stage; and some men who opposed the arming, not to speak
of the freeing, of the slaves obviously opposed, perhaps subcon-
sciously in certain cases, a continuation of the bloody ordeal. The
Richmond *Whig* (March 3, 1865), itself a belated convert to the
experiment, noted this fact before the Barksdale measure was
finally enacted:

A few days ago the Raleigh *Conservative* took occasion to dissent from
the opinion of the *Whig* that a majority of the people of the South
had come to a conclusion favorable to the employment of negroes as
soldiers in the army. Or rather, the *Conservative* applies its dissent
to the people of North Carolina, whom it declares to be generally opposed to the measure. The Goldsboro [N. C.] *State Journal,* on the contrary, supports the views of the *Whig,* even to the extent of asserting
that public opinion in North Carolina, so far from being hostile to, is
decidedly favorable to the project. That paper says, ''Our belief is,
founded upon a pretty general intercourse with the people of North
Carolina, particularly of this [eastern] section of the State, that the

Whig's statement is correct. The only men we encounter opposed to the measure, are those who have steadily opposed every act of the Government and Congress tending to a vigorous prosecution of the war. The men who opposed all the conscription acts, because they preferred submission to a manly effort for independence, now oppose the arming of the negro for the same reason.''

It is undoubtedly true that those who have cherished a latent opposition to our struggle for independence, those who have become hopeless of the cause and wish to abandon it, are opposed to this measure. They very naturally argue against the employment of any means that may contribute to prolong our resistance, or assure our success. Of course they do not rest their opposition on these grounds, because it would then be deprived of any efficacy; but they eagerly seize upon the objections which have been urged against the experiment, and which, though at first entertained by almost all of our people, have at last been abandoned by a large proportion of them. It is a noticeable fact that the very persons who, influenced by this latent hostility to our cause, have taken up and warmly press these otherwise rapidly failing objections, are the very persons who, with the same motives, in the earlier stages of the war, urged as an objection against the Confederate authorities that they did not adopt this very expedient. It was speciously argued to be an evidence of the intrinsic weakness of our system that we did not venture to avail ourselves of the resources offered by a numerous class of our population. Nevertheless, it would be extremely unjust to attribute such motives to all, or even to a majority, of the opponents of the project in question. Most of them are sincere in their opposition. They cling with persistency to the ideas which were certainly dominant, on this subject, throughout the South, but a few months ago. But they do run the hazard of making themselves liable to the suspicion which must attach to those whose objections rest upon other grounds than those of distrust of the efficacy of the measure itself. In other words, there are some people, not many perhaps, but certainly some, who object to employing the negroes in the army, not because they think that the experiment will fail, but because they think that it will succeed. This is, we presume, the class of persons alluded to by the *State Journal.*

But, we repeat, there is no real reason to distrust the patriotism or the sincerity of many who still cling to their old ideas on this subject, and cannot persuade themselves that the exigency demands a new line of policy. It would be simply absurd to accuse a majority of the Senate, voting against the proposition, of any latent purposes inconsistent with their duties to the cause and their country. Senators of distinction, of undoubted patriotism, of recognized ability, cast their votes against the measure. We think that they were mistaken. We think that they failed to comprehend the necessities of the occasion. We think that they did not recognize the force of public opinion; we think that some of them did not reflect the wishes of their constituencies; but we do not think that they were unfaithful. Neither do we believe that sectional considerations influenced the vote; or at least such sectional considerations as would indicate a separation between the Gulf States and the Border States, such as has been hinted at in the public prints, and the assumption of which has already elated the Yankee press with the idea of some innate and irrepressible antagonism between those two sections. In point of fact, the vote shows no such antagonism. If there is any line of separation on this question, it separates the trans-Alleghanian from the Atlantic States, not the Gulf States from the Border States. At least this would be the result of an analysis of the vote in the Senate. A large majority of the Gulf State Senators voted for the bill. A large majority of the Atlantic State Senators voted against the bill. But in reality there is no such sectional division of public opinion. The grouping of votes was purely accidental. In the case of the Virginia Senators, for instance, who voted against the bill, we believe their course to be in direct conflict with the opinions and wishes of the people of the State. But it would be unreasonable to suppose that a great and important question like this, one, too, which is comparatively new among us, could at once find an affirmative solution. In passing from the almost unanimous opposition of yesterday, to the supremacy of to-day, it had to make its way through all the transition stages of heated debate, and final acquiescence. It was settled affirmatively by the public and by the army before it made its way into Congress; and in that body it had to pass through the same phases of opposition and debate. We trust that the indications of public opinion are now so clear and decisive that the Senate will no longer stand in the way, but will retrace its steps and conform gracefully to the wishes of the country.

☞ Despite the importance of the "peace-now" men and the "reconstructionists" in opposing the freeing and arming of the slaves by the Confederacy, the *Whig* was clearly correct in assigning them a secondary role. There were simply too many diehard, zealous Confederates who could never force themselves to agree to any tampering with the cornerstone of the Confederacy. True, just as the Civil War served as a massive catalyst that produced certain changes in northern thought and policy about slavery and Negroes, it was also clearly at work doing the same thing in the South, where, after all, more than 90 percent of the blacks actually were. But in the last analysis, the South as a whole could not summon the intelligence, imagination, and moral courage to begin voluntarily to abandon the peculiar institution.

In the years after the war, Jefferson Davis himself became a foremost exponent of the view that the Confederates had fought and died to vindicate genuine constitutional liberty and states' rights. In fact, in his *Rise and Fall of the Confederate Government,* Davis specifically denied that slavery had ever been the cornerstone of the Confederacy. This sample of Davis' tedious and legalistic argument suggests why his book became a classic dust-gatherer:

With regard to slavery and the slave-trade, the provisions of this [Confederate] Constitution furnish an effectual answer to the assertion, so often made, that the Confederacy was founded on slavery, that slavery was its "corner-stone," etc. Property in slaves, *already existing,* was recognized and guaranteed, just as it was by the Constitution of the United States; and the rights of such property in the common Territories were protected against any such hostile discrimination as had been attempted in the Union. But the "extension of slavery," in the only practical sense of that phrase, was more distinctly and effectually precluded by the Confederate than by the Federal Constitution. This will be manifest on a comparison of the provisions of the two relative to the slave-trade. These are found at the beginning of the ninth section of the first article of each instrument. The Constitution of the United States had the following:

The migration or importation of such persons as any of the States now existing shall think proper to admit, shall not be prohibited by the Congress prior to the year one thousand eight hundred and eight; but a tax or duty may be imposed on such importation, not exceeding ten dollars for each person.

The Confederate Constitution, on the other hand, ordained as follows:

1. The importation of negroes of the African race from any foreign country, other than the slaveholding States or Territories of the United States of America, is hereby forbidden; and Congress is required to pass such laws as shall effectually prevent the same.

2. Congress shall also have the power to prohibit the introduction of slaves from any State not a member of, or Territory not belonging to, this Confederacy.

In the case of the United States, the only prohibition, is against any interference by Congress with the slave-trade for a term of years, and it was further legitimized by the authority given to impose a duty upon it. The term of years, it is true, had long since expired, but there was still no prohibition of the trade by the Constitution; it was after 1808 entirely within the discretion of Congress either to encourage, tolerate, or prohibit it.

Under the Confederate Constitution, on the contrary, the African slave-trade was *"hereby forbidden,"* positively and unconditionally, from the beginning. Neither the Confederate Government nor that of any of the States could permit it, and the Congress was expressly "required" to enforce the prohibition. The only discretion in the matter intrusted to the Congress was, whether or not to permit the introduction of slaves from any of the United States or their Territories.

Mr. Lincoln, in his [first] inaugural address, had said: "I have no purpose, directly or indirectly, to interfere with the institution of slavery in the States where it exists. I believe I have no lawful right to do so, and I have no inclination to do so." Now, if there was no purpose on the part of the Government of the United States to interfere with the institution of slavery within its already existing limits —a proposition which permitted its propagation within those limits by natural increase—and inasmuch as the Confederate Constitution precluded any other than the same natural increase, we may plainly perceive the disingenuousness and absurdity of the pretension by which a factitious sympathy has been obtained in certain quarters for the war upon the South, on the ground that it was a war in behalf of freedom against slavery.[1]

☞ Yet Davis, for all his flaws, was an honest man. And when he came to the portion of his apologia in which he reminisced about the controversy concerning the freeing and arming of the slaves, he had a most revealing flash of memory:

Subsequent events advanced my views from a prospective to a present need for the enrollment of negroes to take their place in the ranks. Strenuously I argued the question with members of Congress who called to confer with me. To a member of the Senate (the House in which we most needed a vote) I stated, as I had done to many others, the fact of having led negroes against a lawless body of armed white men, and the assurance which the experiment gave me that they might, under proper conditions, be relied on in battle, and finally used to him the expression which I believe I can repeat exactly: "If the Confederacy falls, there should be written on its tombstone, 'Died of a theory.'" General Lee was brought before a committee to state his opinion as to the probable efficiency of negroes as soldiers, and disappointed the probable expectation by his unqualified advocacy of the proposed measure.

After much discussion in Congress, a bill authorizing the President to ask for and accept from their owners such a number of able-bodied negro men as he might deem expedient subsequently passed the House, but was lost in the Senate by one vote. The Senators of Virginia opposed the measure so strongly that only legislative instruction could secure their support of it. Their Legislature did so instruct them, and they voted for it. Finally, the bill passed, with an amendment providing that not more than twenty-five per cent. of the male slaves between the ages of eighteen and forty-five should be called out. But the passage of the act had been so long delayed that the opportunity was lost. There did not remain time enough to obtain any result from its provisions.[2]

[1] Jefferson Davis, *The Rise and Fall of the Confederate Government* (1881: repr. ed., with foreword by Bell I. Wiley, 2 vols.; New York, 1958), I, 261–62.
[2] *Ibid.*, 518.

☞ Jefferson Davis spoke more truly and profoundly than perhaps he realized. Presumably his striking remark referred merely to the Confederacy's falling because of the theory that Negro slaves could never make good soldiers. Davis himself probably would never have agreed to an extension and different interpretation of his statement: in truth the Confederacy had in large part come into existence because of the larger theory from which he implied, however unwittingly, that it had died—the majority's belief that Negroes should, as inferior beings, be permanently kept in slavery, where they were happy and subordinated to whites.

A Note on
the Historiography
of the Problem

BECAUSE THE TEXT AND FOOTNOTES clearly show the newpapers and the archival material, largely printed, that I have used in preparing my volume, this brief essay will be limited to certain secondary accounts, and particularly to the question of how the debate on the freeing and arming of the slaves, and Jefferson Davis' role therein, came to be either largely ignored or partly misrepresented.

Nathaniel W. Stephenson's pioneering article, "The Question of Arming the Slaves," in the *American Historical Review*, XVIII (January, 1913), 295–308, has held up remarkably well in some respects and it certainly set the stage for all of the subsequent forays into the area. The title indicates, however, the focus of Stephenson's interest and his main emphasis. Barely mentioning General Cleburne's remarkable proposal, Stephenson seems, strangely enough, to have missed the real point in Davis' pivotal message to Congress on November 7, 1864. He writes (p. 296) : "This message is often misquoted. Frequently it is said that he [Davis] asked Congress to give him 40,000 slaves to be used as soldiers, with a promise of emancipation at the end of their service. His actual request was for 40,000 slave laborers." Having corrected the point about laborers but ignored that about emancipation, Stephenson then proceeds to quote Davis about his disagreement with those who advised a "general levy and arming of the slaves for the duty of soldiers," and suggests, quite erroneously, that after November 7 the matter rested for the next three months. Stephenson then states that sometime between November 7 and March 13, 1865, when Davis wrote his special message rebuking Congress for its tardiness, the Confederate President became converted to "a scheme to enroll slaves as soldiers."

In other words, what Stephenson first reports as being frequently said is quite correct insofar as it refers to emancipation; yet he himself either did not think so or failed to develop the point. The result is that he became confused about Davis and concentrated largely on the roles of Secretary of State Benjamin and especially General Lee. His analysis of Lee's part is quite helpful, but Stephenson may or may not be correct in his elaborate emphasis on Lee's alleged preference for action by Virginia rather than by the Confederate government. Concerning Benjamin, Stephenson misleadingly suggests (p. 295) that the episode confirmed the "impression that Benjamin was practically, during its last stage, the Confederacy's premier, the originator to a great extent of its policy."

Stephenson skillfully traces the course of the Barksdale measure through the Congress, and he corrects various errors that had appeared in a number of monographs and biographies before 1913. But it is not too much to say that, following Stephenson's lead, the large majority of historians who have touched on the matter since 1913 have apparently not read Jefferson Davis' message of November 7, 1864, or if they read it, they did not do so with sufficient care.

Two other early and important articles appeared in 1919. The first of these, by Thomas R. Hay, was "The South and the Arming of the Slaves," *Mississippi Valley Historical Review*, VI (June, 1919), 34–73. Hay goes over much of the same ground as the earlier study but describes more of the antecedents of the movement that came to its climax in February and March, 1865, and he particularly elaborates upon Cleburne's proposal. But Hay was as confused about President Davis as Stephenson had been and, speculating but not admitting it, Hay states (p. 55) that Benjamin "found it difficult to convince President Davis that such a radical step" as liberating and arming slaves was necessary or feasible. A few pages later Hay writes (p. 59) that "General Lee was behind the measure, but Davis was as yet silent," and (p. 68) that Davis had been "forced to acquiescence [in the matter of the Barksdale bill] by circumstances and presumably, in some measure, by the insistent and repeated advice of Benjamin."

In the month following the appearance of Hay's study, Charles H. Wesley, a distinguished pioneer in the field of Negro history, published "The Employment of Negroes as Soldiers in the Confederate Army," *Journal of Negro History*, IV (July, 1919), 239–53. Wesley offers valuable insights about the early phase of the war when Lincoln refused to touch slavery and when, Wesley suggests (p. 241), to "the majority of the Negroes, as to all the South, the invading armies of the Union seemed to be ruthlessly attacking independent States, invading the beloved homeland and trampling upon all that these men held dear." He describes the black state troops in Louisiana and the free Negroes who in 1861 volunteered for service in South Carolina, Tennessee, and elsewhere.

In his article Wesley mentions (pp. 242–43) the Confederacy's impressment of slaves under the law of February, 1864, and adds that Davis "was so satisfied with their labor that he suggested, in his annual message of November, 1864, that this number [20,000] should be increased to 40,000, with the promise of emancipation at the end of their service." No elaboration of the matter follows, and Wesley places his emphasis on the opposition that Davis initially expressed to the arming of the slaves. Wesley concludes his essay (p. 253) with this interesting insight: "The Negro was thus a factor in both the Union and Confederate armies in the War of the Rebellion. These facts lead to the conclusion that the Negro is an American not only because he lives in America, but because his life is closely connected with every important movement in American history."

When Wesley published almost two decades later his valuable book *The Collapse of the Confederacy* (1937; repr. ed., 1968), he overlooked the point about Davis' proposal for emancipation that the article of 1919 had at least mentioned in passing. In the book, which naturally has been more widely used by scholars than the article it presumably replaced and extended, Wesley writes (p. 156): "The position of President Davis was stated in his message to Congress of November 7, 1864, in which he disagreed with the advocates of Negro enlistments, although he asked for the privilege of buying slaves for government use." Then Wesley, nowhere mentioning emancipation, quotes the Confederate leader's statement advising against Negro soldiers at that time.

Why the repeated misinterpretation of Jefferson Davis by these historians? The cautious language he had employed in his appeal for a beginning of gradual, compensated emancipation by the Confederate government was no doubt one important answer. But one must also suspect that because the popular and even the scholarly stereotype of Davis as Confederate President made no allowance for the possibility of change or evolution in the hothouse circumstances of war, as historians have long since understood in the case of Lincoln, emancipation simply became unthinkable in connection with the southern leader.

To trace the long trail of the influence of the above three studies would be pointless. And it is true that not all subsequent historians have failed to go to the documents and thereby have been misled by partly inaccurate or incomplete secondary studies. Perhaps the best and most accurate analysis of the problem, but too brief for any comprehensive treatment, may be found in Bell I. Wiley, *Southern Negroes, 1861–1865* (New Haven, 1938), 146–61. He began his chapter on "Soldiers" by citing the three scholars mentioned above, but Wiley, too, had clearly read the documents he cites, and he presents a concise but lively summary that I found most helpful in preparing this book. Charles P. Roland, in *The Confederacy* (Chicago, 1960), 183–86, also has the essential facts correct, but his treatment was necessarily skeletal because the volume is a short one in the series entitled *The Chicago History of American Civilization.*

Most historians, however, have settled for the studies by Stephenson or Hay or Wesley, or some combination of them. E. Merton Coulter, for example, in *The Confederate States of America, 1861–1865* (Baton Rouge, 1950), a volume in the splendid series entitled *A History of the South* that he edited with the late Wendell H. Stephenson, devotes only a fraction more than two pages (pp. 266–68) to the topic. He not only fails to connect Davis with any idea of emancipation, but the general tone is suggested by this statement: "But, naturally, opposition to making slaves into soldiers was deeply embedded in Southerners. It seemed bizarre and grotesque and wholly at variance with the very essence and character of Southern civilization."

Biographers of Jefferson Davis have not helped much. Robert McElroy in *Jefferson Davis: The Unreal and the Real* (2 vols.; New York, 1937), II, 424–25, mentions the message of November 7, 1864, and gets it straight. But the lack of footnotes, together with McElroy's failure to link the message with the Kenner mission and the legislative battle in February–March, 1865, probably account for the small impact the book has had on Confederate historiography. The most recent biographer of Davis, Hudson Strode, in his trilogy's final volume, *Jefferson Davis, Tragic Hero: The Last Twenty-Five Years, 1864–1889*

(3 vols.; New York, 1964), has certain scattered but useful data, unfortunately not documented. After mentioning the President's message in one place (p. 110), however, Strode jumps to another (p. 120) to mention Governor Smith's message to the Virginia legislature, without suggesting any connection that the latter might have had with the former. When the events of February and March, 1865, are discussed (pp. 151–53) there are several errors of fact plus some simple confusion, and one must conclude that this ambitious attempt to portray Davis has failed to help clarify his role in the Confederacy's last great controversy.

The historiographical situation with respect to Robert E. Lee is little better than with Davis. As earlier mentioned in a footnote, this was a subject that apparently held little interest for Lee's most distinguished biographer, the late Douglas Southall Freeman. Of four massive volumes, Freeman takes one paragraph on page 544 of the third volume of *R. E. Lee: A Biography* (4 vols.; New York, 1946) to discuss what was probably the most important wartime "political" controversy in which Lee allowed himself to take a leading role. Furthermore Freeman's statement that Lee had "previously had a low opinion of the fighting quality of Negro troops" is based on slim evidence: Freeman cites Lee's letter to Davis of September 30, 1863 (*O.R.*, Series I, Vol. XXIX, Pt. 2, p. 736), in which the general responds to the President's information that the Federals were reportedly collecting Negro troops and cavalry in Norfolk for an attack on an important railroad junction at Weldon, North Carolina. Lee wrote: "I do not apprehend that those negro regiments will prove a very formidable body, though unopposed they might do us great damage." This statement hardly gives us clear evidence about Lee's opinion of the "fighting quality of Negro troops," and the general's letters of 1865 to Andrew Hunter and Congressman Barksdale are much more explicit on Lee's positive viewpoint about Negro soldiers than Freeman even hinted. Lee's letters to Hunter and Barksdale, incidentally, are not included in Clifford Dowdey and Louis Manarin (eds.), *The Wartime Papers of R. E. Lee* (Boston, 1961).

With so much confusion and misinterpretation regarding the ideas and attitudes of the Confederacy's two preeminent leaders on the question of freeing and arming the slaves, small wonder that we have not properly appreciated the scope and significance of the controversy that so wracked the Confederacy during its final six months. Perhaps one final illustration may suggest the historiographical vacuum that has existed and certain of its effects.

James M. McPherson placed all students of the Civil War in his debt when he published *The Negro's Civil War: How American Negroes Felt and Acted During the War for the Union* (New York, 1965). Allowing the blacks to speak for themselves insofar as the sources would permit, McPherson compellingly authenticated and dramatized his thesis (p. xi) that the ''Negro was *not* merely a passive recipient of the benefits conferred upon him by the war.'' C. Vann Woodward is quoted on the cover of the paperback edition: ''No other work marshals such massive and impressive evidence about the Negro in this crucial period of his history.'' And one would have to agree with that high praise.

Yet McPherson's title promises a great deal. He states (p. ix) that in addition to the more than two hundred thousand Negroes who fought in the Federal army and navy, an estimated five hundred thousand (Herbert Aptheker's estimate) came within Union lines during the course of the war. As it turns out, the rich documents that McPherson found and convincingly wove together really represent, or tell us about, approximately three quarters of a million Negroes—or less than a fourth of the total number in the South.

In more than three hundred pages of text, McPherson devotes four pages (Ch. 17) to ''The Confederate Decision to Raise a Negro Army, 1864–65.'' While Cleburne, Benjamin, and Lee are represented by excerpts, nothing is said concerning President Davis' proposal, much less about the more important and startling fact that there were Negroes, possibly quite a few, who for freedom and assurances about their postwar future were willing to become Confederates, not only at the beginning of the war but right up to the end of it.

This is certainly not meant in any sense to denigrate McPherson's work nor to deny the validity of his interpretation and conclusion. It is meant to suggest that the whole subject of the ''Negro's Civil War'' is perhaps vastly more complex, and perhaps more ambiguous or paradoxical, than most of us have realized.

To the trailblazing work of Bell I. Wiley, James H. Brewer has now published a valuable addition, *The Confederate Negro: Virginia's Craftsmen and Military Laborers, 1861–1865* (Durham, 1969). Brewer's work is limited to the noncombatant black auxiliaries in one crucial state, but he has made an important contribution toward untangling certain matters about the Civil War that, as his title alone suggests, are yet puzzling if not downright troubling to many.

The Gray and the Black does not primarily deal with the role of the Negro in the Confederacy and does not pretend to do so. But there are obvious implications for that broad subject in this book. I merely hope that this study might help clarify the record about the centrality of the question of emancipation and the role of Jefferson Davis and other Confederate leaders so that more comprehensive work may be done in the future.

Index

Index